Subliminal Treatment Procedures:
A Clinician's Guide

Paul G. Swingle

University of Ottawa
McLean Hospital
Harvard Medical School

Professional Resource Press
Sarasota, Florida

Published by Professional Resource Press
(An imprint of Professional Resource Exchange, Inc.)
Post Office Box 15560
Sarasota, FL 34277-1560

Printed in the United States of America

A CAUTIONARY NOTE

This book is intended to provide accurate and authoritative information about its subject. However, no book is a substitute for scientific study, formal academic/clinical training, and supervised experience in acquiring expertise in using clinical procedures such as those described in this book. Readers are cautioned to carefully assess their professional competence and preparedness for utilizing the procedures described in this book prior to utilizing this material with clients or patients. It shall be the sole responsibility of the reader to insure that he or she is practicing in an ethically appropriate fashion in accord with appropriate practice standards.

Library of Congress Cataloging-in-Publication Data

Swingle, Paul G. date.
        Subliminal treatment procedures : a clinician's guide / Paul G.
    Swingle.
            p.   cm.
        Includes bibliographical references (p. 157) and indexes.
        ISBN 0-943158-77-X (paperbound ed.)
        1. Subliminal perception. 2. Psychotherapy. I. Title
        [DNLM: 1. Subliminal Stimulation. 2. Psychotherapy--methods. WM
    420 S978s]
    RC499.S92S95   1992
    616.89'14--dc20
    DNLM/DLC
    for Library of Congress   90-3857
                                                              CIP

Contents

Introduction

During the era of World War II, Niels Bohr, the Danish atomic physicist, and, at the time, strident pacifist, freely communicated his findings on atomic research. His scientific and political colleagues attempted to persuade him that such free dissemination of this information was very likely to contribute to the Third Reich's development of the atomic bomb. I do not wish to appear to be presumptuous by offering this analogy, for I do not believe that subliminal technology is as potentially destructive as nuclear technology. Early reactions to subliminal procedures, however, did indeed indicate profound disquiet: ". . . the most alarming and outrageous discovery since Mr. Gatling invented his gun" (*Nation*, 1957, p. 206); ". . . take this invention and everything connected with it and attach it to the center of the next nuclear explosive scheduled for testing " (Cousins, 1957, p. 20).

Let me immediately state that subliminal effects are real and it is not my purpose to attempt to persuade any reader of this fact. Readers interested in cogently presented arguments regarding the probity of the phenomenon of subliminal perception should see the reviews by Dixon (1971, 1981), Holender (1986), and Bornstein (1989). What is in question is the *therapeutic* efficacy of subliminal technology. Hence, I feel that a guide is needed to assist clinicians in the preparation of subliminal materials and the necessary methodological procedures for the application and assessment of subliminal treatments. I believe that it will be most beneficial for clinicians to know how to use subliminal technology and to become involved in systematic research investigating the areas of beneficial application. In my judgment, clinical practice will provide the

appropriate research milieu for examining the treatment efficacy of subliminal effects.

Although I review several modalities of subliminal application, the
major emphasis in this guide is on auditory and, to a lesser extent, visual
procedures. The emphasis on auditory procedures results largely from
the greater convenience afforded in clinical application of auditory material. Auditory subliminal material can be readily prepared for easy use by
clients outside of the clinical context. Visual procedures are much more
restrictive and cumbersome, although very useful in clinical settings.

With regard to the general issue of subliminal effects, the scientific and
clinical communities appear to be divided into two highly polarized
groups. This polarization is not along the axis of the traditional experimental–clinical or scientist–professional lines. Rather it appears to be simply polarized across the axis of those who know that subliminal messages
work and those who know that they do not. Those individuals who know
that subliminal messages work form companies. These companies sell
tapes or acoustic devices to government, industry, or the public at large
emphasizing the powerful effects of subliminal treatment, offering testimonials or perhaps demonstrations, but being extraordinarily guarded
with regard to the technical details associated with the preparation of
such materials. Such commercially available materials usually have music with embedded subliminal messages on one side of a tape and relaxing
music on the flip side. Companies that market subliminal tapes to the
general public have experienced remarkable growth. One such company offers more than 175 titles covering everything from weight loss to
attracting love. This company sold more than 600,000 tapes in 1987 at
about $10 each. A different company claimed sales exceeding 450,000
tapes in 1988. The weight-loss market alone accounts for well over
250,000 tapes per year considering the several companies that offer such
titles. Hence, although the debate regarding the efficacy of subliminal
treatment procedures rages on, the potential to sell the products in the
self-help market appears strong indeed. I would not be completely
straightforward if I did not acknowledge that once one discovers how
to reliably elicit subliminal effects, latent entrepreneurial motivations start
to manifest themselves.

On the other hand, there are individuals whose understanding of physiology and cognitive psychology is such that they dismiss the possibility of subliminal effects. They view those individuals who are attempting
to commercially exploit subliminal technology as charlatans as opposed
to opportunists.

Recently, I attended the Behavioral Medicine Society meetings, and
the sentiments expressed by one clinician and one nonclinical health
researcher exemplify the view of those who do not accept the concept of

subliminal effects. One individual was ridiculing subliminal relaxation tapes, indicating that every once in a while you would hear a little whisper on the tape telling you to relax and that this was silly and he had thought that we had put this whole area to bed 30 years ago. The other individual commented at length about one company's recent media blitz attempting to sell their subliminal technology. His criticisms, however, were based on the belief that subliminal technology did not work. He thought that any effects that did occur were based purely on expectation, demand characteristics, and the like and that this particular company, like so many others in the health field, was simply exploiting the public's naivete.

The present guide is divided into four chapters. The first chapter reviews in detail the concept of subliminality, in particular as it applies to the auditory modality. The concept of subliminality, the technical properties of the stimuli, and the technical properties associated with the content of the messages are reviewed. This section also reviews the technical details associated with the preparation of subliminal materials. Although the equipment required for this work is not formidable or expensive, attention to detail is critical so that the subliminal stimuli are presented within certain well-established ranges.

The second chapter of this guide focuses on research on the effects of subliminal material on emotion and behavior. In addition to reviewing the available literature, I report the results of research conducted on nonclinical populations over the past 10 years. This research was supported by the Social Sciences and Humanities Research Council and by research funds maintained by the University of Ottawa.

The third chapter of this book is the one that I consider to be the most important. In this section, I review reseach methodology that is required for the ethical application of subliminal technology. The methods discussed in this section are not limited to the area of subliminal treatment but are appropriate for any clinical research. I believe strongly that clinicians are in the best position to do important research on new treatment procedures. Unfortunately the methodologies that are often used are not only unethical but, more important, are ecologically invalid. Furthermore, clinical research practices must be consistent with the evolving new treatment model, perhaps best captured by the metaphor *mind/body healing*. The old model in which the patient is a passive recipient of treatments administered by the health professional is simply wrong. The evidence that is accumulating that suggests alternative models for health interventions is compelling. Unfortunately, many individuals, although they subscribe to the new concepts of mind/body healing and patient involvement in treatment, still embrace the traditional experimental versus control group metaphor as the gold standard against which treatment procedures should be assessed. Undoubtedly, there are occasions in which this is necessary but increasingly scientist–practitioners are developing research methods that are statistically powerful, ecologically more appropriate, and ethically more acceptable.

The fourth chapter examines research that has been done on clinical populations or research that appears directly relevant to clinical applications. What we know about the potential clinical efficacy of subliminal procedures is limited. However, the research and case studies that are available suggest exciting possibilities for clinical application and important challenges for research-oriented clinicians.

I have been conducting research in the area of auditory subliminal effects for 10 years, and with one exception, I have not published any of my results. There are several reasons for this reticence. My decision to consolidate my work in this form reflects a rather profound change in my own thinking with regard to the compelling evidence that is being accumulated with regard to mind/body healing. Over 10 years ago, I was conducting a workshop for members of various police and military agencies. As is my practice, following the workshop I socialized with the participants, one of whom was moved to unusual candor by spirits. He described a demonstration of subliminal auditory effects in which he had participated. My response to this revelation, consistent with my conservative empirical orientation, was predictably that the whole area was a sham and commercial exploiters of these procedures were, either deliberately or inadvertently, capitalizing on demand characteristics and expectations of participants. I proceeded to relate to this individual what I recalled of the subliminal literature, which generally dismissed subliminal effects as trivial. My informant shook his head and described a procedure which I now know will elicit a subliminal effect. The question is not the effect, the question is whether these procedures have a meaningful clinical usefulness for the treatment of health related complaints.

The reticence of "going public" with this research is obvious given the heated controversy associated with the area. It is reminiscent of the sentiments of the scientific community regarding clinical hypnosis over the last 4 decades or so. The strong bias against a critical assessment of the concept of an auditory subliminal effect is nicely captured by comments I received from a reviewer of one of my grant applications. Although I recognized that it was bad form to complain about specific reviewers of grant applications because one is likely to be characterized as a poor sport or a sore head, I was able to reverse the judgment of the granting committee simply because of the blatant bias of the reviewer. For example, the reviewer's comment about effects in response to a 0 db signal (i.e., a signal at the same sound level as room ambient) as measured at the loudspeaker, which was 8 feet away from the subject, was that "the finding is not that surprising: It may have been a discriminable stimulus.'' The reviewer further commented that a subject in a stressful situation would ''hardly be receptive to a minimal message.'' The reviewer's comments on a lever-pressing situation: ''as S becomes fatigued, how could the stimulus 'faster' possibly have an effect?''

However, the situation has clearly changed. After all, now articles with the word ''subliminal'' and even ''unconscious'' in the title appear in our mainline psychology journals. Now that psychology has regained its mind, the time appears propitious for suggesting that systematic research on applications of subliminal technology with clinical populations is warranted.

Practicing practitioner–scientists who understand the mind/body healing paradigm will be receptive to adding subliminal procedures to their therapeutic armamentarium for the treatment of those human disorders that they find respond in a clinically meaningful manner to subliminal auditory techniques.

CHAPTER ONE

The Concept
of Subliminality

Implicit in our usual understanding of the concept of subliminal auditory influence is the notion that there is some message or stimulus of which we are unaware that gives rise to a predictable and measurable behavior or a change in behavior. Further, we generally conceptualize the relationship of stimulus to response as being, likewise, one of which we are unaware.

In the present section, we focus our attention on three aspects of the subliminal influence process: the properties of the stimulus, the properties of the response, and finally, the nature of the relationship between the stimulus and the response. Before we proceed, however, it is important to keep in mind that our purpose here is to look at the *clinical* relevance of the subliminal auditory technology. From this perspective, it is the clinical improvement in the patient or client that is of paramount concern, as opposed to whether or not the technology that is being applied is in fact subliminal relative to some rigorous definition of that concept. We should also keep in mind that there may be important differences between clinical and nonclinical populations with regard to a number of the factors associated with subliminal influence. We review both of these issues in considerable detail.

The most fundamental issue is whether the target person is aware of the stimulus, the response, or the connection between the stimulus and the response. Further, if the target person is not aware, can the person be made aware of various properties of the stimulus, response, or the connection between stimulus and response?

1

THE STIMULUS

We are constantly being bombarded by a myriad of different types of stimuli that compete for our attention. To some extent we can exercise attentional control over just which stimuli we are going to attend to and which we are not. I can, for example, focus my attention on and become aware of the kinesthetic sensations associated with clothing touching various parts of my body, the tight feeling of my shoes, or the pressure of the arm of the chair against my elbow. Similarly, I can become aware of the auditory sensations of people talking in the corridor, the heating system fans, or the sounds made by my chair as I move around. In short, there are a number of stimuli in our environment to which we are normally not attentive that can be brought to awareness at will.

Although I am generally unaware of many, if not most, of the stimuli in my environment, they may be exerting predictable and measurable changes in my behavior. The fact that I can direct my attention to any one or several of these normally unnoticed stimuli does not mean that I would be aware of the fact that these stimuli are exerting some influence on my behavior. Hence, stimuli that can be brought to awareness and those that can be discriminated on the basis of content, should most properly be called *preconscious* as opposed to *subliminal*. Therefore, the hum from the heating system in my office can be brought to awareness, and I could in turn communicate the frequency of that sound to you by myself humming.

There are other stimuli that may be discernible in terms of being aware that they exist but may not be discriminable on the basis of content. For example, I am aware of people talking in the corridor outside of my office. I can discriminate the gender of the people talking based on the frequency formants of the sounds, but I may not be able to tell you what these people are saying because I cannot discriminate the content of these conversations. Hence, in this case I could communicate to another person some of the technical properties associated with the stimuli such as how many people are speaking, the gender of the speakers, and when they are speaking as opposed to laughing. Perhaps I could even make some guesses about prominent emotional states of the speakers, such as being angry or sad, although I might not be able to determine the content of these conversations. In this case, we can describe some aspects of the stimulus as being preconscious in the sense that I can make myself aware of some of the properties associated with the sounds that I know are speech coming from the corridor. Other aspects of the stimulus may be subliminal in nature in the sense that I cannot communicate to another individual properties of the stimulus which are having a demonstrable effect on my behavior. There are various levels associated with this process in terms of the extent to which I can make myself aware of the content aspects of the stimulus. For example, one of the voices may remind me of a person from my past whom I disliked intensely. Even though I cannot determine the content of the conversation, my mood may be negatively influenced, and I may not be aware of the fact that it was the voices in the corridor that gave rise to this mood change. The major issue is whether I can be made aware of this relationship. One can see that there are various possibilities: I may make myself aware of this property of the stimulus if I focus sufficient attention on attempting to understand the reasons for my mood change; or, on the other hand, it may be possible for some other person to assist me in revealing this property of the stimulus.

Finally, I may be well aware of the fact that a stimulus is, at times, present but I may be unable to detect its presence. For example, if I bring my ear close enough so that I can hear it, I know that the electric clock on the wall emits a low frequency hum. In fact, I can determine my own threshold by moving closer to or further from the clock in a manner similar to the method of limits and determine a range over which the sound is just detectable. If I go beyond that range, I will be in a position in which, although I know that the sound is being emitted, I can not reliably discriminate the presence or absence of that sound. That is, if someone connected and disconnected the clock, I would not be able to determine without looking at the clock whether it was running or not. In previous research, *subliminal* was often defined as the 50% threshold, that is, the point at which an individual could determine the presence or absence of the signal with the probability of 50%. The threshold concept may be used both in terms of the content of the stimulus as well as the presence or absence of the stimulus. So, for example, with a spoken message, I may be able to reliably detect when the stimulus is being presented, but I may not be able to reliably discern the content of those messages. Obviously, the strictest definition of subliminal is that the stimulus must be presented at a level that is beyond the target's ability to reliably detect the presence or absence of the presentation of the stimulus.

In summary, with regard to the stimulus, it is important to specify whether one is referring to the content of the stimulus or the recognition of the existence of the stimulus. Further, one should determine whether the person can be made aware of the existence or content of the stimulus either by his or her own volition or with the assistance of some other person or some other information. If a person can be made aware of the properties of the stimulus, we refer to it as *preconscious*. If the person cannot be made aware of the relevant properties of this stimulus, we refer to it as *subliminal*. The term *subliminal*, then, refers to stimuli that a person cannot discriminate (i.e., become aware of) in terms of content, *or*, cannot detect on the basis of the presence or absence of the stimulus. The strictest definition of subliminality is, of course, the latter.

Just how one determines a target's awareness of stimulus properties is critical. Referring again to the people speaking in the corridor, if you were to ask me what they are talking about, I may not be able to tell you. But, I may be able to tell you that one person is male and the other is female. Further, I may be able to tell you what they first said as opposed to what they subsequently said, or I may be more curious about one part of the conversation as opposed to some other part, even though I am not aware of the content of what was said.

THE RESPONSE

In the previous section we examined some of the properties associated with the stimulus and the conditions under which such stimuli may be considered to be subliminal. We now turn our attention to the second aspect of the stimulus–response process that we must consider, namely, the response. There are several aspects to the concept of response that warrant careful consideration. In the first instance, we use the client's response as an indicator that a subliminal message has been processed. In later sections, in which subliminal influence is examined in considerable detail, some of the problems associated with the response dimension are considered. For our present purposes, however, we are concerned with what properties of the response are associated with our conception of the definition of subliminality. Clearly, if one supposes that subliminal messages are processed at a nonconscious level, one would not expect subjects to be aware of any changes in their behavior. Subjects may simply be unaware of any modification of their cognitive, affective, or motoric behavior. As Nisbett and Wilson (1977) pointed out, people have no privileged introspective access to the causes or determining conditions of their behavior.

We can extend the concept of the limits of introspection in that much that happens in the body is not available to our consciousness. Perhaps more precisely, our behavior differs with respect to the extent to which it is accessible to our selective attention. Some processes we can identify rather precisely, such as the fact that I am now speaking into my tape recorder, breathing, and looking out of the window. Other responses may be less immediately available to selective attention, and the extent to which they are available to selective attention may vary considerably in response to how informed a person is about the processes involved. Premature ventricular contraction associated with anxiety is a good example. It is not uncommon for clients experiencing high levels of anxiety to demonstrate premature ventricular contraction, which is observable on an EKG. Some patients may report that they feel a murmur in their heart or that their heart has sped up. Others report a queasy or uneasy feeling in the chest but do not identify it with a cardiac response. Still others report high states of subjective anxiety but report that they are unaware of any physiological response occurring during this anxious state. By providing the client with some information and focusing his or her attention on cardiac response, we can increase the precision with which he or she can be aware of and monitor premature ventricular contractions.

At another level, however, there are responses of which a person is unaware. There are also ranges within the response dimension below which the person is unable to distinguish differences. Biofeedback is based on the principle that individuals can acquire control over responses when they are provided with a prosthetic enhancement of their sensing capabilities. Hence, changes in peripheral blood flow can be monitored by sensitive surface temperature thermistors, which indicate very slight changes in the temperature of a person's finger. Changes in peripheral blood flow that are too subtle for a client to discriminate are rendered discriminable by providing feedback in another modality (generally visual or auditory). Hence, with regard to the response dimension, one important axis refers to the extent to which a response can be discriminated and thereby become available to selective attention.

The second axis of the response dimension is that of correlated responses. Although a person may be unaware of a particular response, he or she may, nonetheless, be able to discriminate other body states to which that response is related. In the case of the highly anxious client with premature ventricular contractions, the individual may be unaware of any cardiac response but may be able to discriminate subjective anxiety. Similarly, psychic content that is not available to consciousness may nonetheless be related to behavior that the individual can discriminate, that is, become aware of. Analytic psychology is based on the premise that unconscious content, which by definition is unavailable to the person, is directly related to symptomatology of which the person is aware.

Finally, the third axis of importance with regard to the response is the degree to which a person is aware of responses that are available to awareness. Driving a car is perhaps our most classic example of selective attention. Before the behavior is well learned, selective attention is required to perform the behaviors. After the behavior is learned it becomes part of a person's behavioral repertoire. Then the individual's attention to the behavior is determined by the requirements to adjust the behavior (e.g., avoiding a pothole) or if the individual is motivated for some other reason to selectively attend to driving behavior (e.g., enjoying the driving experience).

The concept of the extent to which an individual is aware of his or her response is rather critical in the area of subliminal influence because, by definition, subliminal is not directly available to one's awareness. Hence, asking people if they were aware of a subliminal message, is, of course, not appropriate. For example, if exposed to a subliminal message designed to make me more relaxed, not only would I be unable to indicate whether or not the stimulus had been presented, but I may not even be aware of the fact that I am calmer or less anxious. I may not, for example, be aware of the fact that my pulse rate has dropped or my peripheral temperature has increased (both indicators of decreased sympathetic arousal). In short, if I were interested in determining the efficacy of such a subliminal procedure, I would very likely conclude that the message has no demonstrable effect on sympathetic arousal because I have asked an individual to respond to changes that are beyond the person's discriminable limits.

The research by Zajonc and his colleagues, in my judgment, offers one of the clearest examples of this difficulty (Mooreland & Zajonc, 1979; Wilson, 1979; Zajonc, 1980). The essential feature of this work is that novel stimuli are presented at various frequencies of exposure to subjects (i.e., subjects are exposed to stimuli 0, 1, 3, 9, or 25 times) and then the subjects are asked to identify those they have seen before and those they have not seen before. As might be expected, subjective recognition of the stimulus is correlated with the frequency of exposure of that stimulus with reported correlations in the range of .50. However, for our purposes, the critical aspect of this research relates to those stimuli that were not correctly identified (i.e., those that the subject indicated that they had not seen before, but had in fact been exposed to). Stimulus exposure and subjective affect, as measured by liking of the stimulus, was correlated in the range of .60. This means that stimuli that cannot be cognitively discriminated (i.e., a subject cannot, at better than chance levels, identify stimuli seen versus those not seen previously) can be discriminated on the basis of affect. Liking of the stimulus is positively correlated with stimulus exposure for those stimuli that the subject does not recall having seen. Further, Kunst-Wilson and Zajonc (1980) demonstrated that preference for ambiguous figures can be enhanced by exposing subjects to the figures, tachistoscopically, at durations of 4 msec, a level within the subliminal range.

When working with subliminal technology, the selection of appropriate response modalities is critical. Simply stated, subjects may not be aware of changes in their behavior that have resulted from subliminal influences.

CAUSALITY

The third element in the subliminal influence process is the concept of causality, that is, the extent to which a subject is or can be made aware of the causal relationship between a stimulus and a response. The subject may or may not be aware of a stimulus or the response along a number of dimensions that we have already discussed. Further, the individual may or may not be aware of the extent of the relationship between stimulus and response. Therefore, in terms of our concept of subliminality, it is entirely possible that an individual may be aware of a stimulus and aware of a response but not be aware of the nature of the relationship between stimulus and response.

The issue of the degree of awareness of the causal properties of subliminal influence is of particular importance because we are dealing with the concept of consciousness. Perhaps the most important consideration that will structure any discussion of the unconscious is whether we consider the term *unconscious* to be an entity or a process. Subliminal methodology is of clinical importance regardless of what one's therapeutic metaphor happens to be. Further, I feel most optimistic that subliminal technology may prove to be extremely useful for doing important research on the whole mind/body issue. In particular, the technology could prove to be very useful for research on influences on physical and psychological health behavior and mood states that are, for any number of reasons, outside the person's awareness. Although a number of these issues are discussed in great detail in other sections of this book, for the present purposes, I wish to only look at those aspects of consciousness that are important for our definition of the concept of subliminality.

Let us simply say that the person's awareness of a contingency between a stimulus and a response varies from no awareness to full and accurate comprehension of the nature of the contingency. As Freud pointed out, people are compelled to make connections between psychical phenomena of which they become aware and other conscious material. He also found that such connections are constantly revised if they prove to be incorrect, even though the newly perceived contingency may be incorrect also. As Bowers (1987) pointed out, comprehending a connection between two events is quite different from noticing the events and the contingency between them. There are a number of very interesting demonstrations of this miscomprehension. A device that I use for classroom demonstrations of this effect consists of a panel with four lights and four associated toggle switches. The panel also contains two outcome lights, one indicating that the student correctly solved the sequence problem and the other a fail light that indicates that the sequence was not correct. A trial begins with all of the choice lights illuminated; as the student makes a response the associated light is extinguished. When all four lights are extinguished, either the correct or the fail light is illuminated, indicating to the student the outcome of the particular choice of sequence. Hence, a student might push lever 1, 3, 2, 4 and if that is the correct preprogrammed sequence, the correct light would be illuminated indicating to the student that he or she had correctly solved the sequence problem. Although the students are led to believe that there is a preprogrammed sequence, in fact, the device is programmed so that one particular switch must be depressed in a certain order and all other choices are irrelevant. For example, the device might be programmed so that any sequence in which switch number 2 is pressed first will result in the correct light being illuminated once all switches have been depressed. Even though there are 256 possible sequences, and hence the probability of solving the problem on any particular trial is a bit less than 4 in 1000, students have no difficulty at all accepting the fact that they solved the sequence problem pretty quickly. And, of course, if you ask them they will explain precisely the sequence in which the switches must be depressed in order to correctly solve the problem. There are many variations on this theme, but generally speaking what one finds after revealing the actual contingency is a general reluctance to accept the simple solution to the problem or perhaps a bit of annoyance. The point is that, although the students are aware of contingencies involved, their comprehension of the contingencies is not correct. Further, their incorrect comprehension of the problem may be perfectly effective and they can continue forever "solving" the problem by applying a partially erroneous solution rule.

Nisbett and Wilson (1977) reported an intriguing experiment that exemplifies a similar effect. They asked subjects to judge which of four pairs of identical stockings was superior in quality. Subjects would feel and inspect the stockings and then make a selection. When asked why they had selected a particular pair of stockings, subjects responded in the expected manner by pointing out that the stockings they had selected were superior because of finer weave, better color, and so on. If informed that the stockings were all identical, subjects would continue to insist that the pair that they had selected was in fact superior. Further, it was demonstrated that some subjects had positional biases in that a higher proportion of stockings on the right were selected as being superior. When it was pointed out that they had this bias, subjects again tended to insist that it was in fact the difference in quality that gave rise to their selection, not the positional bias.

Bowers (1975) offered yet another example of such misperception of contingencies in a verbal learning experiment. In his preparation, subjects were asked to indicate preference for a series of paired postcard reproductions of landscapes and portraits. Utilizing a standard verbal learning procedure, subjects were reinforced for selecting either a portrait or a landscape by the experimenter saying "good" following the appropriate selection. Bowers reported that often in these situations subjects were aware of the fact that the experimenter was saying "good" following the subjects' stated preference of the pictures, but they avowed that their stated preferences were not influenced by these contingencies.

In short, with regard to the concept of subliminality, individuals may be aware of two events, such as a stimulus message and a response, but be unaware of any relationship between the two. Second, they may be aware of two events and notice a contingency but not comprehend it. Third, they may be aware of two events but have an incorrect belief about the contingency involved. Finally, they may be aware of the events and fully comprehend the nature of the contingency between these events. Of course, as we have already discussed, a level of awareness or comprehension of contingency should be considered separately from the assessment of the degree to which the person is aware of the stimulus message or his or her response. It is important to keep in mind that although comprehension of the contingency between a stimulus and a response may be incorrect, it may nonetheless be functional. In the example of the sequence-learning demonstration, although the student has to learn only that one response must occur in a certain position in the sequence (all other properties of the sequence are unimportant) he or she is likely to retain a belief about a complex contingency because it works. Similarly, if we intrude upon a belief structure with subliminal procedures, that intrusion is going to influence behavior even if the belief structure is incorrect. For example, if an individual believes in astrology, and we are able to create in that person the belief that their stars are right, that person's risk-taking behavior could well be influenced.

TECHNICAL REQUIREMENTS

Years of experience of dealing with laboratory equipment salespeople has emphasized the utility of a metaphor communicated to me by a computer consultant. He pointed out that if one's objective is to cross downtown Ottawa during rush hour, functionally, it does not matter much whether one is driving a Volkswagen or a Lamborghini. In any area of research where electronic equipment is involved, one can spend considerable amounts of money without dramatic changes in the functional value of the research preparation. The area of auditory subliminal messages is no exception.

With regard to equipment configurations there are two issues of paramount importance. First, because subliminal messages are in fact subliminal, we need a treatment configuration that allows the clinician or technician to reliably determine if the stimulus message is present. In our laboratories we have experimented with a number of different equipment configurations including loudspeakers, headsets, mono and stereo presentations, dichotic presentations, presentations conditional upon EEG states and other physiological states of the body. Our research has demonstrated that the simplest procedure is in fact the best in that it permits one to reliably ascertain (a) that the subliminal message is being presented and (b) that the configuration is best for reliably eliciting subliminal effects.

The second important issue is one that clinicians are often hesitant to acknowledge—from the client's perspective the treatment preparation must look "professional." As will be obvious to the reader after reviewing some of the technical details of subliminal procedures outlined later in this chapter, one can conduct subliminal work with a $25 tape recorder. However, although one can establish a very workable treatment facility at a very modest cost, it is important that the treatment procedures be ecologically valid in the sense that clients' expectations and attributions are that they are going to be exposed to a therapeutically efficacious procedure.

Auditory subliminal treatment procedures may be administered to individual clients, or to groups of individuals, or materials may be prepared for home use. Subliminal effects occur both when clients are aware that subliminal messages are being presented and when they are kept uninformed of this fact. In general, it is my experience that the informed client

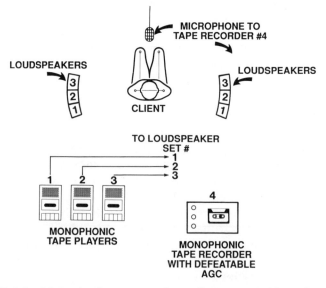

FIG. 1.1. Schematic of treatment and recording preparation for auditory subliminal messages.

procedure is preferable for a number of reasons; therefore, I do not attempt to disguise the purpose of the subliminal preparation. I do not generally tell my clients the exact content of the messages that are being presented, but I do explain that the treatment is effective and just what effects the subliminal messages should have on them.

Important issues associated with the content of the subliminal messages and the nature of the embedding medium are considered in other sections of this guide. For our present purposes we are concerned only with the technical characteristics associated with the physical properties of the stimuli.

In our work, we have found that monophonic recording procedures and monophonic presentation are the most effective and trouble-free procedure for subliminal treatment. Hence, the equipment required for a configuration similar to that shown in Fig. 1.1 includes: (a) three monophonic cassette tape players, (b) a monophonic recorder with a defeatable automatic gain control, (c) three sets of mini 8-ohm speakers, (d) endless loop cassette tapes (the type that are used for telephone answering machines), (e) a sound level meter, and (f) a microphone.

The configuration shown in Fig. 1.1 is used for individual subliminal treatment as well as for the preparation of subliminal tapes for clients to use in their home environments. The speakers are situated at least 1 meter away from the subject's ear and the configuration is symmetrical for both sides of the subject's head. The advantage of this system is that one can always determine that the subliminal message is, in fact, being presented because it is measurable at the speaker. One can control the subliminal range of the stimulus by manipulating the volume level of the message as presented at the speaker, by varying the distance between the speaker and the subject's ear, and by varying the volume of background sound. Further, the ambient sound level in the room can be accurately maintained by controlling the level of white noise being presented through one of the sets of loudspeakers. To determine the actual sound pressure level at the subject's ear, one can make several measurements in the supraliminal range and then extrapolate it to subliminal ranges. Hence, a sound of 42 decibels (42 dB(A)), measured at the speaker drops to about 15 dB(A) at the subject's ear when the speakers are 1 meter from the subject. If the room sound pressure level was 34 dB(A), the subliminal signal would be reported as -19 dB(A) relative to ambient.

Table 1.1 provides examples of three extrapolated dB levels as measured in a room with a background ambient of 34 dB(A). In my facility, I use three tape players, which permits sequencing of different messages, and provide one tape player for presenting ambient or embedding sound. The recorder is connected to a microphone that can be used to make subliminal tapes for clients' home use. Because recording levels are higher for the preparation of tapes, this generally occurs without the client present.

TABLE 1.1
Example of Interpolation of Drop in Sound Pressure Level [dB(A)] as a
Function of Distance from Sound Source. (Room Ambient = 34 dB(A))

	Sound Pressure Level					
			Distance from Source			
Source	1m	Drop (dB)	1½m	Drop (dB)	2m	Drop (dB)
95	69	26	67	28	65	30
90	63	27	61	29	59	31
85	58	27	56	29	54	31
80	53	27	50	30	49	31
75	49	26	47	28	45	30
70	43	27	42	28	41	29
65	39	26	38	27	37	28
Average Drop		26.6		28.4		30.0

Some subliminal messages are presented in the subject's own voice. It is important that the recorder have a defeatable automatic gain control. Automatic gain control adjusts the recording level automatically as the sound levels change. This is not a useful device when attempting to make subliminal materials. If automatic gain control is used and a stimulus is presented at 40 decibels, and then another stimulus is presented at 50 decibels, the automatic gain control feature will modify the recording gain to minimize the differences in the signal. Because the embedding sound is always considerably louder than the subliminal message, the automatic gain control tracks the loudest sound with the attendant potential loss of the subliminal signal.

The procedure one may use for group treatment is shown in Fig. 1.2. As the figure indicates, the procedure is relatively simple. One needs only a loudspeaker connected to a tape recorder with the clients or subjects seated in a fixed position relative to the speaker. Again, by extrapolation, one can determine the exact sound pressure level impinging on the subject who is seated at a specific distance from the loudspeaker. Speakers have a directional range and it is important to determine that range prior to treatment. This is accomplished with the use of a constant tone and a sound level meter. As shown in the figure, the loudspeaker used in this example had a stable directional arc of 60 degrees.

PROCEDURE

It is important to be able to strictly specify the technical properties associated with the stimulus-response relationship in order to provide clinicians with methods for reliably eliciting subliminal effects. The most

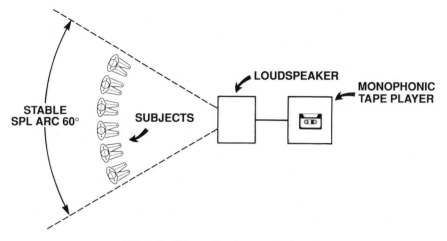

FIG. 1.2.   Schematic of group treatment.

critical aspect is the determination of thresholds. Generally it is the objectively determined thresholds that are of paramount importance when conducting research on clinical populations. Subjectively determined thresholds may, however, be of clinical use or importance. Often we want to present the subliminal messages at a level that is marginally detectable to the client. We do this to enhance credibility, expectation, and placebo effects. Under such conditions, determination of subjective threshold may be useful because, although the client feels as though he or she cannot discriminate, he or she is aware that a signal is, in fact, being presented.

The subliminal stimulus is defined in terms of Sound Pressure Level (SPL) of the signal relative to ambient. The unit of measurement is the decibel (dB) on the A scale. The A scale most closely represents the frequency characteristics of human hearing. Stimulus characteristics are reported in terms of – dB relative to ambient or relative to some objectively or subjectively determined threshold. The most straightforward system is to measure ambient sound level in a room and, as described earlier, determine SPL of the signal by interpolation. The subliminal sound level is reported in terms of – dB relative to ambient dB. The ambient sound level may be the SPL in a room or the SPL in a room with some added embedding medium such as white noise.

When using music as an embedding medium, the music varies in intensity as does the subliminal message. Therefore, one of the more difficult aspects of the preparation of subliminal auditory materials is that of keeping the message at a relatively constant dB level below ambient. The tapes prepared in our sound studios are electronically manipulated to maintain a relatively constant level of signal to ambient. When professional equipment is not available, white noise tends to be an easier embedding medium to work with because it maintains a constant SPL.

When working with equipment that does not have digitizing or electronic clipping capability we present our messages in the − 15 to − 25dB range relative to room ambient. The subliminal and ambient sound levels are adjusted so that the peak maximum subliminal SPL never exceeds − 15 dB relative to ambient. By keeping the subliminal sound at least 15 dB below the embedding sound the message is always maintained below the detection threshold.

There are occasions when one might want the subliminal message to "leak" into the supraliminal range. Leakage can occur when the sound of the embedding music drops but the sound level of the message remains relatively constant (see Fig. 1.3). For research purposes, we are very cautious about leakage. In clinical practice, on the other hand, it may be desirable to develop tapes that have a degree of leakage in them for reasons already stated.

Leakage also varies with the frequency of the subliminal sound. Thus, with a constant embedding sound, detection of the embedded message will vary as a function of the frequency of the embedded message. Therefore, male and female voices of identical sound levels will differ in terms of detectability when embedded in an identical white noise medium.

The two measurements of importance are (a) the ambient sound of the room in which treatment is to take place and (b) the output level of the subliminal message as measured at the loudspeaker. In open environments one always measures subliminal sound level relative to room ambient sound level. Thus if the ambient sound level in the room is 40 dB(A) a subliminal message extrapolated to be 25 dB(A) is reported as a − 15 dB(A) signal. It is important to note that when we are talking about *subliminal* we are not talking about range below a subject's hearing threshold, rather

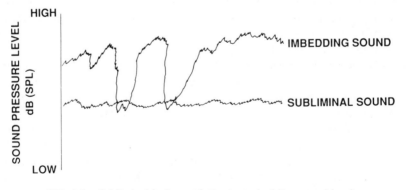

FIG. 1.3.   Subliminal leakage relative to embedding sound level.

we are making our references relative to the ambient or background sound in the environment. Thus, a signal of 25, 50, or 75 dB(A) would be reported as a − 15 dB(A) signal in environments that were 40, 65, or 90 dB(A), respectively. Similarly, when preparing and reporting the details associated with subliminal materials to be used in the home environment, one reports signal levels relative to the embedding background sound. As discussed in another section of this guide, embedding background can vary considerably along a number of different dimensions. If the background ambient is not constant, then further details must be provided. The most straightforward embedding background is white noise that may be maintained at a constant level relative to the subliminal message. When music is used as the embedding medium, a number of issues, discussed elsewhere in this guide, become important. From a technical perspective, however, one must exercise care that the subliminal message does not become supraliminal (leak) when the music stops, pauses, or drops below some critical volume. In practice, I generally listen to the recorded music with a stopwatch so that I can establish just when to terminate the subliminal message during quiet passages in the music. I may adjust the music so that, with the exception of certain specific sections of the music, the minimal sound pressure level as measured at the microphone is 65 dB(A). The subliminal message is then presented at a maximum level of 50 dB(A) as measured at the microphone which, of course, results in the subliminal message being presented at − 15 dB(A). This position of the subliminal message relative to the embedding music is maintained when clients adjust the music to the level that is most effective. Therefore, when providing auditory subliminal treatment to a client in a clinical setting, the message is generally presented at a subliminal level relative to room ambient levels or ambient levels that are adjusted with constant white noise. When preparing subliminal tapes for home use, the signals are always presented at supraliminal levels, and the subliminal property of the message is obtained by embedding the message in background music or some other controllable sound. When recording material for home use, the subliminal message is presented at a level at which it could, in the absence of a background embedding sound level, be recorded at a supraliminal level. We follow this procedure, obviously, to be absolutely sure that a message has in fact been recorded.

For measurement procedures I use a constant 300 Hz (cycles per second) tone or white noise recorded on a 20-second endless cassette tape. By taking readings that are at the supraliminal level at both the speaker and at the position where the subject's ear will be, one can extrapolate into the subliminal ranges. White background noise can be recorded on endless tape or one of the commercially available sound screens designed to mask conversation in psychotherapy offices can be used. One can get an embedding type of white noise by simply recording the sound of rushing air from a fan or from the speaker of a radio or TV that is tuned off a station. Further, one can spend a lot of money on sound level meters. The advantage of using distance from the speaker to the subject as the method for controlling sound pressure level is that inexpensive sound level meters are adequate for measurement purposes.

The preceding procedure for preparing tapes, although relatively economical and effective, is not the procedure that I presently use; my tapes are now studio produced. Research materials, tapes for student projects, and special tapes made from clients' own voices, however, are still prepared following the procedure just described.

THRESHOLD DETERMINATION

Now, although we can very precisely measure the level of the subliminal message relative to ambient sound levels, it must be recognized that a person's auditory acuity is a factor that must be considered. When conducting research with sizeable student populations, in general, one can ignore individual hearing acuity because, with large numbers of subjects in each experimental condition, random assignment will balance differences across conditions so that group main effects of treatment can be determined. In the clinical context, however, the client's hearing acuity becomes an important factor that must be considered. In individual treatment we want to be certain that the subliminal message is presented at a specific level below the client's hearing threshold. The determination of that threshold can be accomplished in several ways, none of which are particularly time-consuming. The first issue, however, is whether to determine the client's threshold for reliable discrimination of the presence or absence of the signal, or to establish the threshold for reliable discrimination of content of the message. Again, this is not as straightforward as it might at first appear. If I present the letters "a," "b," "c," and "d," randomly at, say, 10-sec intervals, the client's ability to reliably identify the presented letter is going to be strongly affected by knowing the message set from which the letter is to be drawn. Similarly, if I present single words such as "happy," "calm," and "peaceful" a recognition procedure will reveal a lower threshold than a blind procedure. Further, if I present a dialogue consisting of, say, 10 sentences, the client may be able to identify some words and may interpret some words incorrectly.

Now to further complicate the issue, clients could identify messages on the basis of affect rather than on the basis of meaning. Recall that Zajonc (1980) reported that subjects could discriminate stimuli on the basis of affect that could not be cognitively discriminated. Similarly, a subliminal message could influence a client affectively and, should the client be attending to affect, above-chance discrimination could occur. One might be inclined to believe that only affectively meaningful stimuli such as the words "happy," "calm," or "shit" could be discriminated affectively. Research has indicated, however, that nonmeaningful stimuli such as pure tones or white noise presented subliminally can enhance performance; this presumably indicates enhanced arousal (Zenhausern, Pompo, & Ciaiola, 1974).

I do not mean to dwell on the complexity of the procedure, but it is important to be mindful of the factors that are likely to be operative when working with subliminal stimuli. In my practice I generally determine threshold by moving the speaker closer to the client's ear and then moving it away from the ear in systematic steps. At each position I present letters of the alphabet randomly with regard to both time and sequence. The client's task is to indicate when the stimulus is being presented, by raising a finger, and to write down on a sheet of paper the identity of the letter if the client believes that he or she heard it. Using this variation on the method of limits I can quickly establish the approximate threshold for detection and the threshold for recognition of content. In practice the detection threshold is used as my reference for presenting the subliminal message. By referring to Table 1.1, I am able to determine the distance the speaker must be from the client to present the subliminal message at the particular level desired.

It is important to remember that hearing thresholds may not be the same for both ears and that the threshold is not static, but varies both in the long and the short term. In practice, within-session variation in threshold is not a concern but the session-to-session variation may be considerable.

For materials that are prepared for the client's home use, threshold determination is not an issue. Likewise, if one uses the embedding procedure in treatment, thresholds need not be determined. Given that the subliminal message is always maintained at a particular level relative to the embedding medium, the subliminal message will always remain at a specified level below the embedding sound regardless of how loudly the tape is played.

The controversy surrounding the concept of subliminal perception centers on the issue of thresholds. Although the influence of stimuli processed outside of consciousness can be demonstrated (Bowers, 1984, 1987; Zajonc, 1980), Goldiamond's (1958) early hesitancy regarding subliminal perception remains. If a subject can detect stimulus presentation, then the possibility of responding to partial cues becomes paramount. It is testimony to the fact that "major breakthroughs" (Goldiamond, 1958, p. 373) in experimental methodology do not herald scientific settlement of important issues. Although Goldiamond pointed out that signal detection methodology would probably find subliminal perception to be an artifact of differences in variance and reliability between semantic and accuracy indicators of signals, the squabble regarding this issue remains (Balay & Shevrin, 1988; Cheeseman & Merikle, 1986; Marcel, 1983 a, 1983 b; Moore, 1989).

Part of the difficulty is that researchers in subliminal perception tend to use the visual modality with tachistoscopic research preparations. Although I strongly endorse the use of visual subliminal stimuli for clinical purposes where client well-being is the dependent measure, it seems to me that visual preparations are least suitable for research on the process of subliminal perception. The research and technical aspects of visual subliminal procedures in clinical contexts are reviewed later in this guide. For present purposes suffice it to say that visual stimuli are rendered subliminal by varying the signal energy or persistence. This is accomplished by varying the duration of stimulus presentation, by varying signal intensity relative to background, and by masking the perceptual persistence of the stimulus by presenting another visual stimulus immediately after target signal offset. Although every sensory modality probably has a subliminal range (Dixon, 1987), in my judgment the auditory modality is most appropriate for research purposes and is certainly most convenient for clinical purposes.

Although there are three aspects of subliminality (i.e., the stimulus, the response, and the connection between stimulus and response) clinicians will generally be concerned primarily with the properties of the stimulus that render the stimulus subliminal. Generally one is concerned with the difference in sound pressure level between an ambient sound in a room or an ambient sound on a tape-recorded presentation and the sound pressure level of the message or signal. The difference between ambient and signal in decibels is the critical technical property associated with subliminal treatment procedures.

Although we specify that for a particular presentation, the subliminal message is, let us say, -20 dB(A) relative to the sound pressure level of the ambient or embedding medium, the concept of subliminality refers to the relationship of the message to some threshold value as determined by the subject's ability to process the information. As shown in Fig. 1.4, there are many thresholds that can be determined associated with the presentation of subliminal material. The ordinant is the dimension of sound pressure level, measured in decibels, ranging from high to low. Again, this can be conceptualized as the range of sound pressure level below that of room ambient or of the embedding medium. The objective thresholds are shown on the left side of the figure, and the subjective thresholds are shown on the right side of the figure. The distinction between objective and subjective thresholds is extremely important. The

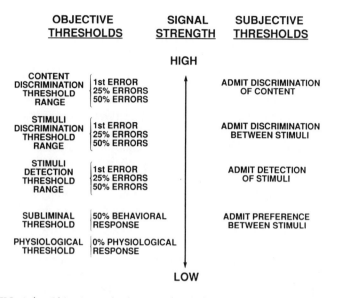

OBJECTIVE THRESHOLDS	SIGNAL STRENGTH	SUBJECTIVE THRESHOLDS
	HIGH	
CONTENT DISCRIMINATION THRESHOLD RANGE	1st ERROR 25% ERRORS 50% ERRORS	ADMIT DISCRIMINATION OF CONTENT
STIMULI DISCRIMINATION THRESHOLD RANGE	1st ERROR 25% ERRORS 50% ERRORS	ADMIT DISCRIMINATION BETWEEN STIMULI
STIMULI DETECTION THRESHOLD RANGE	1st ERROR 25% ERRORS 50% ERRORS	ADMIT DETECTION OF STIMULI
SUBLIMINAL THRESHOLD	50% BEHAVIORAL RESPONSE	ADMIT PREFERENCE BETWEEN STIMULI
PHYSIOLOGICAL THRESHOLD	0% PHYSIOLOGICAL RESPONSE	
	LOW	

FIG. 1.4.   Objective and subjective thresholds for the determination of subliminal range.

subjective discrimination threshold refers to the point at which the subject or client indicates that he or she can discriminate the content of the message. For example, if one were presenting the words "happy" and "sad" the subjective discrimination threshold is the point at which a person indicates that he or she is able to identify the word "happy" and the word "sad." A second subjective discrimination threshold is the ability to discriminate between content but not be able to identify the content. For example, one might present again the words "happy" and "sad" and ask the client to report when he or she feels as though he or she can tell the difference between the two signals but cannot describe the content of the signals. The third subjective threshold is that of detection in which the client reports when he or she can detect that a signal is being presented even though he or she cannot discriminate between signals or discriminate the content of the signal. One should always keep in mind that the subjective threshold is exactly that. It is the point at which clients indicate that, in their judgment, they feel as though they can discriminate the content, discriminate between signals, or identify the presence or absence of the signal.

Objective thresholds are based on the use of a psychophysical method for the purposes of determining chance level thresholds. For the discrimination threshold, for example, one would require that the client choose among the signals that are presented on every occasion in which the stimuli are presented, until the chance level is achieved. For example, if the words were "happy" and "sad," one would randomly present the words "happy" and "sad" and require the client to indicate which word was presented, even if the client has to guess. Clearly when the client is able to discriminate, the hit rate will be at or near 100%. The objective discrimination threshold will be attained when the person's hit rate no longer exceeds chance. It is important to note that one must descend from above-chance performance to arrive at the sound pressure level where discrimination first falls to chance level. Clearly if one continues to reduce the sound pressure level of the signal using a forced-choice method, discrimination will remain at 50%, regardless of how low the sound pressure level becomes. The 50% discrimination level for content will be at a higher sound pressure level than the 50% discrimination threshold between stimuli. For example, one might ask the individual to respond in a yes/no fashion to a discrimination between a stimulus and to the immediately preceding stimulus on the basis of whether it is the same or different. Again one will arrive at a point at which the client's ability to discriminate whether a signal is the same or different from the signal that had immediately preceded it does not exceed chance. The third threshold is the threshold of detection in which the client is required to indicate the presence or absence of the signal on any particular trial. One will arrive at a 50% level in which the client's accuracy and ability to detect when a signal is being presented will be no better than chance. Finally, we have the behavioral threshold in which the effect of the stimulus on some designated behavior of the client first arrives at the 50% or chance level. As is discussed in detail later in this book, we have found the most effective range of subliminal messages to be below the objective detection threshold.

Fisher (1975, 1976) developed a straightforward method for assuring that auditory messages were present and subliminal. He varied the sound volume until the content of the message could be distinctly heard when one's ear was directly in contact with a loudspeaker but could not be detected at a distance of 1 meter from the speaker. Independent judges could not detect when the message was being delivered, thus, they were at or below the detection threshold. Fisher reported that this procedure resulted in a message of approximately 42.5 dB in an ambient environment of 40 dB. This procedure appears to be ideal and, as we discussed earlier, presents messages in the effective subliminal range of -15 to -25 dB(A) when the subject's ear is about 1 meter from the speaker.

In practice, one generally uses the detection threshold of either the objective or subjective variety. There are occasions when one might prefer to use the subjective threshold, but for research purposes one should always use the objective threshold. The work to be reported from our laboratories makes use of the objective detection threshold as reference. Hence the messages are clearly subliminal: The subject cannot detect when the message is being presented. I should add, again, that this threshold is determined under forced-choice conditions. Thus, with this technique we can put to bed the partial-cue explanation of subliminal effects.

Borgeat, Elie, Chaloult, and Chabot (1985) reported a study on the effect of auditory subliminal stimuli on psychophysiological responses. Following a taboo-word design, subjects were presented with two sets of three words each: one set was emotional with the words "rape," "whore," "penis," and the second set contained neutral words—"veil," "skates," "tennis" (this study was conducted in French and these words were reported to be phonetically balanced with comparable utilization frequencies in French). Physiological measures were obtained from the frontalis muscles (electromyographic signals), skin conductance response, and heart rate. The experimental procedure involved having the subject listen to either the emotional or the neutral words repeated twice at each of 7 sound pressure levels. The subjects were asked to respond by pushing a button to indicate whether they could identify the content of the stimuli or whether they could detect the presence or absence of the stimulus. Skin conductance and frontalis EMG physiological effects were noted in the range of − 15 dB(A) up to identification threshold.

It should be kept in mind that these thresholds are subjective thresholds. The heart rate data reveal the possible contaminating effect of using a subjective threshold in subliminal research. Figure 1.5 shows the heart

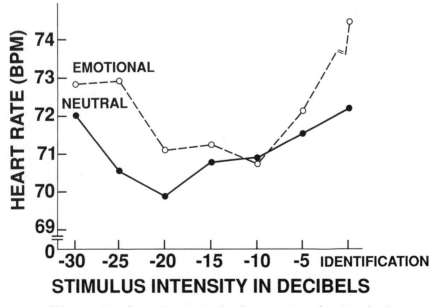

FIG. 1.5.   Mean heart rate associated with presentation of emotional and neutral words (from Borgeat et al., 1985).

rate data for the emotional and the neutral stimuli. Note that effects appear in the − 25 dB and − 30 dB range and then reappear in the − 10 dB and above range. Because subjective thresholds were used, it is possible that subjects were able to discriminate content at the levels considered to be subliminal even though they could not articulate this. The physiological differences between the emotional and the neutral set in the − 25 dB and − 30 dB range appear to be a true subliminal effect. Subjects are most probably below the objective detection threshold when in the − 25 dB range relative to the subjective identification threshold. Borgeat and his colleagues (Borgeat, Boissonneault, & Chaloult, 1989; Borgeat, Chabot, & Chaloult, 1981; Borgeat & Goulet, 1983) reported several studies in which subliminal suggestions for activation and/or relaxation deactivation were found to differentially influence the level of activation as measured by an adjective checklist and increased physiological response to a stressful task.

An honors thesis research project conducted in our laboratories by Steve Hutchinson determined the critical ranges of subliminal susceptibility for males and females utilizing the 75% objective recognition threshold as reference. Using a forced-choice guessing paradigm, 15 males and 13 females participated in an auditory letter-detection task at 8 subliminal intensities ranging from objective detection threshold to − 40 dB(A). The study involved auditory presentation of the letters "a," "e," "l," and "n" in random order at 5-sec intervals, five times each at every sound pressure level. The auditory intensities of the 4 letters were within a 3-decibel range. Subjects, seated at a table, wore headphones through which the white noise embedding medium and the subliminal letters were presented. The room was equipped with an intercom system so that the subject could communicate with the experimenter. Each trial consisted of the presentation of one of the letters simultaneously with a light signal following which the subject was required to guess which of the four letters had been presented. Individual objective detection thresholds were determined by the method of limits. Subjects were required to indicate whether they heard "something" through the white noise and secondly to guess which of the letters had been presented if they indicated that they had heard something. Signal level was adjusted until a threshold of approximately 75% stimulus identification was achieved with the provision that the subject could not identify the presence or absence of the signal at − 5 dB(A) relative to that 75% threshold. Thus, two thresholds were obtained, separated by 5 dB(A). The first threshold is that at which the subjects achieved approximately 75% stimulus identification (i.e., were able to correctly identify the letter with approximately 75% accuracy). The second threshold, 5 dB(A) below the first, was that at which the subject could not detect the presence of the signal with greater than chance accuracy.

All data are presented relative to the first threshold (defined as zero), at which the subject was able to correctly identify the letter with 75% probability. Each of the other levels is at – 5 dB stages relative to that zero threshold. It should be recalled, however, that the – 5 dB range would be at or close to the objective stimulus detection threshold at which presence or absence of the signal could be detected with a probability no greater than chance.

Subsequent to threshold determination, the eight subliminal intensities (– 40 dB through – 5 dB, at – 5 dB intervals) were tested for percent accurate letter identification. At each level, each letter was presented five times with a total of 20 trials per level. The sequence started at – 40 dB and progressed up through and including – 5 dB. Using the multiplication theorem of probabilities (Ferguson, 1981) the probabilities associated with obtaining greater than chance accuracy at each level were determined. Chance expectation, of course, is five correct identifications. Seven correct identifications has a probability of .063 and eight correct identifications has a probability of .016. For the purposes of the present study, subjects who obtained a level of eight or more correct responses during a sequence were considered to have better than chance performance. Individuals who had at least one performance at better than chance level were tested again at a later date to determine the reliability. A total of 28 subjects completed the experiment. Five of 15 males (33%) and 10 of 13 females (77%) scored better than chance at one or more subliminal intensities. The mean detection level at threshold was 79%, satisfying the requirement of approximately 75% accuracy at threshold level.

Of the individuals who had greater than chance subliminal performance in Phase 1, 66% of the males and 75% of the females retested had a greater than chance performance at one or more subliminal intensities. Further, all retested subjects had greater than chance accuracy at threshold with an overall accuracy rate of 78.5%. The data for the males and females who achieved greater than chance accuracy levels at one or more subliminal intensities are shown in Fig. 1.6 plotted in terms of percent of subliminal hits (i.e., performance that was greater than chance accuracy). Figure 1.7 shows the combined data for males and females who demonstrated greater than chance accuracy at one or more subliminal intensities.

Peak subliminal performance occurred at – 15 dB for males and – 25 dB for females. These percentages were calculated on data from both the original test and the retest. It is interesting to note that no hits were scored at – 40 dB or – 5 dB and that 77% of all subliminal hits occurred at – 15, – 20, and – 25 dB. Although males' peak susceptibility level is approximately – 15 dB, whereas females' susceptibility level peaks at about – 25 dB, both males and females do appear to be susceptible over the entire – 15 to – 25 dB range.

The fact that there were no hits at the – 5 dB level is of particular interest. As is discussed later, it has been postulated that there may be two separate or at least discontinuous processing systems for information

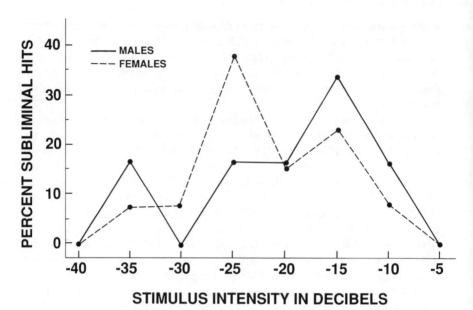

FIG. 1.6.   Percentage of total subliminal hits for females and males as a function of stimulus intensity.

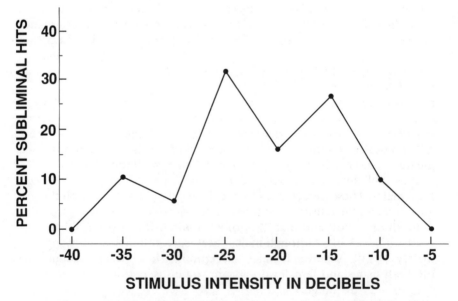

FIG. 1.7.   Percentage of total subliminal hits as a function of stimulus intensity.

presented to the auditory system. In terms of a dual processing theory, a "dead zone" at about the detection level threshold would appear to be functional to facilitate some degree of independence between supraliminal and subliminal influences.

As the data from this study indicate, the determination of thresholds is of critical importance when applying subliminal stimuli in treatment context. Although the use of subjective threshold determination may be useful in a clinical context, objective threshold determination is required if we wish to be certain that we are presenting our stimuli in subliminal ranges. Subjectively determined thresholds lead one to question the accuracy of statements about subliminal influence given that partial discrimination of marginal stimuli may be apparent and responsible for subject's behavior.

DICHOTOMOUS PROCEDURES

Subliminal procedures vary considerably. In addition to the auditory and visual procedures of clinical usefulness that are the focus of the present guide, subliminal research preparations include dichotic listening, dichoptic viewing, and theta state conditional listening. In dichotic listening, material is presented to one ear with instructions to perform a task that forces the subject to attend to that channel. For example, the subject might be asked to echo (i.e., repeat out loud) letters that are rapidly presented to one ear. While the subject is attending to the one channel, material is presented to the other nonattended ear. This material is outside of subject awareness but has been found to influence ongoing tasks and such subliminally presented information is stored in memory (see Corteen & Wood, 1972; Fowler, Wolford, Slade, Tassinary, 1981; Lewis, 1970; MacKay, 1973; Marcel, 1983a, 1983b). Similarly, visual material presented to the nonattended channel in a dichoptic viewing situation also appears to be out of awareness, but nonetheless exerts demonstrable influence on material presented in the attended visual channel (Somekh & Wilding, 1973).

CHAPTER TWO

Research on the Effects
of Auditory
Subliminal Messages

Now that subliminal perception is again respectable, research on some intriguing issues is appearing in our main-line journals. The evidence for subliminal influence on cognitions and behavior is compelling. It is apparent that attention to threshold determination is most critical. Very different effects of low energy messages will be obtained with very minor alterations of the signal energy. The difference between detection and discrimination thresholds may be less than 5 dB(A) in the auditory modality and less than 5 msec in the visual modality. Groeger (1986a, 1986b, 1989) showed that subjects are more likely to process different aspects of the stimulus depending on level of stimulus presentation.

SUBLIMINAL INTRUSIONS
INTO THOUGHT PROCESSES

To determine if auditory subliminal stimuli can intrude into thought processes, individuals were asked to simply write down anything that came into their minds while being exposed to subliminal messages. The study took place in a large room equipped with a tape recorder and two loudspeakers. Subjects were seated 2.5 meters or 4.5 meters from the loudspeakers. All subjects knew that subliminal messages were going to be presented.

The study consisted of playing 4-minute sections from 12 audio cassettes. The ambient SPL was 60 dB(A) and the signals were 62 dB(A) peak as measured at the speaker. Of the 12 tapes, 9 were blank and 3 contained subliminal messages. Tapes 3, 6, and 9 contained the subliminal messages. On Tape 3, the word "hair" was repeated at the rate of 13 repetitions every 20 seconds. On Tape 6, the numbers "2," "4," "6," and "8" were presented at 3-second intervals. The total number sequence was repeated 4 times every 20 seconds. On Tape 9, the word "war" was presented at the rate of 13 repetitions every 20 seconds.

After each tape was inserted and started, the subjects were required to sit silently for 2 minutes and then for the following 2 minutes to jot down, in point form, anything that crossed their mind. The responses were anonymous and subjects were encouraged not to filter or censor their thought processes.

The results indicate that there was some restraint, in that there was virtually no rude language and, on average, less than one sexual item per subject over the entire 48-minute study. However, analyzing the data for the presence of the words and numbers presented in the subliminal messages, it was apparent that the messages did, in fact, intrude upon thought processes. Given that the subliminal messages were presented on Tapes 3, 6, and 9, the frequency of "hair" and hair-related words on Tapes 1 and 2 was compared with the frequency of "hair" and hair-related words on Tapes 3 through 12. Similarly, the frequency of numbers appearing in the responses to Tapes 1 through 5 was compared with the average frequency of numbers responses for Tapes 6 through 12. Finally, the average frequency of "war" and war-related words occurring in response to Tapes 1 through 8 was compared with the average frequency of "war" and war-related words to Tapes 9 through 12. This procedure offers a good comparison because one is looking at the average frequency of response both prior to and following the subliminal message, which was equally distributed throughout the 12-tape study. Figure 2.1 shows the average frequency of response prior to and after the subliminal presentation. In all cases, the frequency during and after the subliminal message exceeds the frequency prior to the subliminal message. For the word "hair," on average, there was one response per subject prior to the introduction of the stimulus and 1.6 following. For numbers it was .2 prior and 1.4 following the subliminal message. For the word "war," the average frequency was 2.2 prior and 3.2 following the presentation of the subliminal message. The probability that any target word would appear in a subject's listing prior to subliminal presentation was .32 whereas the probability following subliminal presentation was .57 ($t(14)$ = 2.08, p = .027).

The previous study indicates that thoughts appear to be influenced by one-word subliminal messages. The following studies were designed to determine if such simple messages could influence the content and emotional tone of thought processes as reflected in written fiction. In all three of the following studies, subjects who were unaware of being

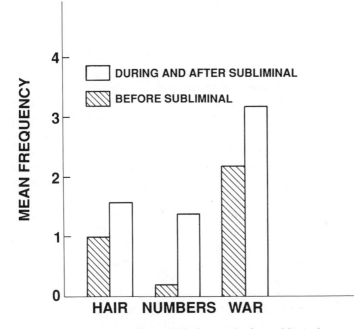

FIG. 2.1. Frequency of words before and after subliminal message presentation.

exposed to subliminal messages were asked to write a brief story suitable for children. The frequency of occurrence of the words that had been presented in the subliminal message appearing in the stories, as well as the emotional tone of the stories as rated by independent judges, were the dependent measures.

Thirty-one male and female college students were asked to participate in a study "designed to determine the nature of children's stories stimulated by certain types of pictures." Groups of subjects were exposed to one of three conditions in which they viewed a slide-projected picture of a painting for 30 seconds. The slide was then turned off and they were asked to write a story appropriate for children between the ages of approximately 7 and 10 years. Subjects were only permitted 3 minutes to write the story. Prior to presentation of the slide, the subliminal stimulus was presented for 45 seconds so that, in total, the subliminal stimulus was presented for 1 minute and 15 seconds.

Subjects were seated in a single row at a distance from the loudspeakers that resulted in the subliminal message being 15 to 18 dB(A) below room ambient. The loudspeakers used for this study were those that were recessed into the walls as a permanent part of the room's audiovisual system.

Three conditions were introduced in the study. In Condition 1, three words, such as *friends, clothes*, and *letter*, were presented by a male voice, followed immediately by a female voice repeating three different words. Condition 2 was a reversal of these conditions with the female voice preceding the male and the Condition 3 was a white-noise control. Stimulus words were repeated at the rate of one per second.

After writing the story, the subjects were given a list of 25 words which contained the 6 words that had been presented subliminally. They were asked to rate each of the concepts or objects as to the degree of appropriateness for a children's story. Subjects rated each word on a 100-point scale where 0 indicated that the word or concept was *not appropriate* for a children's story and 100 indicated *very appropriate*.

Even with this severely time-limited protocol, evidence of subliminal intrusion on thought processes was evident. The results of this study are interesting in that all of the effects were specific to the female voice and the effect appeared to be limited to the male subjects. The frequency of inclusions of the subliminal words showed no difference between experimental and control conditions for the female subjects (23% versus 27%). For the male subjects, the difference between experimental and control conditions was significant (27% versus 5% of the stories contained target words for the experimental and control groups, respectively, $p = .001$).

Ratings of the subliminally presented concepts in terms of their appropriateness for children's stories also indicated a superiority of the subliminal female voice for both male and female subjects. The superiority of the female voice was, however, greater for male subjects (for females: 74.5 versus 81.1 for the male and female voice, respectively $p = .11$; for males: 70.1 versus 85.1 for the male and female voice, respectively $p = .06$). Overall, however, there were no significant differences in the ratings of the appropriateness of the words between experimental and control conditions.

David Mibashan conducted a pilot study in our laboratories using a similar story-writing procedure. Female subjects were asked to write a story suitable for a child of about 10 years of age. Subjects were asked to take 5 minutes to think about the details of the story they were going to write and then were allowed 15 minutes to actually write the story. The subliminal messages "happy, fast, courageous" or "sad, slow, coward" were presented to the subjects in the *happy* or *sad* group, respectively. The messages were presented continuously over the 20-minute session with each word being separated by a 5-second interval. The messages were presented via loudspeakers located approximately 1 meter from the subject. The subliminal SPL at the subject's ear was approximately -18 dB(A). Subjects were not aware that subliminal messages were being presented.

Judges rated the affective tone of the stories on a *happy-sad* bipolar scale, ranging from 0 to 99: the higher the score, the happier the rating.

The agreement between judges was $r = .86$. The results indicated a reliable effect of the subliminal messages. The average rating of the stories of subjects in the happy group was 71, whereas the stories of the sad group received an average rating of 27 ($p = .004$).

Examples of the first three sentences of a story taken from each of the two conditions leads one to conclude that the effect of auditory subliminal messages on creative thought processes may be considerable. The following is from the happy message group: "Once upon a time there was a little monkey named Mikey. Mikey was a happy, active little monkey. He was always trying something new in his spare time." A subject in the sad message group, on the other hand, wrote: "It was Sten's birthday. He was 6 years old. 'What an awfully long time to be alive,' was his first thought when he woke up."

SUBLIMINAL INFLUENCES
ON PROBLEM SOLVING AND MEMORY

Many of our studies, as well as those in the literature, indicate quite persuasively that subliminal messages can intrude into a person's thought processes. An interesting question that derives from this research is the extent to which this intrusion might aid in more efficient or selective retrieval of information from short- and long-term memory or aid in problem solving. That is, if the solutions or hints to solutions to problems are presented subliminally, can people solve puzzles more rapidly? Several studies (unpublished) that address this issue have been conducted in our laboratories. Kim De Champlain and Christine Gibson, for example, had male and female subjects solve a puzzle that required them to identify seven minor differences between two very similar schematic pictures. The puzzle was taken from a series entitled "Eye Twister" published daily in the local newspaper. Half of the subjects completed the task in the presence of white noise whereas the experimental subjects were exposed to white noise plus -15 dB(A) subliminal hints as to the location of the differences (e.g., words such as *antenna*, *footsteps*, and *crater*).

The time required to solve the puzzle (i.e., finding seven of eight actual differences) was the dependent measure and indicated no effects on male subjects (M = 4.93 and 4.90 minutes) but an effect on female problem-solving time (M = 5.66 and 3.47 for the control and experimental groups respectively; $t(8) = 1.52, p < .09$). Whether these results indicate a greater receptivity of females to subliminal influence or a ceiling effect for male problem-solving speed, of course, cannot be determined.

A similar study conducted in our laboratories by Tanto Battisti, Wendy Ryan, and Annu Wadehra was designed to determine if anagram solution time could be influenced by subliminal primes. Research on anagram solving (Marx, 1982; Seidenstadt, 1982) demonstrates that supraliminal priming (e.g., presenting word lists containing solutions) decreases solution time for difficult anagrams. Further, primer words not recalled in a free recall test were more effective as solution facilitators as compared with recalled primes.

Male and female undergraduates who were aware of the possibility that subliminal messages might be presented solved five 5-letter anagrams of either a high level of difficulty (e.g., ITVLA—VITAL) or a low level of difficulty (e.g., KCLER—CLERK) under timed conditions. Half of the subjects completed the anagram task under conditions of exposure to white noise, whereas the second half of the subjects completed the anagram task while exposed to white noise plus a -15 dB(A) prime of the five solutions to the anagram. The solution words were presented continuously at 1-second intervals by a female voice.

The results were quite consistent with research on supraliminal primes of anagram solving. Overall, the subjects exposed to the subliminal primes solved the anagrams faster than the subjects exposed to the white noise only (M = 21.1 seconds and 53.4 seconds, respectively; $F(1,28) = 13.9$, $p < .001$). A two-way interaction revealed that the effect was reliable only for the difficult anagrams. Time of exposure to the subliminal primes prior to the start of the anagram solving task was not rigorously controlled and varied from approximately 46 to 168 seconds. Although reanalysis of the data with exposure time as a covariate had no effect on the results, it was found that solution time was negatively correlated with time of exposure to the subliminal primes ($r(13) = -42, p = .059$).

Dixon (1981) maintained that external stimuli of which a person is totally unaware may exercise a selective function on memory and influence conscious recall. Further, such influences may bring about the emergence into consciousness of material in long-term memory. We have all had many experiences of memories arising into consciousness without apparent stimulus prompting. Often we can analyze the sequence of external events that stimulated recall. On the other hand, we are often unaware of the conditions that gave rise to recall of a previous experience. Further, internal stimuli can often evoke memories of a particular emotional motif. When we are tired, sad, or anxious, for example, our thoughts are likely to be complementary to our emotional state.

A question of interest is the extent to which subliminal prompts may influence selective retrieval of information in short-term memory. A study conducted in our laboratories by Marek Senkowski and Chantal Mazur was designed to determine if information incidentally learned could be influenced by presentation of a subliminal category prompt during encoding and/or retrieval of information relevant to a word puzzle task.

Subjects (48 males and females) were given a list of 75 three- or four-letter words and asked to perform four simple tasks which involved counting the number of words containing certain letters and the total number of words in the list. This procedure required the subjects to review the list four times to complete the four tasks. No reference was made to the content of the lists that would encourage subjects to attempt to recall the words. After completion of the tasks the list was removed and a second list of 25 incomplete words was given to each subject with the instruction to fill in the missing letters (e.g., C__PE). Seven of the 25 incomplete words could be completed with letters that would result in an animal word or an inanimate object word (e.g., deer or door). The initial list of 75 words contained all of the solution words for the inanimate objects but two solutions for the seven critical items, one animal (e.g., deer), and one inanimate (e.g., door).

The experimental manipulation consisted of the presentation of the word "animal" at 15 dB(A) below the imbedding white noise medium, whereas control subjects were exposed to the white noise only. The subliminal prompt was presented at a rate of 14 times every 20 seconds.

Four conditions were created. Condition 1 received the subliminal prompt during both the encoding and the test; Condition 2 received the white noise during both phases. Conditions 3 and 4 received only the puzzle-solving task; Condition 3 received the subliminal prompt during the puzzle solving phase; Condition 4 subjects were exposed to the white noise during the puzzle phase.

The results, shown in Fig. 2.2, indicate that subliminal presentation of the word "animal" during both the incidental learning and the puzzle-solving phase resulted in more animal solutions to the puzzle

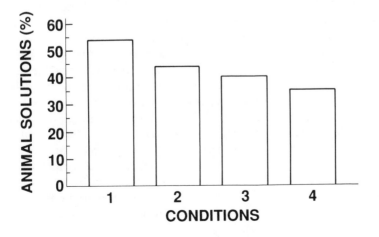

FIG. 2.2.   Average percent animal solutions.

(Condition 1 is significantly different from all other groups ($p < .05$)). Although Conditions 3 and 4 are in the expected direction of superiority of the subliminal, the difference between the two conditions is not significant. The design of this study permits us to conclude only that category of response in the puzzle task can be influenced by subliminal presentation of the response category. It may be that it is important for this subliminal manipulation to occur during incidental learning or it may be that longer presentations of the subliminal message are required to have an effect on the category of puzzle-solving response. Also, given that priming is important for subliminal effects (Fisher, 1976), it is possible that the incidental learning task had the effect of priming the subjects who were therefore more susceptible to the subliminal message.

SUBLIMINAL INFLUENCES ON AESTHETIC JUDGMENTS

The author (Swingle, 1979) designed a study to determine if aesthetic judgment could be influenced by auditory subliminal messages. Eighteen subjects were asked to rate 40 slides of paintings borrowed from the Art Department of the University of Ottawa. Subjects were asked to rate each painting on six bipolar adjective scales: *beautiful-ugly, dull-exciting, strong-weak, bad-good, warm-cold,* and *awkward-graceful.* Each bipolar adjective set was separated by a 100-millimeter line. Subjects were asked to indicate their ratings by simply drawing a line through the line at the point that corresponded with their assessment of the picture.

Slides were presented for 30 seconds during which time the subjects were asked to look directly at the picture followed by 30 seconds in which the screen went blank. During the 30 seconds when the screen was blank, they were asked to complete the scales. The auditory message was simply a repetition of either the positive or the negative adjectives from the previously mentioned scales, or a set of neutral words. For the positive message, a female voice repeated "beautiful, exciting, strong, good, warm, graceful." For the negative condition, the female voice repeated "ugly, dull, weak, bad, cold, awkward." The neutral message was "slide," "room," "projector," "student," "desk," and "table." The neutral words were all items present in the room during the experiment. This list of positive, negative, or neutral words was repeated continuously at approximately 1-second intervals during the course of the 30-second slide presentation. During the 30 seconds when the screen went blank and subjects were required to complete their scales, white noise at a comparable dB level was presented.

The auditory stimuli were presented through a single speaker mounted in the center of the ceiling of the classroom. The tape recorder was in another room and, hence, subjects were unaware of the fact that auditory stimulation was being presented. The ambient noise level in the empty room was 66 dB(A), although with subjects in the room the dB level was somewhat higher. The added sound levels measured at the speaker never exceeded 70 dB(A). Subjects were a minimum of 8 feet from the speaker.

In total, subjects rated 30 slides and the order of presentation was randomized. Analysis of all slides indicated a very trivial difference between positive, negative, and neutral conditions (positive M = 57.2: negative M = 54.5: $t(11)$ = 1.30, $p < .15$).

Henley (1975) reported that such subliminal cues maintain an influence over time and affect later judgments. Hence the data for only the first slide presentations were analyzed with rather startling results. The mean ratings for the first two slides in each condition are 64.6, 57.7, and 53.8 for the positive, neutral, and negative conditions, respectively. The positive condition differs from the negative ($t(11)$ = 3.60, $p < .005$), and the neutral ($t(11)$ = 1.99, $p < .05$). The difference between the neutral and the negative condition is not reliable ($p > .20$).

This study indicates that, in addition to intruding on thought processes, it is possible with subliminal influence to modify aesthetic judgment. The aesthetic qualities attributed to paintings can be influenced in a direction advocated by the subliminal message.

A similar study was conducted with female subjects using brief exposure times for the slide projected pictures. A male or a female voice repeated the adjectives during the post-exposure rating period. Six slide-projected pictures, with exposure times varying from .05 to 2.0 seconds, were rated on a 100-point scale of masculinity. Results indicated that pictures rated during the presentation of male-voice subliminal adjectives were rated as more masculine in content (M = 53.1) as compared with those rated during the female-voice subliminal presentation (M = 47.0) ($F (1,11)$ = 4.87, $p < .05$).

A study by Joanne Egan, Karen Narduzzi, and Anne Kerridge conducted in our laboratories also demonstrated that aesthetic judgments of ambiguous figures could be influenced by auditory subliminal messages. Male and female subjects were asked to sort 40 Rorschach-like inkblots into one of two piles, one labeled *peaceful*, and the second labeled *disturbing*. Half of the subjects performed the sorting task while exposed to white noise, whereas the experimental group of subjects completed the sorting task while exposed to white noise with the − 15 dB(A) embedded subliminal message, "These are very peaceful pictures; peaceful, calm, relaxed, pleasant. These pictures are very pleasant." One half of the subjects from each group was delayed in the start of the sorting task for 3 minutes, during which time the white noise or white noise plus subliminal message was presented. The other half of the subjects from each group started the task immediately upon entering the testing room. Subjects were told that they had 10 minutes to complete the task, and they were encouraged to reevaluate their decisions if they completed the task early.

The results indicate that, overall, more inkblots were placed in the *peaceful* pile when exposed to the subliminal message ($M = 57.5\%$) than in the control condition ($M = 45.2\%$) ($F (1,38) = 10.33, p < .01$). Delayed start (i.e., incubation) apparently had no effect, probably because of the generous time allotment and encouragement to reevaluate decisions.

An interesting gender effect was found. Although both males and females on average place more inkblots in the *peaceful* pile when exposed to the subliminal as compared to control conditions, the effect was most pronounced in the male groups. In the absence of the subliminal message, males rated 38.7% of the pictures as peaceful whereas females rated 51.8% of the pictures as peaceful. When exposed to the subliminal messages the average peaceful sortings increased to 56.5% and 58.5% for the male and female subjects, respectively. Whether this reflects a ceiling effect, basic differences in quiescence, and/or subliminal susceptibility differences between male and females in this task remains to be determined.

From a treatment or clinical perspective, it is interesting that decisions regarding stimuli designed to discriminate projective content (Rorschach, 1942) can be influenced by subliminal stimuli. If we accept that inkblots tap unconscious processes, then we have an intriguing theoretical issue to contemplate. Do subliminal messages intrude into unconscious processes with the result that the content or structure of these processes are changed (i.e., males see less disturbing material because the unconscious dynamics fundamental to this process are altered)? On the other hand, we know that subliminal prompts can influence retrieval from memory. If we accept the unconscious in its psychoanalytic sense, that is, a place where psychodynamic material resides, then subliminal messages might operate to alter retrieval or emergent processes. Thus, peaceful prompts might enhance the retrieval or emergence of peaceful content from the unconscious without altering the content of the unconscious in any way whatsoever.

On the other hand, the percept may be changed or influenced in some way such that more peaceful percepts appear. For example, biphasic illusions such as the old woman/young woman illusion are strongly influenced by being told what to look for. If self-talk is more peaceful in content, then it is not unreasonable to assume that one will "see" more peaceful objects in the inkblots. Further, the meaning of the perceived content could be influenced. For example, if one sees a bee in the inkblot, the bee could be framed within a cognitive structure that is more or less disturbing. The bee could be perceived as the peaceful cartoon character seen in TV advertisements for honey or as a disturbing image of a dangerous and frightening insect.

Finally, we also know that emotional state influences memories as well as the interpretation or evaluation of thoughts. If one feels sad, then one remembers sad events and is sensitized to perceive more sad events as well as interpret events as being sad. Therefore, if subliminal stimuli induce a peaceful feeling, one may see more peaceful images or interpret images as more peaceful. It should be recalled that this study used ambiguous inkblots under conditions of fixed decision categories. The imposed structure was "peaceful" or "disturbing," which serves as a pre-induction prime for the subjects. The subject is therefore rehearsing the peaceful–disturbing theme as he or she is going through the decision-making process. This type of preparation is maximally effective for subliminal influence.

Our research has indicated that short-term memory material can be influenced by subliminal procedures. Research is required to determine the relative effects of subliminal procedures on the encoding versus the retrieval processes in short-term memory. However, relevant to the issue of the unconscious, Dixon (1981) proposed the very intriguing notion that long-term memory may include a repository for material of which the recipient has never been aware. Further, this repository appears to be characterized by large capacity and slow rate of loss or decay (Bryden, 1971; Martin, 1978). From the perspective of the psychoanalytic conception of unconscious psychodynamics it is not unreasonable to postulate that this long-term memory repository for material received, processed, and stored without being routed through selective attention resides as a structurally separate entity. Material with which a person cannot cope (i.e., trauma) could be transferred to this unconscious domain. Just how this might be accomplished is not at all clear. A template-matching metaphor might help us conceptualize just how this might happen. If, for example, material is deprived of categorizing labels, it is not captured by any encoding template and therefore ends up in a repository of material structured by some alternative organizing principle such as sensory modality, affective tone, sensory image, physiological pleasantness, hedonic tone, or whatever. A conceptual model of this process might be that of the popular notion that retrievable memory of one's childhood is directly related to the development of language. As the child acquires language, labels or categories are established that serve as encoding structures for retention of memories that are available to consciousness. Psychodynamically oriented theorists maintain that the early experiences (including intrauterine and birth experiences) are not simply lost but are present in a repository of unconscious material. Although not directly available to consciousness, such material, according to this view, does exert important influences on our ongoing physical and mental life.

Thus, the repository that Dixon (1981) and others postulate may also function as a catchment for all mental material that survives template filtering due to lack of labels, input below the sensory threshold that triggers labeling, or denial of a label. Once in the catchment access to the material is not direct because the operating principle of consciousness is not compatible with (or in computer jargon—"can't shake hands with") the operating principle of the catchment.

An alternative notion is that of the organizing possibility of cognitive images. An adult who was sexually traumatized as a child may only have snippets of images regarding the traumatic event. In hypnotic work with such clients, I have found that such images may be composed of information from various sensory modalities. The person may be aware of frightening sounds, smells, bodily sensations, kinesthetic sensations, visual images, emotional states in various combinations and in various degrees of form and vividness. The information regarding the trauma is available to selective attention when accessed by means of a relevant image or images. A subliminal stimulus, therefore, is not available to consciousness because it was not encoded by or in the presence of a cognitive image or, as Dixon (1981) termed it, a phenomenal representation.

There are interesting possibilities for understanding maladaptive memory processes such as traumatic flashbacks characteristic of Post Traumatic Stress Disorder (PTSD). There is some evidence to indicate that arousal or anxiety or, conversely, boredom or underactivity may serve as a trigger for flashbacks. It does appear likely that stimuli outside of awareness will influence recall of material in long-term memory. Whether or not subliminally presented material can be used to alter either access or emergence of traumatic memories is an intriguing issue that warrants careful study.

We have demonstrated that subjective judgments can be influenced by subliminal stimulation. An interesting question addressed by Josie Geller, Daisy Wong, and Kinkini Premachandra in our laboratories was whether judgmental certainty could be influenced by the presentation of auditory subliminals suggesting confidence in judgments. We know that one can increase the positivity and negativity of aesthetic evaluations, the masculinity and femininity of ratings of picture content, the happiness and sadness of stories, but what about the certainty of those judgments?

Twenty-four male and female undergraduate students participated in a picture-sorting task while exposed to either white noise or white noise plus the -15 dB(A) auditory message "I know, I trust myself, I am sure," repeated twice every 20 seconds. The task involved sorting 27 rather neutral pictures of persons taken from magazines such as the *National Geographic*, into one of two piles. Pile 1 was marked with the label *definite feelings*, whereas Pile 2 was labeled *unsure feelings*. Subjects were instructed to sort the pictures by placing them in one of the two piles depending on whether or not the picture evoked a definite feeling, either positive or negative, or only rather vague feelings. The subjects were allowed as much time as required to complete the task.

The dependent measure was the number of pictures placed in each pile. Of the total 27 pictures, the average number placed in the *definite feelings* pile was 12.8 and 16.4 for the control and the experimental groups respectively ($p < .01$). Considering only the last 15 pictures, the averages were 5.3 and 7.5 for the control and experimental groups respectively ($p < .001$). The pattern of results was identical for both males and females.

Mood rating scales taken before and after the experimental session indicated that subjects exposed to the subliminal message were more likely to report enhanced happiness and feelings of dominance as compared to subjects in the control group, where the opposite pattern was observed. In the experimental group, 75% increased their happiness ratings and 82% increased their dominance ratings. In the control group, on the other hand, 67% reported a decrease in happiness and 70% reported a decrease in subjective dominance. These differences between experimental and control groups are both significant ($p < .05$). Although one should be most cautious about generalization from these data, it does appear as though subliminal methods may be useful for enhancing certainty of feelings with attendant positive changes in feelings of subjective well-being and control.

THE EFFECTS OF AUDITORY SUBLIMINAL MESSAGES ON PERFORMANCE

The next series of studies was designed to determine if output quantity could be influenced by auditory subliminal messages. Zuckerman (1960) demonstrated that written output could be influenced by visual subliminal messages. Subjects viewed slides of pictures and were asked to write stories about the pictures. After establishing a baseline, the message "Write more" was presented at 20 msec exposure for 15 repetitions. This was followed by the message "Don't write," also presented at 20 msec exposure for 15 repetitions.

Zuckerman reported that subjects wrote more during the "write more" message, and that a significant drop in output occurred when the "don't write" message was presented. The don't write message had a greater influence than the write more message. Further, presenting these same messages supraliminally had no effect on output.

Although the methodology of this study was criticized (Moore, 1982), the fact that different results were obtained between the subliminal and supraliminal presentations suggests nonconscious processing. The first study in our series was conducted on a group basis with subjects who knew that a subliminal message was being presented. This procedure again made use of a tape recorder with two loudspeakers. The subjects were seated from 2 meters to 5 meters from the loudspeakers. The ambient sound pressure level in the room was 46 dB(A), the tape peak was 50 dB(A) as measured at the speaker.

The study consisted of presentation of four Rorschach-like cards, each of which was presented for 4 minutes. Subjects were asked to sit and observe the card for 2 minutes. They were then given 2 minutes to write their responses to the card.

The study consisted of two manipulations. One was the presentation of a subliminal message, a control condition, and a subliminal message. The second manipulation was the presentation of a Rorschach-like image when it was obvious that no tape was placed in the tape recorder.

Tape 1 contained the subliminal message "Write more, more." This was presented in a male voice at a rate of 4 repetitions every 20 seconds. The second tape was the control condition in which the statement "The book is blue, blue" was repeated at a rate of approximately 4 repetitions every 20 seconds. Tape 3 was a repetition of Tape 1 with the same "Write more, more" message. On Trial 4, the tapes were taken out of the machine, the cassette cover was left open and no tape was put in.

The data are shown in Fig. 2.3. What is immediately obvious is that when there was obviously no tape and therefore no subliminal message being presented, subjects wrote considerably more responses to the stimulus than when they believed that a subliminal message was being presented. It is, of course, possible that, given that the stimuli were not counterbalanced or randomized, the last image generated a higher output than the others. Nonetheless the results indicate, in agreement with the previous studies, that when subjects expect to receive a subliminal message, their behavior may be constrained or controlled in some fashion.

Considering the subliminal and control conditions, the data indicate that subjects wrote more in response to stimuli that accompanied the "Write more, more" subliminal message than they did to the neutral stimulus. On average, subjects generated 17.4 words to the "write more" signal versus 15 words to the neutral stimulus (t (12) = 2.42, p = .042).

A replication of the "write more" study was conducted in our laboratories by Louise MacMillan and Mafalda Urbanyi. Two groups of 10 subjects each were asked to write a story about a picture under con-

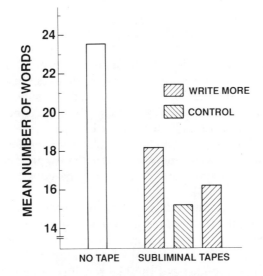

FIG. 2.3. Average number of words written in response to stimulus cards as a function of treatment condition.

ditions of noise distraction. The picture, taken from a magazine, was in color and depicted a man holding a heart-shaped box, and looking at his watch. Ten of the subjects wrote under the control condition of exposure to 80 dB(A) white noise, whereas the 10 subjects in the experimental condition also received the –15 dB(A) message, "Write more, smart people write more, write more to describe what you see, smart people write more. Keep on writing more, smart people want to keep on writing more, write some more. Keep on writing more and more. Smart people will write more." The subjects were given 15 minutes to complete the task and the white noise or white noise plus subliminal message was presented continuously during the writing task. The results are consistent with previous findings. Subjects in the control condition wrote an average of 110.2 words whereas the experimental group subjects wrote an average of 167.8 words (t (19) = 3.88, p < .01).

Yet another replication of this effect involved having Anglophone and Francophone subjects write associations to stimulus words projected on a screen. The words were "association," "exposition," "force," and "service." The subliminal message "Write more, more" or "Ecrire plus, plus" was presented through the public address loudspeaker system. The tape recorder was situated in an adjacent room, and hence, subjects were not aware of the fact that subliminal messages were being presented. In the experimental group the subliminal message was presented during the presentation of the first and the third slides, and no subliminal message was presented during the presentation of the second and fourth slides. Control group subjects were never exposed to the subliminal messages. The session lasted for 10 minutes. Each slide was shown for 15 seconds and then the screen went blank for 2 minutes during which time the students wrote the associations to the stimulus word. After 2 minutes the subjects were instructed to turn the page of their response packet. After a 15-second pause the next slide was presented. For subliminal trials, the message was presented at the beginning of the 15-second pause and remained on for the entire 135-second trial.

The results of this study again indicate that a greater number of experimental group subjects wrote more during subliminal presentations relative to nonsubliminal presentations (60%) as compared with control group subjects (28%) ($p < .05$).

The consistency of this finding with both auditory and visual (Zuckerman, 1960) subliminal messages indicates that output can indeed be manipulated without a person's awareness. The implications of this influence on other factors such as quality of output, fatigue, interest in the task, subjective mood, and the like remains to be determined.

These studies indicate that subliminal messages can influence the quantity of output. The following series of studies was designed to determine whether the speed of response could be influenced with auditory subliminal messages. The following series of studies made use of a standard lever-pressing preparation. Subjects were seated in ventilated 4×6 foot cubicles acoustically isolated from the recording apparatus. Each cubicle contained a standard 19×21 inch relay rack upon which a light and a cam key were mounted.

The experimental session consisted of a series of twenty 10-second work trials, each separated by an intertrial rest period of 15 seconds. When a trial began, the light mounted on the console would light up indicating that the subject's key was operative and he or she was instructed to respond as rapidly as possible. Once the "go" light was extinguished, there was a 15-second rest period. Subjects were involved for 20 trials without a subliminal message. A 4-minute rest period followed, during which time a subliminal message was presented over loudspeakers at an effective range of -15 dB(A). Following the presentation of the subliminal message, the subject responded for another twenty 10-second lever-pressing trials during which time the subliminal message continued to be presented.

In the first study, two groups of male undergraduates were exposed to either a white noise control condition or a subliminal message designed to slow down the subject's lever pressing. The slow message was "Slow down, go slower."

The data in Fig. 2.4 show the mean difference in response rate between

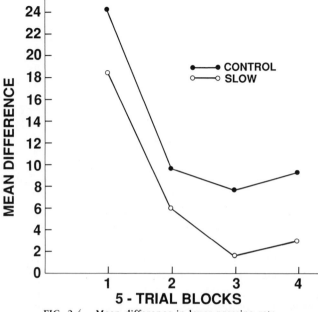

FIG. 2.4.   Mean difference in lever-pressing rate.

the last four five-trial blocks relative to the average base response rate obtained during the subject's initial 20 lever-pressing trials. As the data indicate, the mean difference curves for both the control and the slow group are virtually identical in shape but the group receiving the slow message is slower, relative to base rate, at every one of the five-trial block periods ($F(1,10) = 5.36, p = .041$).

A similar study was conducted with a group of 12 male undergraduate subjects divided into those who received the subliminal message "Slow down, go slower" versus those who received the subliminal message "Fast, go faster." The data indicate that subjects receiving the "go faster" subliminal message had a greater increase in lever pressing rate relative to baseline ($M = 33.6\%$) as compared with the individuals in the "slow down" subliminal message condition ($M = 11.1\%$) ($t(10) = 2.52, p < .03$).

A master's thesis study conducted in our laboratories by Brian McLean used a similar design. Male subjects lever pressed 5 periods of 10 seconds each separated by 15-second rest periods. They then lever pressed for twenty-five 10-second trials. The lever pressing trials were separated by 15-second rest periods. Subliminal messages were presented continuously during the last 25 trials. The messages were in a female voice, repeated approximately 90 times, and the message length was approximately 7 seconds in duration.

The message was presented across the effective range of −2.5 to −30 dB(A), relative to ambient at the speaker, with the subject positioned 1

TABLE 2.1
Average Lever Pressing Responses Per Second

Condition	Total Average Responses Per Second	Fastest 10 Second Responses Per Second
Fast	6.8	7.9
Slow	6.4	7.3
Backward	6.6	7.6
No Subliminal	6.2	7.0

meter from the speaker. Four conditions were created. The first was a fast message, which was "Go faster, this is enjoyable, do better, this is fun, press quickly, speed up." The second group was exposed to a slow message, which was "Go slower, this is boring, this is tiresome, do worse, press slowly, slow down." A third condition was a sound pressure control condition in which these two messages were played backwards so that the sound pressure level was constant, but the message was deprived of meaningful content. Finally, a no-noise condition was included.

The total average responses per second and the fastest single 10-second response rate are shown in Table 2.1. As the data indicate, the fast group had the fastest lever-pressing rate, followed by the backward message, followed by the slow, with the slowest performance being that of the group exposed to no subliminal message. When the fastest single average five-trial rate is examined, exactly the same ordering is apparent with the fastest group having the highest fastest single rate, followed by the backward, followed in turn by the slow message, with the no message conditioning having the lowest single fastest response time. The difference between the fast and slow conditions is reliable ($p < .025$); the fast and no-noise differ ($p < .01$) and the backward and the fast differ ($p < .10$). These probabilities are associated with analysis of covariance with the first five trials serving as the covariate.

What is interesting in this particular study is not so much that the fast–slow manipulation was replicated, but rather that the introduction of subliminal sound deprived of content may have an arousing or activating effect. This is consistent with the work of Zenhausern and Hansen (1974), among others, who found that the introduction of a subliminal signal, deprived of meaningful content, has an arousing or activating effect on performance. Hence, this offers an explanation of why the slow message appears to give rise to a higher response rate than the no-message condition, although these differences are not significant.

A study was conducted using a slightly modified preparation to determine whether subjects would attribute influence to novel tones when exposed to performance-relevant subliminal messages. This study also varied the performance task. Rather than lever pressing with feedback (i.e., points accumulated on a fixed ratio displayed on the console counter), subjects finger tapped without performance feedback. The finger-tapping mechanism was a contact relay circuit that detected each finger contact with a 9 mm metal disk.

The study consisted of six five-trial blocks of 10-second finger-tapping periods separated by 10-second rest periods. Two pure tones of 300 Hz and 310 Hz were alternated every five trials. During Trial Blocks 3 and 4 (i.e., Trials 11 through 20) auditory subliminal messages were embedded in the pure tones at − 15 dB(A). The finger-tapping procedure was used because it is quieter and therefore potentially less interfering with the subliminal messages. Further, the procedure is less harmful to those subjects, particularly males, who appear so highly involved in lever-pressing self-competition that they respond vigorously enough to cause skin lesions on their fingers (Swingle, 1970b). Indeed, we always find that males rate lever pressing as more "interesting" or "enjoyable" than do females. This enjoyment factor is also found for finger tapping. In the present study, for example, males rated the task as more interesting than did females (Ms = 55.1 and 39.7 on a 100 point scale, p < .02, for males and females, respectively).

The finger-tapping study involved 126 male and female students. They were exposed to the pure tones, as described, and were told that we were interested in investigating the influence of "sound on motor performance." Subjects were exposed to subliminal messages in either the same-sex or opposite-sex voice. The message was either "Go fast, faster, fast" or "Go slow, slower, slow." One group of males and one group of females in the control conditions were exposed to the pure tones with white noise embedded at − 15 dB(A).

Subjects' finger-tapping rates during the last five trials were compared with the pre-subliminal message base rates. Overall, the results again indicate an effect for the *slow* message but no effect for the *fast* message, relative to control. In the slow condition, 83% of the subjects had slower rates during the last five trials relative to base rate. The values for the control and fast groups were 43% and 45% respectively. The slow group differs from the control and the fast groups (p < .01 in both cases), which do not differ from each other (Z < 1.0). The effect, however, appears to be entirely associated with the cross-sex conditions in which the subliminal message was presented in a voice opposite in gender to that of the subject. The percentage of slower final finger-tapping rates for the cross-sex conditions were 52%, 81%, and 43% for the control, slow, and fast groups respectively. Although the fast group had a lower proportion of subjects who had slower rates than the control group, this difference in proportions is not significant (Z < 1.0). For the same-sex conditions the comparable percentages were 33%, 43%, and 48% for the control, slow, and fast groups, respectively ($Z < 1.0$ in all cases, NS).

The greater effect of the slow message, relative to the fast, may again simply reflect a ceiling effect inherent in this research preparation. Subjects asked to respond as rapidly as they can may be performing at close to maximum levels and hence are less likely to demonstrate the influence of a subliminal designed to increase performance.

At the conclusion of the finger-tapping session, subjects were asked to complete a questionnaire. One question asked the subjects to rate, on a 100-point scale, the extent to which they felt that the tones influenced their performance. We were interested to determine if subliminal influence might be reflected in greater attribution of influence to a salient feature of the research setting.

The mean rating for subjects who responded in the direction advocated by the subliminal message (i.e., faster in the fast condition and slower in the slow condition) was 45.2. The average rating for subjects who responded in the direction opposite to the subliminal message was 35.3. This difference is not significant ($t(65) = .95, p = .35$). Furthermore, the proportion of subjects in each of the categorizations who responded with ratings over 50 on the 100-point scale was .472 for the former and .357 for the latter groups ($Z = 1.33, p(1t) = .092$). Thus, it appears as though the tendency to attribute greater influence to salient features of the situation when influenced by a subliminal message is marginal at most.

An honors thesis study conducted in our laboratories by Wendy Braid examined the use of subliminal messages to alter the meaning of lever-pressing behavior. Specifically, rather than issue an imperative message to go slow or speed up, or a message suggesting boredom or fatigue, Braid presented subjects with messages implying that going fast or going slow was clever or stupid.

Male and female subjects lever pressed for twenty 10-second work trials followed by a 10-second rest period. For the first 10 trials, no subliminal messages were presented. There was then a 4.5-minute rest period during which the subliminal messages were presented. The subliminal message was presented continuously from the beginning of the 4.5 minute rest period until the end of the last lever-pressing trial. Subjects then lever pressed for an additional ten 10-second trials, each one separated by a 10-second rest period. The messages were repeated at a cadence of eight repetitions every 20 seconds at a maximum peak of -18 dB(A) relative to ambient.

Four conditions were created: In Condition 1, the message was "Going fast is stupid"; Condition 2 was "Going slow is clever"; Condition 3 was "Going fast is clever"; and Condition 4 was a 500 Hz tone. The overall data for each of the four conditions are shown in Fig. 2.5. The data

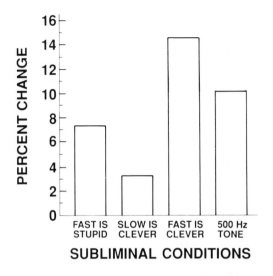

FIG. 2.5.   Percent change in lever-pressing rate as a function of subliminal
messages.

presented are the percent change of the second lever-pressing rate relative
to the first.

As the data indicate, the group that speeded up the most was Condition
3, which was exposed to the message "Going fast is clever." The group
that increased its lever-pressing rate the least was the group exposed to
the message "Going slow is clever." The overall analysis indicates that
Condition 1 differs from 3 ($p < .05$), 2 differs from 4 ($p < .025$), 2 differs
from 3 ($p < .005$), and 3 and 4 differ ($p < .10$) ($F(3,36) = 3.85, p < .02$).

An interesting note is that, when the data are divided according to male
and female subjects (see Fig. 2.6), the effects on males and females appear
to be consistent. The family of curves for the males is displaced upward,
indicating a higher overall lever-pressing rate relative to females. However, the impact of the subliminal messages appears to be consistent for
both males and females. This study indicates that performance can be
influenced by subliminally manipulating the meaning associated with
certain types of performance. In other words, if, as a result of a subliminal
message, a person feels that high effort is clever or stupid, that subliminal
message will influence the individual's output accordingly.

Our research indicates that speed and quantity of output can be
influenced by simple auditory subliminal messages. Subjects lever press
more rapidly when told to do so (e.g., "Go faster") or when the meaning
of the behavior is manipulated (e.g., "Going fast is clever"). Subjects also
output more when told to do so (e.g., "Write more"). There is also reason
to believe that the addition of subliminal sound devoid of meaningful

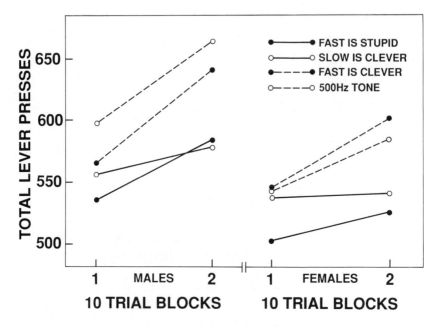

FIG. 2.6. Average total lever-pressing responses before and after exposure to subliminal messages.

content enhances performance. For example, Zenhausern and Hansen (1974) and Zwosta and Zenhausern (1969) showed that subliminal sound enhances performance, and in our own research we often find that a content-free subliminal control (e.g., white noise or backward message) gives rise to enhanced performance relative to that of a no-sound control.

We also know that music can be used to increase or decrease arousal (Fisher & Greenberg, 1972) or to influence subjective mood (Nielzen & Cesarec, 1981). The following study was conducted by Ray Alyman, Philip Fleurian-Chateau, and Michael Wyman as part of a requirement for my course on auditory subliminal perception. During six aerobic workouts of approximately 1 hour each, participants were exposed to either music, as usual, or music with a short auditory subliminal message (i.e., "Great, energetic, happy, improving") repeated continuously or a long message (i.e., "This workout will fulfill all my physical and emotional needs. It will develop my body and clear my mind. I'm getting in shape and look great. This is the way I want to be. I'm on top of the world and feel exhilarated. Life is energy, energy is life. To improve myself I must work harder.") also repeated continuously throughout the session. The subliminal messages were presented at an average of − 15 dB(A) below the music used for the exercise sessions. Persons required to attend the sessions (e.g., varsity athletes) were not included in the analyses. Following each aerobic session a questionnaire was administered that contained items relevant to mood or performance. Presentation of the short message, long message, and control conditions were randomly determined and resulted in the order: control, long, and short with 68, 81, and 71 subjects in each condition, respectively. It should be noted that some subjects were represented in more than one condition. The aerobic instructor was blind to the condition but was aware of the experimental procedure and could, of course, have been himself influenced by the subliminal messages.

The results of this study are interesting and suggest that field applications of subliminal messages are indeed potentially viable. The short message appears to be superior to the long message. Relative to the control group, subjects in the short message condition rated themselves as more energetic following the workout ($p < .10$), felt that their performance was better (compared with previous workouts) ($p = .02$), and looked forward more enthusiastically to their next workout ($p < .03$). Overall, summing the ratings of all nine questions, the results indicate an effect for both the long and the short subliminal messages relative to control, with superiority of the short message ($M = 23.4$, 25.4, and 26.9, $p = .03$ for the control, long message, and short message conditions, respectively).

THE EFFECTS OF AUDITORY SUBLIMINAL MESSAGES ON INTERPERSONAL BEHAVIOR

We turn our attention now to the impact of subliminal messages on interpersonal behavior. A study (Swingle, 1979), conducted in collaboration with Kerry Lawson and Louis Renaud, was designed to determine the effects of subliminal auditory messages on behavior in a two-person, two-choice, power game situation (Swingle, 1970a).

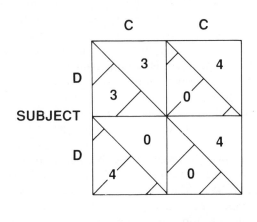

FIG. 2.7.   Non-zero-sum game matrix for the opponent in power condition.

Three groups of 15 and one group of 16 female college students played the weak position in the power game shown in Fig. 2.7. Subjects played the game for 100 trials against an opponent programmed to respond cooperatively (Response 1) on 80% of the trials. On each trial, signalled by a go light, the subject and the computer made Response choice 1 or 2. After both responses were registered, a light came on behind one of the four quadrants of the matrix indicating the results of that trial. Hence, if both choices were 1, the top left quadrant would light up indicating that both the subject and the other player (computer) received three payoff units. The payoff points were accumulated automatically on two counters on the console. Subjects were kept unaware of the fact that the opponent was programmed and were told that points would be redeemed at 2.5 cents per point for subjects whose names were drawn in a lottery of the subjects who participated in the project.

This game is a power game in which player B is in absolute control. By playing Response two 100% of the time, player A would receive zero payoff, whereas player B would receive four payoff units per trial. Previous studies (Swingle, 1989) indicate that highly cooperative opponents tend to be exploited by weak opponents.

Three subliminal messages and one control condition were included in the study. Sound levels were varied over an effective range of −15 dB(A) to −45 dB(A). The subjects were seated 1 meter from the sound source and the ambient sound level in the room was 70 dB(A). The decision to use multiple sound levels was guided by research reports indicating effects of subliminal sound as low as −30 dB(A). However, we now know that, contrary to reported findings, subliminal influence below −30 dB(A) is unlikely. The messages were recorded through a gain control circuit which reduced peaking dB levels.

For Condition 1 (+C) a male voice repeated "Be nice, be kind, do not be selfish, your opponent is wise, your opponent is strong, your opponent is successful, your opponent is realistic, push 1, hit 1, press 1."

For Condition 2, the competitive condition (+D), the subliminal message was "Your opponent is failing, your opponent is foolish, your opponent is naive, your opponent is weak, your opponent is stupid, push 2, hit number 2, press 2."

The third subliminal condition was a white noise control (WN). The white noise was presented at the same average dB levels as the other messages.

The fourth condition (NS) was a no-subliminal-sound control condition.

The average number of Response 2 choices (noncooperative) for the +C, +D, WN, and NS conditions are shown in Fig. 2.8. The differences between the cooperative and competitive conditions, the cooperative and white noise conditions, and the cooperative and no-sound conditions are all significant ($p < .02$). The white noise and the no-sound conditions and the competitive and no-sound conditions did not differ significantly.

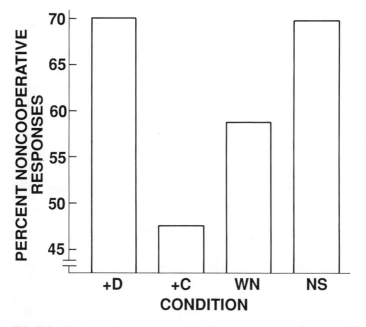

FIG. 2.8.   Average percent noncooperative responses as a function of
treatment condition.

There are several interesting results of this experiment. In the first instance, because the power game, under cooperative opponent conditions,
gives rise to a high level of competition (Swingle, 1970a), the potential
for the competitive induction to enhance cooperation was minimized.
This is shown quite clearly in Fig. 2.8 in which the no-sound and the
competitive induction situation give rise to virtually identical levels of
noncooperation. The principal difference as shown in the figure is the
cooperative induction in which subjects' cooperative responses were considerably below those generally expected (i.e., the no-sound condition).

A recent study by Neuberg (1988) using visual subliminal messages
replicated this finding. Neuberg presented competitive words (e.g., *competitive, hostile, unfriendly, combatitive, war-like*) or neutral words (such
as *something, might, should, people, would*) at visually subliminal levels
to subjects, prior to their playing the Prisoners' Dilemma Game. Subjects
were divided in terms of their initial move (i.e., those who made a
cooperative first move versus those who made a competitive first move)
as an indication of their cooperative behavioral predisposition. It was
found that competitive subliminal words increased the competitiveness
of competitively predisposed subjects, whereas there were no differences
in terms of the primes for cooperatively oriented subjects.

An interesting study was reported by Sheffler and Brody (1989) in
which they demonstrated the influence of subliminal stimuli on dyadic

interaction. Mixed dyads were videotaped while involved in a 7-minute discussion. Prior to the discussion, subjects in one half of the dyads were exposed to hostile words presented visually at subliminal levels. The remaining subjects were exposed to neutral words. The hostile stimulus words included "hostile," "rude," "punch," "beat," and "hate." The neutral words were selected from the 200 most frequently appearing words in the English language (Carroll, Daview, & Richman, 1971) and included "what," "together," "little," and "always."

The stimulus words were presented for 17 msec, followed immediately by a 100-msec backward pattern mask. The pattern mask was a series of randomly arranged repetitions of all of the letters of the alphabet in various orientations. The mask was 1.5 times as long and four times wider than the stimulus word to completely mask the subliminal stimulus. Stimuli were presented at 3.5 second intervals. This backward pattern masking procedure apparently does not impede visual processing but does block availability to consciousness of the masked stimulus (Marcel, 1983b). The videotapes were scored for four nonverbal measures: foot movements, gestural size, body lean, and distance between subjects; and five verbal measures: speaking turns, interrupts, filled pauses, silent pauses, and silence time. Further, a subjective rating of the hostility of the partner was obtained.

The results indicated that subjects who had been exposed to the hostile primes interrupted more, had more filled and silent pauses, and a greater total silence time. Furthermore, they leaned farther back from their partners and there was a greater distance between them as compared with subjects who had received the nonhostile primes. This study further corroborates our work that indicates that subliminal messages can have an influence on interpersonal behavior.

An interesting study that purported to demonstrate the effect of unconscious conflict on competitive behavior was reported by Beisser (1961). Male subjects involved in a dart-throwing competition were exposed to a tachistoscopically presented subliminal message, "Beating Dad is wrong" or "Beating Dad is OK." The psychoanalytic rationale for this study is that activating oedipal conflict results in an association between winning and symbolic defeat of the father. In turn, this defeat is associated with the unacceptable desire for the mother. The "OK" message on the other hand alleviates oedipal conflict which all college-age males have to some degree. Briefly stated, the results of this study indicate reduced accuracy following the "wrong" message but enhanced accuracy subsequent to exposure to the "OK" message. As might be expected, there have been studies that failed to replicate this effect (Heilbrun, 1980).

SUBLIMINAL PROCESSING

Although there appears to be ample evidence to indicate that subliminal stimuli affect behavior without awareness, many questions remain as to just how this process occurs. One can focus on the neurophysiology of the processing of information or on the cognitive–affective aspects of this process. For our purposes, the latter is of considerably greater importance to the clinical applications of subliminal procedures. As Dixon (1981) pointed out, the meaning of a stimulus, although it does enter conscious awareness, may nevertheless be processed unconsciously and evoke consciously experienced emotional tone. One can question, as did Dixon, whether the subliminal stimulus evokes an emotional response, which is in turn attributed or projected onto some salient, proximal, or appropriate object, or, conversely, if the subliminal stimulus directly alters the perception of the supraliminal stimulus. In any event it is clear that there is scope for potential processing of information at several levels of consciousness in many exquisitely complicated patterns. It is also possible that the subliminal message intrudes on self-talk or labelling procedures in a predominantly mechanical fashion. For example, it has been demonstrated that subliminal prompts can influence problem solving in tasks such as anagrams and picture discrimination. Subjects might have an auditory representation of the subliminal message in their self-talk which in turn gives rise to classification or labeling of stimuli to which the subject is currently attending. This might be particularly probable in a laboratory experiment with undergraduate participants involved in an ambiguous task of sorting pictures into groups based on some imposed categorization system. So, for example, if a subject is asked to sort pictures of landscapes into two piles based on a masculine versus feminine categorization, repetition of subliminal prompts such as *masculine, male, man*, and the like may find auditory representation in consciousness (i.e., self-talk) with the result that the subject accepts this auditory representation as his or her decision. This is, of course, reminiscent of Jaynes's (1976) interesting thesis regarding the development of the bicameral mind in which auditory representations might have been interpreted as words from God by early humans. Once humans developed to the point of recognizing that the auditory representations were produced from within, then they no longer sought an external explanation for their self-talk.

An alternative metaphor for conceptualizing subliminal processing is that of single-channel serial processing versus multichannel, parallel processing systems. The former is that which is engaged by selective attention that imposes a serial, linear structure on experience processed in consciousness. Unconscious or preconscious processing on the other hand is characterized by multichannel, parallel processing of material simultaneously (Neisser, 1963; Posner, 1982; Posner, Klein, Summers, & Buggie, 1973). However, even though a system is multichannel and characterized by parallel processing of information, some mechanism for structuring and prioritizing the incoming stimuli is required. Organisms are constantly bombarded by millions of bits of information and some filtering system must be postulated to make sense of the research that demonstrates specific effects of finite sets of stimuli that are processed out of consciousness.

The affect-memory-learning research offers an indication of one possible mechanism operating to impose organizing structure on unconscious information. Research has shown that threatening stimuli are processed differently, in terms of latencies, as compared with non-threatening stimuli (the perceptual defense model). In addition, certain arousal states of the organism, whether state or trait in nature, influence susceptibility to material presented subliminally. Further, an individual's subjective mood state, as measured on the hedonic tone axis, also influences learning and retrieval of information. Now all of these states or conditions can be at various levels of consciousness. Even when we are not aware of or attending to our mind/body state, our affective state alters the accessibility, salience, or priority of stimuli received at energy levels below the level necessary for selective attention. We can postulate a vigilance model, an attribution model, or a defense model, to name but three, as possible organizing principles characterizing the unconscious processing systems. In vigilance, the system is enhancing the processing of material that poses some threat to the organism. In attribution, the system is enhancing the processing of material that aids in understanding of the state of the organism, and in defense, the system either reduces the access of threatening material or enhances sensitivity to material inconsistent with the threat.

It is useful to recall the original studies by Eriksen (1954), Bruner and Postman (1947), Postman, Bruner, and McGinnies (1948) that found that the recognition thresholds for words varied inversely with the value rating given to the words by each subject. Words of higher value had lower thresholds (perceptual sensitization) than words of lower value. This concept of the perceptual threshold being responsive to the subjective value of the perceptual object stimulated considerable debate regarding the preconscious properties of this precognitive process. Further, perceptual objects (i.e., words) classically conditioned to a painful stimulus (i.e., electric shock) were found to have higher thresholds than words not so conditioned even though words not consciously processed did nonetheless evoke an autonomic (i.e., SCR) response (Lazarus & McCleary, 1951). Much confusion regarding this issue of perceptual defense surrounds the notion that such a process would seem to be maladaptive in that early detection of threat would seem to be of paramount importance. However, from our evolutionary perspective the inherent value of a few milliseconds would seem to be inconsequential when avoiding a tyrannosaurus, when more intellectual strategies might be of greater value. With the advent of the six-shooter, a few milliseconds might be critical to life or death but our biological apparatus has not had time to catch up. On the other hand, such duel-in-the-sun scenarios might be the product of creative cinematographers and not relevant survival considerations in any event. Similarly, ego-threatening material results in increased perceptual thresholds. This concept would, at first glance, not seem to pose the same problem of biological survival relevance as compared with the notion of heightened thresholds from recognition of biologically threatening stimuli. The point, however, is that we know that mood, object valence, thresholds for selective attention, and nonconscious processing are all interrelated. Our ability to make sense out of the "purpose" of some of these relationships, once we agree on just what they are, is an issue that may never be resolved.

Now, as we discussed earlier, any part of the processing system can be subliminal or unconscious. We may not be aware of our affective state or the state of bodily arousal (Zillmann, 1971). On the other hand, we may be aware of subjective mood but be unaware of stimuli that we are selectively processing. Or we may be aware of both our mood state and our attention to specific stimulus material but be unaware of the nonrecursive relationship between our mood and the material to which we are attending.

The challenge from a clinical perspective is that of the development of an understanding of the psychodynamic processes that operate to transfer information (i.e., moods, images, memories, apprehensions, affective judgments, body states) from one system to the other. If a child is traumatized how does the material get transferred from the consciousness-accessible to the consciousness-inaccessible systems? Further, what is the relationship of the system(s) that contains such repressed material and the system(s) that is accessible through subliminal presentation procedures? Does the information reside in the same system? Or do the two systems directly correspond with each other? Again a computer analogy is probably helpful. In the first instance we are conceptualizing the systems as residing in the same memory area and although the information is discrete, the same rules of access apply. In the second case, we conceptualize the two types of information as residing in different areas of memory with different rules of access but with the rules of intersystem access being compatible (i.e., the two memory systems can "shake hands" with each other, but the rules of getting information into or out of each system are different). Silverman's (Weinberger & Silverman,

1987) intriguing work on the psychodynamic activation procedure suggests that the latter conceptualization may be most parsimonious. He presented disorder relevant or disorder irrelevant (as defined by psychoanalytic theory) material to persons with three forms of psychological disturbances. The three conditions were stutterers, male homosexuals, and paranoid schizophrenics. Disorder relevant material designed to enhance unconscious conflicts associated with the disorders was: anal material for the stutterers (i.e., the words "Go shit" and the pictorial image of a person defecating); incest material for the homosexuals (i.e., "Fuck Mommy" with the pictorial image of an elderly woman in a sexually suggestive pose); familiarly aggressive material for the schizophrenics (i.e., "Kill Mommy" with a pictorial image of an elderly woman being stabbed). The written and pictorial images were presented visually at subliminal levels. When material relevant to the disorder was presented, increases in pathology (disorder relevant symptoms) were apparent. No such increase in symptoms was observed when the material was not relevant to the disorder. It is also interesting to note that Silverman studied disorders that varied in terms of the measurement of the symptoms. Stutterers were assessed in terms of speech disruptions, homosexuals were assessed in terms of self-reported homosexual erotic feelings, and schizophrenics were assessed in terms of ward attendants' ratings of pathological behavior patterns.

Silverman further demonstrated that the use of a single psychodynamically unifying message "Mommy and I are one" has a quiescing effect on symptomatology across a number of disorders. The theoretically interesting aspect of this work is that of the questions associated with just how the specificity property of the disorder-relevant material operates. Is disorder-irrelevant material processed, but because it is not relevant it does not interact with the psychodynamic conflict? Or, on the other hand, is the selective process operative during the encoding process and therefore the disorder-irrelevant material is not processed in the first place? I think it is perfectly clear that the research required to understand these processes is going to be theoretically exciting and methodologically challenging.

The relationship between affective state and memory processes offers an interesting example of a process that appears to have many of the structural properties of the unconscious catchment notions discussed earlier. Network theory (Bower, 1981; Gilligan & Bower, 1984) maintains that emotions are central to the semantic network and that interrelationships exist among ideas, events, memories, autonomic activity, emotion, affective valence of material, and muscular and expressive activity. According to this view, subjective mood and memory can be related in four important ways. Memory is facilitated when mood state at learning and recall are comparable; material with affective tone that is congruent with current mood is more easily retrieved from memory; material with affective tone consistent with current mood is learned most readily; and affectively intense material is learned more readily than affectively less intense material. There are many studies that demonstrate that the person's subjective mood and the affective valence of the material to be learned or retrieved from memory are nonrecursively related. Natale and Hantas (1982), for example, found that free recall of personal memories was selectively influenced by the subject's subjective mood state, which had been hypnotically induced. Bower, Gilligan, and Monteiro (1981) hypnotically induced happy or sad moods in subjects who were then asked to read a story describing positive or negative events and characters. Subsequently, subjects were asked to recall information about the story. The results indicate enhanced recall for information that was affectively congruent with the subject's mood state when reading the story. The effect appears most pronounced for sad mood states and the effect was more pronounced for information about incidents as compared to information about characters in the stories. Further, Clark and Teasdale (1985) reported that the effect of mood on retrieval of trait words appeared to be greater for females in comparison with males. In addition, Isen and Shalker (1982) reported that the effect may result from an interference process as opposed to an enhancement process in that sad moods appear to interfere with the encoding of positively valenced material but do not enhance encoding of sad valenced material.

Research Methodology

There are three aspects to any treatment procedure. The first is how to do it, the second is how to assess it, and the third is how to improve it. Clinical settings provide the context for conducting important research with a view toward improving treatment procedures. All competent therapists are researchers; they could hardly be otherwise. Where good therapists differ profoundly from each other is in their ability to conduct research in a systematic manner that permits them to communicate their findings. Simply stated, in my view, therapists of any professional orientation who are not methodologically and analytically competent are simply bad therapists.

Many clinicians have an aversion to research because of fundamental misconceptions about what research is. If we conceptualize research as large groups of individuals, some of whom are treated while others are deprived of treatment, then clinicians are very likely not to see themselves as capable of conducting research. They take this view either because they find such procedures ethically unacceptable or because they feel as though they are not in a position to obtain large populations of subjects. Further, they may believe that they lack the methodological and statistical skill to conduct meaningful research. Let me say, simply, that I consider this view to be inaccurate. One need not choose between research and practice. This reflects an old view of the health professions which is no longer relevant. Unfortunately some of our professional training programs are structured in a manner that fosters this inaccurate view. The unfortunate result of this is not only poor training of clinicians, but an erroneous view that research must be conducted in a manner that com-

promises patient welfare by fostering a callousness, on the part of the
researcher, to patients' well-being. We have all heard or read about
repugnant examples of immoral or unethical behavior on the part of
researchers who attempt to justify their behavior by hiding under the
mantle of science.

The purpose of research, in my view, is to discover similarities or
regularities in processes. Once these similarities or regularities are identified, the structure of the process can be defined and isolated. The
scientist-practitioner thereby gains an understanding of the essence of
the process and a related appreciation of the physical and psychological
processes involved in the treatment procedure. In other words, the
scientist-practitioner while discovering regularities is able to better understand how and why something works. More importantly, the clinician
can determine which aspects of the process might be fruitfully examined
for the purpose of improving treatment procedures.

The other important feature of systematic research is the facilitation
of communication with a community of colleagues, which creates an
environment in which skills are enhanced. I might also add that knowing
how to do research in a proper manner renders clinical work intellectually
challenging and, frankly, fun.

ETHICAL CONSIDERATIONS

I suspect that most practitioners would agree that all clinical decisions
are investigative in nature. A client provides details associated with a
complaint and, based on the client's responses to our queries, we make
a decision about just which of a number of treatment options we will
try in any particular situation. Ideally, treatment choices are based only
on the practitioner's concern for the client's well-being in a holistic sense.
In effect, we are conducting a mini-experiment to test the efficacy of a
particular treatment procedure with a particular client with a particular
set of characteristics associated with a particular complaint. Should the
client's complaint not respond well after some period of time to the treatment we have chosen, then, generally, we try another mini-experiment
with another treatment procedure. Clinical research, following the scientist-practitioner model, is nothing more than a formalization of treatment
procedures used by competent practitioners each and every day in their
clinical practices. It does not include considering people to be numbers,
depriving them of treatment, behaving in a callous manner, treating them
like "guinea pigs," nor does it mean spending hours at a calculator or
a computer. What it does involve is structuring one's treatment program
so that how, when, and why a treatment procedure was used can be

documented. Further, it involves collecting information on clients in a manner that permits categorization or dimensionalization.

The issue of ethics as it applies to clinical research is a topic of such overwhelming importance and complexity that it could easily fill several volumes. For the purposes of the present book, my comments and suggestions are restricted to research procedures appropriate to subliminal treatment procedures. By way of introduction, let me reiterate that I consider research and treatment to be inseparable, or perhaps more accurately, that I conceptualize research as treatment because it is designed that way. The procedures that are recommended here are powerful and statistically sensitive, yet they are consistent with our growing understanding of mind/body healing. In short, not only are they ethical and morally acceptable, but they are ecologically valid.

There are many influences on our behavior. Many of these influences are so subtle that they escape our ability to fully comprehend the nature of the influences and the effects that these influences are having upon our cognitive and emotional behavior. The influence of one's discussion partner on temporal properties of speech is a good example. We found (Swingle, 1984; Swingle & Hope, 1987) that the frequency of pauses in a person's speech that exceed a particular duration (say 100 msec) is a relatively stable characteristic within individuals over relatively long periods of time. This pattern of hesitation (known as the hesitation index) is related to emotionality and it is influenced by such things as induced negative mood, the type of conversational task the discussants are involved in, the content of the discussion, and so on. Furthermore, and most interesting, we know that under certain circumstances discussants' hesitation indices converge, that is, become more similar to one another. Because of the subtlety of this effect, people are not aware of the fact that their hesitation index is becoming more similar to that of their conversational partner. People are generally not aware of such changes, of course, because the temporal properties of the characteristic are such that they are below the person's ability to discriminate such changes. An interesting possibility is that if the hesitation index reflects the dysphoric mood of the speaker, it is conceivable that dysphoric influence from one conversational partner to the other may, to some extent, occur at the nonlexical level (Swingle & Hope, 1987).

When conducting research in the area of subliminal influence, we are faced with much the same sort of problem. Individuals may be being influenced by the subliminal treatment, but the effects of that influence may not be available to the individual in any direct form. In short, we may not be able to ask the individual to tell us what effects are experienced from exposure to a subliminal treatment condition. A second important consideration with regard to subliminal treatment research is the distinction between demonstrating that subliminal auditory messages are processed by the individual versus demonstrating that the subliminal auditory messages have clinical efficacy. This is the usual sort of distinction that is often made in clinical terms between significance and meaningfulness. We may, for example, be able to demonstrate that subliminal stimuli are processed by the organism, with a very high degree of statistical significance, but we may find that a particular subliminal treatment is not clinically meaningful in terms of contributing to the betterment of the client's condition.

It is no secret that many researchers have behaved in a totally unconscionable manner with respect to the pain, suffering, dignity, and well-being of the subjects of their research. Subjects have been exposed to diseases without their awareness, their conversations have been recorded without their approval, physiologically damaging stimuli have been presented to children, and so on. I have a number of examples of incompetent, unthinking, uncaring, and downright immoral behavior of researchers toward human subjects that I present to students in some of my courses. Perhaps my favorite example is that of a study designed to determine the side effects of birth control pills (Fake pills, 1977), which was conducted on a group of women who presented themselves at a clinic for birth control advice. The physician in charge of the research project created two groups, one experimental and one control. He then provided the women randomly assigned to the experimental group with bona fide birth control pills whereas the control group was given placebos similar, of course, in all respects to the bona fide birth control medication but lacking the essential active ingredients. As one might expect, a number of pregnancies resulted. However, because of the *purity* of the design, the researcher was able to determine the extent to which side effects associated with birth control pills were in fact attributable to the active ingredient. The level of incompetence associated with this research design is almost laughable, but it is important to note that it took place in a clinic and the research was funded by a government agency.

Ethical decisions in clinical research are never easy, and the problem is often compounded by ethics committees who are charged with the responsibility of reviewing research procedures. Unfortunately, many of these committees are composed of individuals who do not know how to do research and this compounds an already difficult problem. There are, of course, many examples of silliness in this domain also.

There are a number of very straightforward principles for the conduct of important clinical research. As I assume any clinician would agree, the well-being of the patient takes absolute priority over any other consideration. Although we are likely to agree with this statement in an unqualified manner, it is important to keep in mind that the patient's welfare may often cause compromises in the search for an understanding of how a process works. In the clinical context, we often are most concerned with achieving a goal even at the expense of our fully understanding just why what we did worked. Marriage counsellors, I presume, are more concerned with having their clients emerge from therapy sessions with better marriages than understanding just how they brought about that improvement. Further, I trust that all peace researchers value peace more than they value an understanding of war. The practical implication of the principle of incontrovertible priority of patients' welfare is that it forces clinicians to use research designs that provide some understanding of the nature of the processes involved without depriving the clients of therapeutic benefit. The second major principle to which I subscribe is that under no circumstances should a client be deprived of treatment for experimental purposes. I am reminded of a statement that I recently heard from an AIDS sufferer and patient advocate. He said, "The one thing we do know about AIDS, and which need not be tested further, is that AIDS sufferers who are given inert substances, as part of control procedures, die."

The concept of experimental versus control groups is so fundamental to the folklore of scientific research that burying that concept is going to be extraordinarily difficult. Much of the aversion that caring clinicians have to scientific research is based on the concept that in order to understand how a treatment works, some clients are going to have to be deprived of the benefit of that treatment. Let me say at the outset that I consider this concept to be nonsense. Anyone who cannot design a better method for determining the side effects of birth control pills than the one described previously should simply stop doing research and probably should stop doing clinical practice as well.

The problem with the experimental versus control conception of the research process is not only that it is morally repugnant, but, more importantly, it is often ecologically invalid. Further, the procedure is so at variance with our growing realization of mind/body healing that results from such experimental designs are very likely to be irrelevant, in the long run, to clinical practice. An excellent example of the problem associated with the experimental versus control group research design is a study that was recently conducted in the Ottawa area. The purpose of the research was to test the efficacy of a drug on a particular heart disorder. Designed according to conventional wisdom, patient volunteers were randomly assigned to experimental or control conditions. The double blind was strictly enforced in that both groups took the same number of capsules at the same time each day. Neither the patient volunteers nor the drug administrators knew which patients had the active capsules and which patients had the placebo capsules. Following conventional ethical practice, patients were told prior to random assignment that they would be in either an experimental or a control condition and that the medication they were taking would be either one that contained the active ingredient or one that contained no active ingredient. They were fully informed before they participated and signed consent forms.

As someone once said, damning the darkness is easier than lighting a few candles. But I think it is important for us to examine clinical research of this nature in very intricate detail with the view of developing research strategies that are more appropriate in clinical contexts. The first problem with the research design just described is that it is ecologically invalid. Furthermore, it is ecologically invalid from either the traditional model of acting upon a passive patient or the more contemporary behavioral medical model of engaging the client as a participant in the healing process. The reason that this particular approach is ecologically invalid is that one cannot think of any conceivable therapeutic context in which a client would be dealt with in a manner comparable to the research setting. When a client seeks assistance for any type of complaint, practitioners take special efforts to enhance the client's expectations of the efficacy of the treatment procedures. Further, health practitioners make a special effort to minimize uncertainty associated with treatment procedures and, finally, one always does what one can to alleviate client anxiety. In the experimental–control context, on the other hand, clients are in a state of uncertainty and very likely they are in a state of heightened arousal, if not stress, due to the fact that they are in a state of cognitive uncertainty with regard to treatment procedures. It is important to point out that such procedures also give rise to the problem of self-selection of participants. People who volunteer for such programs are different from people who refuse to participate, so that the generality of the results is immediately questionable. Finally, we add the ethical issue of the deprivation of treatment of individuals in the control conditions, even though individuals have been informed of the probability of being placed in the deprivation condition.

Criticism is, of course, easy. Offering positive alternatives is an entirely different issue. I am not a cardiologist, and I would not presume to redesign the previously described experiment without a much more substantial understanding of exactly what the cardiologists were attempting to accomplish. Further, I think it goes without saying that there are conditions under which ethically harsh decisions must be made, but it is critical that we understand the very serious limitations of the conventional experimental–control design, particularly when these difficulties are strongly exacerbated by informed consent requirements. I am not suggesting that we do away with informed consent. Rather, I am emphasizing that efforts to make an ethically problematic design less morally repugnant may be rendering the entire research context far more ecologically invalid.

THE ROLE OF DECISIONS AND EXPECTATIONS

Clinical research designs that require some compromise associated with client welfare are most problematic. The conventional wisdom is that whenever a design requires such compromise, the client must be informed of the nature of this compromise and offered a choice. That choice is usually whether to participate in the clinical research program or to refuse participation and seek treatment elsewhere. We must keep in mind that individuals who participate in this research have health complaints often of an extraordinarily serious nature. Frequently these clients have chronic conditions and have been exposed to multiple treatment efforts by any number of health professionals. Presumably the research is being conducted because the researchers are looking for safer, more thorough, faster, cheaper, and/or less dangerous treatment procedures. The reason a client would agree to participate in the first place is that he or she has a condition that needs attention that has not responded to conventional, conservative, or readily available treatment.

Now, if we look first at the traditional passive-patient treatment model, we immediately recognize the problem of creating a condition in which the patient has a pessimistic expectation about treatment outcome. There is an overwhelming literature available that indicates that the patient's beliefs and expectations activate very real mind/body healing mechanisms. Traditionally viewed as a placebo response, and often as a nuisance factor (Cousins, 1979), positive attitudes, emotions, and a firm belief in one's ability to activate mind/body healing mechanisms are critical to health and healing. This orientation is the fundamental distinction between the traditional passive-patient model and the more contemporary behavioral medical concept of establishing a close partner relationship between the client and the health care provider.

What is striking in the literature with regard to psychosomatic healing processes is the consistency of the statistics. In the considerable social psychological literature addressed to conformity, yielding, and compliance, we find that approximately one third of virtually any subject population will show a yielding or conforming response to a wide variety of manipulations. Often these requests for compliance are totally outrageous but, even so, compliance rates in the region of one third of the population are quite frequent. Studies of the placebo response show a similar pattern. Beecher (1959) and Evans (1985), in reviews of a total of 26 studies, reported that about one third of patients with a wide variety of pain conditions found significant relief with placebos. As Rossi (1986) pointed out, carefully controlled clinical studies of placebos consistently find that about one third of the patients receive more than 50% pain relief.

Rossi (1986) also pointed out that the placebo response is not limited to pain relief but has been found to be a mind/body healing factor in a wide variety of complaints including hypertension, blood cell counts, headaches, diabetes, colitis, asthma, and cancer. Such findings indicate that belief structures implicate the autonomic nervous system, the endocrine system, and the immune system. Further, the placebo response has been shown to be implicated in a variety of treatment procedures including surgical, biofeedback, and psychotherapeutic.

Now, although about one third of clients will show a placebo response, it is something else again to determine exactly how much of the variance associated with the change in the client's condition is attributable to the placebo. Evans (1985) also found a remarkable consistency in the degree of the placebo response, which averages about 55% of the therapeutic effect. What is even more remarkable is that the effectiveness of the placebo compared to standard doses of a variety of different drugs remains relatively constant, namely about 55%. Furthermore, the effect is not limited to analgesics but has been found in studies of psychotropic drugs, such as tricyclics (Morris & Beck, 1974), lithium (Marini, Sheard, Bridges, & Wagner, 1976), and nonpharmacological treatments.

There are several implications that are important with regard to the research on placebos. First of all, I do not like the term *placebo*. The dictionary defines a placebo as an inactive pharmaceutically inert compound given to a patient to satisfy the expectation for medication. Further, we have long criticized different healing methodologies on the basis that they merely activated the placebo response. This criticism is based on the observation that if a health professional behaves in a manner that fosters the client's expectation of improvement (the placebo response), then about one third of the clients will improve regardless of the treatment procedure used. This critical analysis continues with a further observation that if one has a well-established procedure for selecting out those individuals who do not respond well to the placebo response, then one can have a thriving practice and enjoy the reputation of a miracle worker, when in fact one's therapeutic methods have no particular efficacy.

We tend to think of the susceptibility factor as being a relatively stable factor, comparable to a personality trait. It is entirely possible, however, that the "magic third" that we find in placebo, conformity, and yielding studies does not reflect an individual difference but rather reflects a normal fluctuation or cycle of the individual. In short, at times an individual may be more susceptible to influence or placebo effects than others. This may be due to factors such as fatigue, autonomic arousal, hemispheric dominance, and the like. Thus, all individuals may well be susceptible about one third of the time with the result that research studies demonstrate that about one third of the population responds to various forms of influence. I find that this is a particularly useful operating principle in clinical practice. It encourages practitioners to look at combinations of treatments. The treatment finally judged effective by the client may well be the one that was potentiated by the placebo response (which, again, accounts for 50% to 60% of the effectiveness, irrespective of the nature or potency of the treatment).

It is also widely known that shamans, witch doctors, voodoo priests, faith healers, and the like do in fact strongly influence people's physical and emotional states. A voodoo priest's curse can be more lethal than a bullet if the victim believes it to be so. Believers do spontaneously remit all types of physical and emotional complaints when they strongly believe that they are in the presence of a person who has the power to cure them. Such procedures usually involve ritual, initiation, or changes in physical state which presumably enhance belief and confidence in the efficacy of the treatment procedure.

In short, I think it goes without saying that research procedures that jeopardize or minimize clients' expectations regarding treatment efficacy are open to criticism on a number of grounds. First, I think all the health professions are becoming aware of the fact that the most powerful tool in their armamentarium is likely to be the "doctor who resides within" (Cousins, 1979, p. 69). Clients who are shown how to help cure themselves do so. And any treatment procedure or research procedure that compromises this process is likely to yield results that are ecologically invalid and to create a treatment environment that compromises client well-being.

However, the overwhelming problem with such random-assignment controlled clinical trial procedures is that they do not seem to resolve the questions posed by the investigators. This results largely, I believe, from the clinically invalid procedures used to investigate clinical treatments. Research methods that randomly assign clients to treatment procedures that are administered in a manner at variance with proper clinical methods are simply invalid on many grounds. To ask the question "Is thermal biofeedback superior to a relaxation exercise for the treatment of migraine headache?" is to ask the wrong question. Defining this problem in meaningful researchable terms requires that we determine who improves with which type of treatment and why.

The literature abounds with ongoing controversies regarding the relative efficacy of competing treatment procedures that have been studied in widely varying contexts. Research in the area of biofeedback provides some good examples of this problem. Raynaud's disease and syndrome have been treated with thermal biofeedback, autogenic training, progressive muscular relaxation, and so on. The controversy regarding relative efficacy of these treatments has at least a 15-year history and still no resolution (e.g., Blanchard & Haynes, 1975; Freedman, Ianni, & Wenig, 1985; Guglielmi, Roberts, & Patterson, 1982; Jacobson, Hackett, Surman, & Silverberg, 1973; Keefe, Surwit, & Pilon, 1980; Rose & Carlson, 1987). Some reported that thermal biofeedback is superior; others reported that there was no difference among the various treatments; still others reported that treatment combinations are important. Of course, they were all correct.

Similar squabbles continue with regard to the efficacy of various types of muscle biofeedback training for tension headache (Holroyd, Andrasik, & Noble, 1980) and the research on the merit of progressive muscular relaxation relative to other relaxation techniques is likewise enjoying a protracted life. Apparently the score in 1978 was 60% to 40% (of the 25 studies reviewed) in favor of progressive muscular relaxation (Borkovec & Sides, 1978).

Similarly, the relative efficacy of live versus recorded relaxation exercises remains a controversial issue. Some researchers found a difference, some no difference, and some perhaps a difference (see Beiman, Israel, & Johnson, 1978; Bernstein & Borkovec, 1975; Borkovec & Sides, 1978; Hamberger & Schuldt, 1986).

Outcome studies of the treatment of unipolar depression (see McLean & Carr, 1989) as well as meta-analyses comparing psychotherapy with "placebo" (see Prioleau, Murdock, & Brody, 1983; Smith, Glass, & Miller, 1980) further indicate that there are many effective treatment procedures to which clients respond differently.

The point is that research methods that do not apply treatment in a clinically meaningful way are inappropriate for several reasons. Such methods may be ethically unacceptable because client well-being is compromised. They may be logically unacceptable because they are ecologically invalid. Further, such procedures may give rise to equivocal results because client variables are ignored, albeit randomly.

We come now to the other problem associated with the experimental–control research design. The second problem is the harmful effects of inappropriate use of informed consent. I believe it was Sigmund Freud who once pointed out that all processes must go to their logical absurdity, and I have heard of a number of outrageously foolish ethics committee requirements imposed on researchers. Asking subjects to give informed consent in an inappropriate context can not only invalidate many research procedures, but also can cause unnecessary distress on the part of participants. However, there is a more important aspect associated with the informed consent problem. The first issue is the problem of the syndrome of too much choice. If you have a client who presents with an anxiety-exacerbated disorder, asking that person to choose among treatment procedures, or telling (or implying to) him or her that he or she is involved in a research project in which treatment is being manipulated for research purposes jeopardizes client well-being. Granted, there may be circumstances under which such procedures are required, but we should always keep in mind that the way we set up treatment procedures is often going to dramatically affect the efficacy of the treatment itself and, subsequently, the well-being of the client.

Finally, what are our obligations to the patient who has volunteered under an informed consent methodology, once the experiment is completed? In even the simplest of the two by two designs, there are a number of outcomes that are problematic. There is, of course, no problem if a patient had been put on an active pharmacological compound and his or her condition improved. The person would simply be told that he or she had received a drug of choice and that his or her condition improved accordingly. If the condition has not improved, and the patient has been on the pharmacologically active ingredient, we are faced with a dilemma. Namely, did the patient's condition not improve because of the ecological invalidity of the treatment procedure (i.e., patient's expectations and belief structures were affected by the research design), or is the patient one of the individuals who is routinely found not to respond to conventional and traditional treatment procedures for a particular malady. Do we tell the patient we will try it again, but this time let them know that the pharmacological agent is in fact the drug of choice? What will the patient's belief structure be at that time? Cautious? Suspicious? Angry? Frustrated? Treating a patient with a drug of choice after lack of desired response to that same pharmacological agent during an informed consent clinical trial may understandably seriously limit the potential for the medication to be effective in the more traditional usage.

What if the patient had been in the placebo group and his or her condition had not improved? This is perhaps the easiest condition to deal with given that it is consistent with patient and researcher's expectations. The patient is informed that the condition did not improve because as luck had it they had been placed in the control condition and that now once the researcher has gained the information required, proper treatment will be provided. If the researchers have attended to the interpersonal aspects of any research procedure, the patient is very likely to accept this good naturedly and may in fact respond more dramatically to the drug of choice treatment because expectations regarding the drug's efficacy have in fact been enhanced by the experience with the placebo.

Dealing with informed consent and the responsibilities associated with informed consent subsequent to a patient remitting a symptom on placebo is an ethical dilemma that many researchers must face. Do we tell the individual that even though he or she was on an inactive pharmacological agent the symptoms remitted? What does that communicate to the patient? Hopefully the researchers are sensitive enough not to communicate "Ha, ha, it was all in your head." If the researchers can communicate to the patient that the bodily defensive mechanisms had been mobilized by the patient's expectations and that these defenses had "cured" him or her, the outcome is likely to be a satisfactory one to everyone involved. If, however, the patient experiences apprehension regarding the permanence, stability, or actuality of the "cure," then relapse may be potentiated. It is for this reason that many researchers choose not to reveal to patients who have improved under placebo conditions that they were in fact in the placebo group. They argue that patients' well-being would be jeopardized more by being informed that they were in the placebo condition than if they were led to believe that they were in the active pharmacological agent condition.

CONTROL GROUPS AND CONTRAST GROUPS

The ethical conundrum that researchers face is the necessity for treatment deprivation, which is a requirement of conventionally controlled procedures. In order to design such treatment in a more ethically acceptable form, researchers often make use of the delayed treatment control procedure. Using this procedure, clients are randomly assigned to immediate or delayed treatment. Those on the "waiting list" receive treatment after some specified period of time, and the change in their condition relative to the change in the condition of those individuals exposed to the treatment condition is the measure of treatment efficacy.

The delayed treatment procedure, as one might imagine, is not free of ethical dilemmas. In the first instance, we have the problem of random assignment to treatment versus waiting list and the extent to which individuals should be so informed (i.e., that assignment is on a random basis). Second, how does one deal with the problem of treating waiting-list clients if it is determined that the treatment is not efficacious? Researchers often circumvent this problem by delaying analysis of their research until everyone has been treated, but the ethical dilemma remains. Of course we have the fatigue factor or habituation factor in many treatment procedures in which practitioners lose their enthusiasm or interest or arousal for the waiting list clients relative to the first clients treated.

There are other procedures that are designed to treat clients more equitably in the sense that everyone is equally deprived of treatment. One design, called the reversal design, can only be used for procedures that are in fact reversible or subject to relapse. As the name implies, this procedure involves presenting and then terminating a treatment procedure alternately over some period of time. Changes in the client's complaint during the treatment on–off cycles determines the relative efficacy of the treatment procedure. It is obvious, of course, that the ethical dilemmas associated with this procedure are indeed formidable. If one imposes informed consent requirements on this design, one can readily see that confounding is almost inevitable. Furthermore, allowing a condition to relapse also creates a number of moral and ethical problems. At a recent behavioral medicine conference, a researcher presented a paper on comparing a number of treatment procedures with regard to relapse rates. The procedure very simply was to provide one of several treatments to groups of clients for a specified period of time. The treatment was then terminated and the clients were followed up for another specified period of time and relapse rates among the groups were compared. This, of course, is a treatment-deprivation design and has all of the ethical pitfalls of any procedure that compromises client well-being.

An example that I like to offer my students with regard to the problems associated with clinical designs is borrowed from peace research. In peace research, the goal is the reduction of lethality, however one cares to measure it. To a peace researcher, following a relapse design allowing a conflict to increase in lethality would be unconscionable given the value structure of peace research (assuming, of course, that one had adequate control over a conflict to use a relapse design).

A variation on control group procedures designed to be less ethically objectionable is the use of contrast groups. In contrast procedures, treatments are contrasted against one another as opposed to against an inert placebo. The argument in favor of such a procedure is that clients are not deprived of treatment, the placebo response may be strongly engaged or activated, and the procedure is not at variance with normal clinical procedure in which a clinician often must choose among a number of different treatment regimens for a particular client. Thus for the treatment of a certain type of arthritis, a rheumatologist may randomly assign patients to conventional clinical doses of indomethacin versus naproxen. Or, if attempting to examine the most effective dosages, contrast groups may be defined in terms of dosage of a specific compound.

Although perhaps less objectionable, contrast procedures still pose many ethical and moral dilemmas for the practitioner. As soon as allocation to treatment condition is made random the problem arises of whether or not the client should be informed. Furthermore, if one is rigid with regard to formal contrast procedures in which treatment duration is fixed and contrast made at a particular point in time, then the requirements of the research design are defined in terms of the treatment as opposed to the treatment being modified or titrated relative to the changes in the client's condition. The latter is a most serious ethical dilemma.

A control procedure that I find very useful and ethically acceptable is the historical control group (Patterson, Questod, & de Lateur, 1989). As the term implies, the historical control group refers to clients treated in the past who are compared with present clients to whom different (or additional) treatments are applied. Adequate data must be obtained on all clients for historical comparisons to be meaningful. In addition to systematic measures on the dependent variable, data on other important client characteristics should be routinely obtained to permit the matching of the historical controls to present treatment subjects.

As with all procedures, the historical control design is vulnerable to error. Previously treated clients may vary as to time of year, economic climate, sociopolitical climate, differences in treatment and support personnel, therapist enthusiasm, and the like. Also, unless one's data are unusually complete, important issues such as client attrition are likely to be difficult to analyze or control. In addition, other characteristics of treatment such as timing or structure are likely to be difficult to match or control.

However, although this control procedure, like all others, has some problematic features, it is a powerful and, more importantly, an ethically appropriate clinical research procedure. The intention to utilize historical control procedures forces clinicians to be organized and systematic. To be viable as a control procedure, predispositional as well as outcome data collection must be well-conceived and systematic.

CUMULATED SINGLE-N RESEARCH DESIGNS

A concept from physics of particular relevance to the social and health sciences is the Heisenberg Uncertainty Principle (Heisenberg, 1971). The essential feature of the Uncertainty Principle that is of importance for our purposes is that measurement affects the phenomenon under investigation. A number of examples of this principle may be offered. In obtaining blood for clinical analysis, venapuncture modifies the substance under investigation, however trivially. A person's mood, attitude, and emotional state are modified by the process of measuring those conditions either with questionnaires or interviews.

In behavioral medicine, measurement of the complaint is part of the treatment procedure. In fact, some highly successful weight control programs use periodic weighing and recording of weight as the principle feature of the program. Cigarette smoking is modified by keeping daily records of the amount smoked, physiological measurements are affected by efforts to obtain baselines, pain perception is influenced by systematic self-recording, and so on.

Now, the Heisenberg Principle, or, in our language, the measurement-treatment concept, fits very nicely with cumulated single-n research-treatment designs, particularly from the behavioral medicine perspective. The important distinction between the traditional passive-patient model and the active-client behavioral medical model is that the client and the health provider form a partnership as coinvestigators dealing with the client's complaint as the subject matter. The client is always involved in decision-making but in a therapeutically relevant context. The measurement as treatment concept is fundamental to replicated single-n research designs.

At a recent conference, I attended a remarkable address by psychiatrist George Engel. Engel reported on a 15-year study of his bleeding hemorrhoids. He pointed out that from time to time hemorrhoids bleed and the biomedical reasoning ascribed such random bleeding to local trauma related either to straining or stool consistency. Over a 15-year period of self-observation, Engel found no relationship to trauma. Instead, in a 4-year prospective study, he found that bleeding occurred significantly more often around dates directly and indirectly related to his father's death almost 70 years earlier. Although Engel was concerned with contrasting the biomedical and the biopsychosocial conceptual models, for our purposes, his single-n study exemplifies a number of the features of research designs that appear most suitable for clinical studies. The single-n design is based on the notion that, as Engel pointed out, it is not how many subjects one has, but how much data one has collected that is critical for understanding biopsychosocial processes as related to health and wellness.

Case study has constraints but these constraints need not compromise investigative rigor provided the researcher reorient his or her approach to scientific research. Again, the overriding principle is that the client's well-being takes absolute precedence over any other objective. Under such circumstances, multiple treatments are often simultaneously administered if the practitioner has reason to believe that withholding any element of the treatment regimen may jeopardize the client's well-being. Further, the practitioner must apply the treatment procedures in a manner that maximally marshals the client's optimistic belief in the potency and/or efficacy of the treatment to which he or she is being exposed. In addition, again from the perspective of mind/body healing, the client must be made to feel as though he or she is in a partnership with the health provider in an investigation designed to efficiently deal with the complaint.

Even with these constraints the practitioner can apply the treatment procedures in a manner that permits the determination of the potential efficacy of particular components of a treatment regimen. The basic procedure is that the practitioner and the client collect quantitative evidence of the concordance of changes in a treatment procedure with changes in the client's biopsychosocial state.

The contrast between the biomedical and the biopsychosocial approaches to clinical research are nicely captured by the squabble between the homeopathic and allopathic physicians with regard to research procedures designed by the latter group to demonstrate the lack of efficacy of homeopathic procedures. In one such study, following conventional design procedures, three groups were formed of persons afflicted with osteoarthritis of the hip and knee. One group was administered a conventional analgesic and the anti-inflammatory drug, fenoprofen. A second group was administered a homeopathic dose of the poison oak extract, rhus toxicodendron. The third group was administered a placebo. The purpose here is not to argue for or against allopathic or homeopathic treatment procedures, but it is worthwhile to point out that single-n replicated research designs are markedly different from the type of research procedure characterized by this example. Critics of the multiple and experimental control group design point out that the problem with such procedures, other than the ethical and moral problems discussed previously, is that the research requires that one treat the disease rather than the client. From the mind/body healing perspective, one wants to involve the client in the decision-making, create a situation in which the patient is sensitive to changes in his or her condition, and modify or change the treatment regimen accordingly. Outcome research is then based on the concept of cumulated single-n studies or the replicated single-n design. In cumulative single-n research, one categorizes clients on the basis of similarities in the structure of the treatment procedure. This is the direct extension of the concept of construct validity in which treatment regimens are categorized and compared on the basis of prototypes. A treatment procedure is represented as a prototype in order to formalize the properties that are common to certain treatment situations without becoming enmeshed in the details unique to each. Regularities observed in the prototypical treatment procedures in turn contribute to our understanding of the efficacy of treatment, the processes by which treatment effects change, comparison between and among treatment procedures, and so on.

PATIENT MODULATED TREATMENT PROCEDURE: THE TREATMENT-CHOICE DESIGN

Specific examples can be useful to exemplify just how research can follow a single-n format in the context of the involved patient model. One of the problems that clinicians face when attempting to treat clients is that of selecting among a wide variety of treatment options. Even if one is settled into the practice of providing only a single type of treatment for a particular complaint, issues such as timing, potency, frequency of treatment administration, individual differences of clients, risk factors, and so on, are important considerations and every practitioner must make such decisions. The underlying concept of the client modulated single-n design is that the practitioner makes the choice among treatments to administer but the client makes the determination of which treatment or treatments are efficaciously impacting his or her complaint. After that determination is made, further refinements in the treatment regimen can be introduced by the practitioner with the client consistently making the determination of efficacy. Embedded within this design is client and practitioner assessment of the properties of the complaint, namely severity, periodicity, frequency, variance, and the like. The following examples of the use of this methodology for subliminal treatment and for pharmacological treatment should help to clarify the procedure.

In the flow diagram shown in Fig. 3.1, the treatment proceeds as follows: At time of initial contact, once the nature of the client's complaint has been delineated, a regimen of data collection is provided for the client and thoroughly explained. When dealing with a pain problem, for example, one of the standard pain measurement procedures might be used. A client might be asked to record the level of subjective pain on a 0-to-5 scale during every waking hour. The subjective values of the

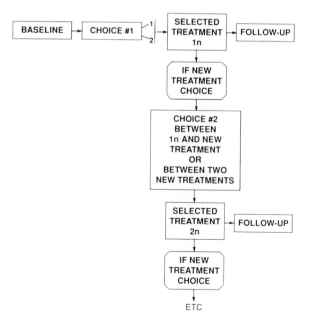

FIG. 3.1.   Flow diagram of treatment choice procedure.

numbers are thoroughly explained to the client: 0 indicates no pain at all; 1 indicates that the client is aware of pain but the pain is not a serious distraction; 2 indicates a level of annoying pain to which the client is frequently attentive but not at a level of severity that interferes with social or work situations; 3 is a level of pain that is severe enough to interfere with social and occupational functioning but not to the extent of debilitation; 4, a level of pain that is a severe limitation to social and work situations; 5 is the most severe or highest intensity pain the client has experienced associated with his or her complaint. Some practitioners prefer to use more widely spaced measurements such as at mealtimes and bedtime; other variations are, of course, possible.

In addition to measuring subjective pain, one would generally also monitor amount and frequency of analgesic use, subjective mood, and other aspects of the client's condition that are relevant to treatment. Often at this time, a recognized treatment package is prescribed. For example, in psychological intervention for pain, it is not uncommon for clinicians to prescribe some sort of relaxation training such as progressive muscular relaxation, visualization, focusing, cognitive tension reduction, and the like. During this time the health service provider may also obtain other clinical measurements that are relevant to the client's complaint. For pain, such clinical measures may include range of movement, peripheral blood flow, electromyographic measurements, and so forth, which should be obtained on a multiple measurement per visit basis.

The treatment-choice design is imposed on any other treatment regimen that is applied in a systematic fashion. This is characterized in the flow diagram in terms of treatment choice. When working with subliminal messages, I inform the individual that he or she is being exposed to several different types of subliminal treatment. What I want him or her to do is try all of the treatments for as long as he or she likes and to decide which single treatment makes him or her *feel* the best. There are several important characteristics associated with this instruction. First, it builds expectation of positive therapeutic benefit by orienting the client toward expecting to feel better. Second, it is important to point out to the client that you are not asking which treatment he or she likes the best (with subliminal messages embedded in music or noise patients cannot tell the difference anyway), but rather you are focusing the client's attention on feelings. Third, we are doing what is necessary to mobilize the therapeutic benefit of placebo. If one of the treatment choices is, in fact, a placebo condition and the client benefits from it, then one has proceeded in a manner that is not detrimental to the client. In my own use of subliminal messages, for example, I often embed the subliminal messages in background music. There is considerable evidence to indicate that music in and of itself can have a therapeutic benefit.

Subsequent to treatment choice the client is exposed to continuous treatment of the selected option and, of course, the client maintains the data record on his or her condition. Should a new treatment or modification of present treatment be warranted, another treatment-choice procedure can be implemented following exactly the same procedure as for previous treatment selections. One can consistently refine a treatment package by combining previously chosen treatments with a contrast treatment with the client being instructed to select the treatment that makes him or her feel the best. It is important that any new treatment choice be designed so that the subject cannot determine the previously chosen treatment, to control for demand characteristics, expectation, habituation, and so forth.

Now let us take a few examples. Assume that I have 20 clients who complain of a particular form of migraine headache to whom I plan to present a treatment choice between two different subliminal messages. Initially, and prior to subliminal treatment, I provide the clients with a relaxation program that they are instructed to use in their home environments. After the first visit I may find that my population has dropped to 15 because 5 of the clients report that their migraine headaches are considerably improved. This improvement may have resulted from the relaxation package they used at home. These 5 clients would receive the support procedure designed to maintain the gains they have made. Because their condition had improved to an extent that they defined as successful, they would not be exposed to any further treatments. Of the 15 whose discomfort continues at a level at which further treatment is warranted, the two subliminal treatments are given to the clients for home use. Usually these treatments are on each side of an audiocassette, which the client can play at will in the home environment. During this phase I generally ask clients to keep a running record of just how often they have used each side of the tape (i.e., how many times they have used each treatment) and each time I see them I ask them if they have decided on which treatment (which side of the tape) makes them feel the best. Obviously, there are three possible outcomes from a design with two choices. Namely, the client can indicate that either one of the two treatment procedures was most beneficial or they can indicate that they were unable to choose between the two. Hence, one has three groups of clients made up from cumulated single-n designs: Those who chose Treatment 1; those who chose Treatment 2; and those who could not make a choice between the two treatments.

During the treatment phase, clients are instructed to use the treatment of choice chronically for a specified period of time. Clients who have not yet decided are asked to continue to alternate between the treatments. Concordant measures provided by the client as well as concordant clinical measures give us an indication of the efficacy of each one of these treatment packages. It is important to know that this treatment package can be applied over any other treatment procedure that the clinician feels is appropriate. In the previous example, biofeedback treatment could be used concurrently with the subliminal choice treatment procedure. That is, subjects do not have to be deprived of treatment for meaningful comparisons to be made.

One can make use of multiple-baseline designs in conjunction with the treatment-choice design by introducing the treatment choice after various lengths of baseline measurement. In short, the treatment-choice procedure maintains all of the properties of patient involvement, recruitment of optimism, and marshaling of potential placebo effects all to the benefit of the client without sacrificing experimental rigor.

This procedure can be used for determination of efficacy of drug versus placebo. The client is simply given two bottles, one containing the experimental compound, the other containing the placebo compound and told to take one of either A or B but not both at appropriate times until the client is able to determine which compound makes him or her *feel* best. After treatment choice is complete the client is offered the chosen treatment chronically. Again, this may include the use of placebo, an active compound, or a combination of the two. Obviously, there are many variations on this theme, but again it sustains all of the necessary properties associated with meaningful mind/body approaches to client care.

The chance probability of a person selecting the subliminal side of the tape or the active ingredient in a two-choice situation, of course, is .50. Thus if five clients sequentially picked a specific treatment, the probability of that choice is .031 (i.e., $.5 \times .5 \times .5 \times .5 \times .5 = .031$). However, more generally one is likely to find various combinations of clients choosing a particular treatment or unable to make a choice between two treatments.

In practice, some clients will indicate that they cannot choose between the two treatment procedures. That is, they report that they cannot discriminate between which one of the treatments makes them feel better. This could indicate that any benefit the client is receiving is attributable to placebo, but, of course, other possibilities exist. For example, it is possible that clients benefit from the interaction between the two treatments or from reduced level of frequency of treatments maintained by alternation and so on. However, from a statistical perspective, we must recognize that even if we do not offer the client the option of no choice, clinically in fact some individuals will indicate that they are unable to make such a choice. Clinically one tends to find that the frequency of no choice is relatively low, or at least that has been my experience. It is important to note, however, that when applying any binomial statistic, the number of "no-opinion" clients excluded from the analysis must be very small relative to the total sample size. A choice ratio of 12 to 2 may be both statistically and clinically meaningful if there was one "no-opinion" client excluded from the analysis, but would certainly be meaningless if 100 "no-opinion" clients had been excluded.

Let us return to the example of the 15 migraine clients who were offered a two-treatment choice protocol. If two clients picked treatment A, and one client could not make up his or her mind about which treatment to choose, then 12 clients picked Treatment B. Eliminating the one client who was unable to make a choice between Treatment A and Treatment B, reduces the cumulative single-n to 14. Two choices of Treatment B and 12 choices of Treatment A has a one-tail probability of .006 and a two-tail probability of .012. One would generally apply one-tail probability when considering an active treatment versus a placebo and a two-tail probability when considering two active treatment conditions. The table of probabilities associated with binomial comparisons is shown in Table 3.1.

These probabilities only determine the client's ability to discriminate between treatment procedures. That is, the clients in the migraine situation, for example, are able to indicate that Treatment A makes them feel better at a frequency that is beyond chance. This does not in any way indicate the clinical efficacy of the treatment. The clinical efficacy of the treatment is determined by examining the client's monitoring of his or her complaint in conjunction with the clinical measurements that are taken during visits. Again, we have a number of possibilities. It is entirely possible that a client indicates that a particular treatment makes him or her feel better, but in terms of subjective evaluation of pain, there is no significant difference between individuals selecting Treatment A versus those selecting Treatment B. On the other hand, we may find that the nature of the complaint changes differently, in terms of the frequency or time of onset, the duration of the migraine, the number of migraines suffered, the amount of analgesic medication taken, or an increase in the variance associated with the severity of the migraine for individuals who have selected Treatment A versus those who have chosen Treatment B. Individuals who are unable to select between treatment conditions are often interesting contrast groups. In one of my studies, for example, it became obvious that individuals who did not make a selection between two treatment procedures were not compliant with home treatment regimen as indicated by other indicators of compliance. Hence, their inability to choose between Treatment A and Treatment B was a reflection of their compliance and presumably the amount of exposure they had to the treatment procedures rather than a property of the treatment procedures or the treatment-choice design.

TABLE 3.1
Table of Binomial Probability Distribution*

One-tailed probabilities associated with values as small as observed values of X or N-X (whichever is smaller) when $P = Q = 1/2$. Decimal points are omitted (e.g., .046 is shown as 046).

N \ X	0	1	2	3	4	5	6	7	8	9	10	11	12	13	14	15	16	17	18	19	20	21	22	23	24	25
5	031	188	500																							
6	016	109	344	656																						
7	008	062	227	500																						
8	004	035	145	363	637																					
9	002	020	090	254	500																					
10	001	011	055	172	377	623																				
11		006	033	113	274	500																				
12		003	019	073	194	387	613																			
13		002	011	046	133	291	500																			
14		001	006	029	090	212	395	605																		
15			004	018	059	151	304	500																		
16			002	011	038	105	227	402	598																	
17			001	006	025	072	166	315	500																	
18				004	015	048	119	240	407	593																
19				002	010	032	084	180	324	500																
20				001	006	021	058	132	252	412	588															
21					004	013	039	095	192	332	500															
22					002	008	026	067	143	262	416	584														
23					001	005	017	047	105	202	339	500														
24						003	011	032	076	154	271	419	581													

25	002	007	022	054	115	212	345	500													
26	001	005	014	038	084	163	279	422	577												
27		003	010	026	061	124	221	350	500												
28		002	006	018	044	092	172	286	425	574											
29		001	004	012	031	068	132	229	356	500											
30			003	008	021	049	100	181	292	428	572										
31			002	005	015	035	075	140	236	360	500										
32			001	004	010	025	055	108	188	298	430	570									
33				002	007	018	040	081	148	243	364	500									
34				001	004	012	029	061	115	196	304	432	568								
35					003	008	020	045	088	155	250	368	500								
36					002	006	014	033	066	120	202	309	434	566							
37					001	004	010	024	049	094	162	256	371	500							
38						003	007	017	036	072	128	209	314	436	564						
39						002	005	012	027	055	100	168	261	375	500						
40						001	003	008	019	041	077	134	215	318	437	563					
41							002	006	014	030	059	106	174	266	378	500					
42							001	004	010	022	044	082	140	220	322	439	561				
43								003	007	016	033	063	111	180	271	380	500				
44								002	005	011	024	048	087	146	226	326	440	560			
45								001	003	008	018	036	068	116	186	276	383	500			
46									002	006	013	027	052	092	151	231	329	442	558		
47									001	004	009	020	039	072	121	191	280	385	500		
48										003	007	015	030	056	093	156	235	333	443	557	
49										002	005	011	022	043	076	126	196	284	388	500	
50										001	003	008	016	032	059	101	161	240	336	444	556

*Adapted from Tables of the Cumulative Binomial Probability Distribution. Harvard University Press, 1955.

Obviously this single-n research design could be expanded for any number of refinements of a treatment or the number of treatment choices could be expanded. One could have a client choose between three or four different treatments, but I believe that there are important limitations to expanding the number of decisions a client must make and the ability the client might have for successful discrimination. In my own experience the two-choice treatment procedure appears to be extremely sensitive.

COMBINING TREATMENTS

The important property of the treatment-choice design is that it permits powerful research within the context of maximally efficient therapy. In my practice, I often embed the subliminal message in background music. There is ample evidence to indicate that music alone can have an important therapeutic effect. Combining the benefits of certain types of music in conjunction with the therapeutic benefit of a subliminal message might give enhanced therapeutic impact. This procedure also provides a powerful method for determining the magnitude of the therapeutic effect of the subliminal message in competition with a background of demonstrated therapeutic efficacy.

The procedures are, again, quite straightforward. First, one presents the client with a tape with 15 minutes of recorded music on each side. The client is given the same instruction as when testing the efficacy of subliminal messages, namely to select the side of the tape that makes the client feel best. The client is again reminded to select the side that makes him or her feel best as opposed to selecting the music he or she favors. This procedure emphasizes the focus on subjective feelings. After the client selects the music sequence according to these instructions, the subliminal message is embedded in the music sequence on one side of the tape, and some contrast condition is put on the subliminal track in the same music sequence on the other side of the tape. The client is then instructed to again select the side that makes him or her feel the best. It is explained to the client that, in contrast to the first choice procedure in which they could hear the difference between each side of the tape, the music for the second choice procedure will sound the same. Therefore, it is important for the client to focus his or her attention on his or her feelings and select the side of the subliminal test tape that makes him or her feel the best. It should further be explained to the client that getting in touch with his or her feelings might require a bit of time. Hence, he or she should not feel obliged to make a rapid selection, but simply keep alternating the tape from side to side while attending to his or her feelings.

The client is to expect that both sides of the tape will give rise to a sensation of feeling better, but one side will have a more potent effect on the psychological sense of contentment and well-being than the other. Once convinced of an emotional preference for one side of the tape, the client is instructed to use the preferred side exclusively.

The combined-treatments design permits one to determine whether certain treatment conditions have higher selection rates when in competition with other treatments. Furthermore, by collecting systematic data on the client's mind–body states that are relevant to the client's presenting complaints, the therapeutic efficacy of each treatment can be determined. It is important to note that the treatment procedure used on any particular client is always the treatment selected by that client. That is, the client is never told to use Treatment B when he or she has selected Treatment A in an A–B choice procedure.

Let us consider the following example. Assume that each of 10 clients, referred for treatment of essential hypertension, is given a tape consisting of two musical selections, one on each side, each lasting 15 minutes. Each client is instructed to play the tape, wherever, whenever, and as often as he or she chooses and to select the side that makes him or her feel best. Of the 10 clients, assume that 8 select Side A, 2 select Side B. The probability associated with an 8 out of 10 outcome in a binomial choice situation is .055.

The music selected by each client is then used as the background embedding medium for the subliminal treatment. One side of the tape contains the embedded subliminal message whereas the other side of the tape contains a comparable sound pressure level of embedded white noise or other contrast material. The clients are again told to play the tape, whenever, wherever, and as often as they wish while focusing attention on their feelings and to select the side that makes them feel best.

Assume that of the 10 clients, 6 select Side A and 4 select Side B. The probability of such a departure from chance is .377. Hence we would conclude that the choice of the subliminal treatment procedure does not exceed chance levels in competition with an affectively preferred treatment as the embedding medium. However, it should be recognized that in all cases, the client has been exposed to a combination of two self-selected treatment procedures with the expectation of and the experiencing of positive beneficial impact on his or her complaint.

Now, we turn to the data that the client has been recording on dimensions related to his or her presenting complaint. If one finds, for example, that the 6 people who selected the subliminal treatment had greater declines in mean arterial pressure over the course of treatment relative to the 4 individuals who selected the alternative treatment condition, one has information that, although the affective detection threshold does not statistically exceed chance, the therapeutic efficacy of the treatment can be demonstrated. At this point, of course, treatment for clients not responding as desired could be modified.

If one repeats this entire process with another 10 clients, and again finds that 8 out of 10 select the same musical sequence as those in the first group of 10 clients, the combined probability now decreases to .003 (i.e., .055 × .055). One then embeds the subliminal messages in the client's preferred music selection and again presents this to the 10 clients. If one finds that 7 out of 10 picked the same subliminal treatment as the 6 out of 10 in the first study the probability of affective detection exceeding chance decreases to $p = .065$ (i.e., .377 × .172 = .065).

If, rather than considering the preceding as two experiments of N = 10 each (i.e., an experiment and a replication), one pools the clients and considers the N to be 20, the binomial probability would be approximately double that calculated on the basis of two independent studies with N = 10 (see Table 3.1). That is, the probability associated with 16 out of 20 is .006 and the probability associated with 13 out of 20 is .132 (see Note 1).

It should also be recognized that one has additional important information available. From the total sample of 20 clients, 16 people picked a particular musical sequence and 4 people picked the alternate. One can ask the same questions of this division of the data as well. Namely, what is the affective detection probability for the subliminal message when the embedding medium is Musical Sequence A versus Musical Sequence B. Of the 20 people tested, 14 picked the subliminal treatment. Therefore on average, we would expect that 70% of individuals who selected Music Selection A would choose the subliminal treatment and likewise, 70% of the sample of individuals who selected Music Sequence B would select the subliminal treatment. If, for example, we find that no one who selected Music Sequence B chose the subliminal treatment in the second choice-treatment stage, that indeed may be interesting and worthy of further research.

It should be obvious that one can collect extremely interesting and important data with relatively small samples in a treatment situation that is ecologically valid, therapeutically efficient, and ethically proper.

Note 1

The obtained probability level of combining the two probabilities of the independent samples will be lower than that obtained if one combines the population and then determines the probability. This results from the difference in possible outcomes from these two procedures. For example, if 5 clients make the choice, there are 6 possible outcomes (i.e., 0, 1, 2, 3, 4, or 5 clients choose X). Combining the probabilities from two 5-client samples then gives a probability based on 12 possible outcomes. If on the one hand, the two 5-client samples are combined prior to determination of probability level, the number of possible outcomes is 11 (i.e., 0, 1...9, 10 clients choose X).

Hence, if one has two 6-client samples and in each only one client chooses X, the binomial probability for each sample is .109. If combined on the basis of independent samples this becomes .012 (i.e., .109 × .109 = .012). If the samples are combined and then the probability is determined, the probability is .019. The former level will be close to the probability level that would be obtained if the sample size was increased by one while retaining the same level of X choice (i.e., 2 X choices from a population of 13 has a probability of .011).

In practice-based research one is likely to have several small logically created groups. For example, a new procedure may be used for a small group of clients. After determining that a beneficial effect appears likely, a second small sample of clients may be exposed to the same procedure. These client samples are independent and may differ on other dimensions such as time of year, the therapist's expectations regarding treatment efficacy, client gender, and the like. Combining the probabilities on the basis of independent samples therefore, is a reasonable procedure for assessing effect likelihood based on binomial choice.

Note 2

Some of the comparisons discussed in the preceding section lend themselves to tests of the significance of difference between proportions.

A. *Test of the significance of an observed proportion.* If one had an expected or comparison proportion against which to test an observed proportion, the following formula may be used:

$$Z = \frac{P_o - P}{\sqrt{\dfrac{P(1 - P)}{N}}}$$

where P_o = observed proportion
    P = expected or comparison proportion
    N = number of clients in group from which P_o is determined

For example, if 14 out of 20 clients selected Treatment A (P_o = 14/20

= .70) and one wants to determine the probability that the proportion .70 is *greater than* an expected chance outcome of .50 then:

$$Z = \frac{.70 - .50}{\sqrt{\dfrac{.50(.50)}{20}}}$$

$$Z = \frac{.20}{.1118}$$

$$Z = 1.79$$

Refer to the table of Normal Curve Areas (Table 3.2) and find that for a Z of 1.79 the proportional part of the curve beyond the obtained Z value is .463. Therefore, the one-tail probability that the proportion .70 is *greater than* the comparison proportion .50 is .037 (.500 − .463 = .037).

B. *Test of the significance of the difference between two observed proportions.* If one had two groups of clients each of which were given the treatment choice procedure, the significance of the difference between the proportions of clients choosing a particular treatment can be determined using the following formula.

$$Z = \frac{P_1 - P_2}{\sqrt{\dfrac{P_1(1-P_1) + P_2(1-P_2)}{N_1 + N_2}}}$$

where P_1 = proportion observed in Group 1.
P_2 = proportion observed in Group 2.
N_1 = number of clients in Group 1.
N_2 = number of clients in Group 2.

For example, to determine the effects of the embedding medium on the selection of the subliminal treatment one could expose Group 1 to the treatment-choice procedure with Medium A and Group 2 to the choice procedure with Medium B. If both groups contained 30 clients and 18 of the 30 Group 1 clients selected the subliminal treatment (18/30 = .60) whereas 24 of the 30 Group 2 clients selected the subliminal treatment (24/30 = .80) then:

$$Z = \frac{.80 - .60}{\sqrt{\dfrac{.80(.20) + .60(.40)}{30 + 30}}}$$

$$Z = \frac{.20}{.082}$$

$$Z = 2.43$$

TABLE 3.2
Normal Curve

Z	.00	.01	.02	.03	.04	.05	.06	.07	.08	.09
0.0	.000	.004	.008	.012	.016	.020	.024	.028	.032	.036
0.1	.040	.044	.048	.052	.056	.060	.064	.068	.071	.075
0.2	.079	.083	.087	.091	.095	.099	.103	.106	.110	.114
0.3	.118	.122	.126	.129	.133	.137	.141	.144	.148	.152
0.4	.155	.159	.163	.166	.170	.174	.177	.181	.184	.188
0.5	.192	.195	.199	.202	.205	.209	.212	.216	.219	.222
0.6	.226	.229	.232	.236	.239	.242	.245	.249	.252	.255
0.7	.258	.261	.264	.267	.270	.273	.276	.279	.282	.285
0.8	.288	.291	.294	.297	.300	.302	.305	.308	.311	.313
0.9	.316	.319	.321	.324	.326	.329	.332	.334	.337	.339
1.0	.341	.344	.346	.349	.351	.353	.355	.358	.360	.362
1.1	.364	.367	.369	.371	.373	.375	.377	.380	.381	.383
1.2	.385	.387	.389	.391	.393	.394	.396	.398	.400	.402
1.3	.403	.405	.407	.408	.410	.412	.413	.415	.416	.418
1.4	.419	.421	.422	.424	.425	.427	.428	.429	.431	.432
1.5	.433	.435	.436	.437	.438	.439	.441	.442	.443	.444
1.6	.445	.447	.446	.447	.450	.451	.452	.453	.454	.455
1.7	.455	.456	.457	.458	.459	.460	.461	.462	.463	.463
1.8	.464	.465	.466	.466	.467	.468	.469	.469	.470	.471
1.9	.471	.472	.473	.473	.474	.474	.475	.476	.476	.477
2.0	.477	.478	.478	.479	.479	.480	.480	.481	.481	.482
2.1	.482	.483	.483	.483	.484	.484	.485	.485	.485	.486
2.2	.486	.486	.487	.487	.488	.488	.488	.488	.489	.489
2.3	.489	.490	.490	.490	.490	.491	.491	.491	.491	.492
2.4	.492	.492	.492	.493	.493	.493	.493	.493	.493	.494
2.5	.494	.494	.494	.494	.495	.495	.495	.495	.495	.495
2.6	.495	.496	.496	.496	.496	.496	.496	.496	.496	.496
2.7	.497	.497	.497	.497	.497	.497	.497	.497	.497	.497
2.8	.497	.498	.498	.498	.498	.498	.498	.498	.498	.498
2.9	.498	.498	.498	.498	.498	.498	.499	.499	.499	.499
3.0	.499	.499	.499	.499	.499	.499	.499	.499	.499	.499
3.1	.499	.499	.499	.499	.499	.499	.499	.499	.499	.499
3.2	.499	.499	.499	.499	.499	.499	.499	.499	.499	.499
3.3	.499									
3.4	.499									
3.5	.499									
3.6	.499									
3.7	.499									
3.8	.499									
3.9	.499									
4.0	.499									

Referring to Table 3.2, we find that the proportional part of the normal curve beyond the obtained Z value is .493. Therefore, the one-tailed probability that the two proportions are significantly different is .007 (.500 − .493).

These statistical procedures are particularly suitable for use with the historical contrast group design described earlier. If one has been systematic regarding determining the proportions of clients who, in the past, responded favorably to particular treatments then one can determine the relative efficacy of a new procedure relative to historical contrast groups.

For the aforementioned methods to be appropriately interpreted as a deviate of the normal curve, an arbitrary rule has been suggested (Ferguson, 1981). Take the smallest value of *each* choice ratio and multiply that value by the appropriate N. If each product exceeds 5, the test may be used. For example, if 12 out of 20 clients choose treatment A, P would equal .60 and Q would equal .40 (Q = 1 − P). The smallest proportion (.40) multiplied by N (20) equals 8 and therefore the test may be used.

In the second test (B) described, P_1 is .80 and, therefore, $1-P_1 = .20$. The product of .20 multiplied by the N_1 of 30 equals 6. The P_2 is .60 and, therefore, $1-P_2 = .40$. The product of .40 multiplied by the N_2 of 30 is 12. Because *both* of these values exceed 5, the test of the difference between proportions may be used.

CHAPTER FOUR

Clinical Treatment Procedures

During the era of concern regarding the commercial use of visual sub-liminal advertising, Goldiamond (1958) pointed out that the issue was not one of ethics but rather of efficacy. He maintained that if subliminal perception does not exist, then there is no ethical issue. Although I disagree with this pragmatic view, I do agree that the important issue is efficacy.

As discussed in previous sections of this guide, we know that veridical subliminal effects can be demonstrated. Stimuli below detection threshold do influence choice, aesthetic judgment, motor performance, subjective mood, memory, cognitive processes, certainty of judgment, and creative performance. Although we know that an effect can be demonstrated, we are less certain about the clinical efficacy of subliminal procedures.

Mindful that the overriding priority is client well-being, clinical efficacy is a complicated issue. In the first place, we may find that the most clini-cally efficacious procedure requires that one abandon a strict definition of subliminality. In chapter 1 of this guide, we discussed the notion of "leakage" with regard to auditory subliminal treatments. Leakage, again, refers to detectable snippets of the subliminal message emerging through the embedding or ambient medium. It may be, for example, that such detectable leaks, although not discriminable on the basis of content, may strongly contribute to the clients' expectations of positive treatment effects. If this proves to be the case, it would be foolhardy, if not unethical, for any clinician to persist in the use of detection threshold procedures.

Much of the controversy surrounding the clinical use of subliminal messages centers on the issue of partial discrimination of the stimulus. Part of the problem rests with the modality commonly used for clinical subliminal work. When visual procedures are used, the problem of remaining below discrimination threshold is more serious than when auditory procedures are used. Visual procedures require that subjects focus at a specific point on the visual field. Often such procedures involve the use of a tachistoscope or a tachistoscopic shutter on a slide projector. To remain below discrimination threshold, such procedures often require the use of multiple projection devices to maintain a relatively constant level of illumination. Furthermore, the procedure that appears most successful for preventing discrimination is that of backward pattern masking. Backward masking involves presenting a stimulus word or phrase for a short duration (e.g., 17 msec) followed immediately by a mask of randomly arranged and randomly oriented capitalized letters of the alphabet for a longer duration (e.g., 100 msec). Of course, with so many structural features of the stimulus presentation procedure being varied, the controversy regarding subliminality could enjoy a significant life expectancy. Some of the main players in this debate are or were Brody, 1988; Cheesman & Merikle, 1986; Henley, 1984; Holender, 1986; Lewicki, 1986; Marcel, 1983a, 1983b; Silverman, 1985.

Another problem is that the backward masking procedure may alter the effective properties of the subliminal message in important ways. A series of five studies reported by Dixon and Henley (1984) indicates that although not discriminable, masked words have different effects than totally subliminal verbal stimuli that are visually presented.

This problem is not unique to the visual modality. Auditory subliminal messages are always embedded in some masking sound such as room ambient, white noise, pure tones, or music. There are advantages and disadvantages of each embedding medium, discussed later.

Although, in my judgment, certain forms of visual subliminal procedures may be very useful in clinical settings, on balance I strongly prefer auditory preparations. There are several advantages of the auditory modality. First of all, one can present rather long statements to clients. This could be of considerable importance. Our data indicate that multiple related word presentations are superior to single word presentations. As discussed previously, this could simply reflect an advantage of redundancy correcting the misunderstanding of a word. More importantly, however, longer statements allow the practitioner to cover a greater range of content associated with a particular treatment objective. By analogy, if one were using hypnosis to treat obesity, the simple intervention "Don't eat" would seem to be less efficacious than an intervention that stressed health, loss of cravings, custodianship of one's body, interpretation of the meaning of food, and the like. Similarly, subliminal treatments incorporating broader content may prove to be of considerably greater benefit than short presentations.

The issue of just what is getting into the fovea when verbal material is presented visually remains a problem. When a person fixates on a point, the words nearest that point may be processed more thoroughly than more distant words. Similarly, the stimulus size, the viewing distance, the levels of illumination of the room, and the viewing field are all important in determining just what is processed and whether or not the message is subliminal. A complete account of some of these difficulties may be found in Fudin (1986, 1987). The interesting aspect of these squabbles from the clinicians' perspective is that treatment efficacy appears to be ignored. The problems associated with longer presentations using the visual modality are formidable and hence auditory methods are preferable.

On the other hand, the proverb "One picture is worth one thousand words," seems relevant here. As we discuss later in this chapter, Silverman (1976, 1985) and his associates are able to package significant psycho-dynamic content in written and pictorial visual combinations. The impact of the words "Fuck Mommy" and an attendant picture of an older woman in a sexually suggestive pose or, conversely, the words "Mommy and I are one" with an attendant picture of two individuals joined at the shoulders, would seem to be considerable. Given the considerable therapeutic benefit of imagery, we may find that subliminally presented pictures have important clinical uses. Silverman (1978) cited evidence (Kaplan, 1976) indicating that the effects of the subliminal messages are, in fact, more powerful if presented in association with a relevant picture.

Our own research leads me to suspect that auditory procedures are superior for verbal material. However, the effects of visual images for diagnostic as well as treatment purposes warrants intensive clinical investigation. Later in this chapter we review some interesting research indicating that subliminally presented images do, indeed, have effects of considerable clinical interest.

A second advantage of auditory procedures is that they can be omni-directional. If messages are embedded into background ambient sound, the client can be exposed to the subliminal content virtually anywhere. Furthermore, given that focused attention is not required, the client may be receiving subliminal content while engaged in a wide variety of activities. It remains to be determined, however, just how the predispositional and concurrent state of the client is associated with the efficacy of treatment. Clients may, for example, be less susceptible to subliminal messages if they are physically active or distracted by other stimuli. Or we may find that certain concurrent activities are best for specific treatments. We return to this issue later in the present chapter.

A third advantage, although an ethical quagmire, is that auditory procedures may be applied more easily without alerting the client that subliminal messages are being presented. Visual procedures require that clients be focusing on some visual field. Hence, bringing clients into contact with the visual field without their being made suspicious of intent may require elaborate deceptions. My own clinical experience and research has convinced me that informing clients that subliminal messages are being presented does not in any way interfere with treatment. Indeed, as we discuss shortly, informed clients, those that elect to receive subliminal treatment, appear to respond more dramatically to treatment, at least as compared to laboratory preparations with nonclinical populations. I should indicate at this point that, although clients may be informed about the purpose and methodological issues associated with subliminal treatment, they are not made aware of the verbatim content of the message.

The major advantage of auditory procedures, however, is that of the facility with which one can establish thresholds and critical effective ranges. The extrapolation method described in the previous section can be very quickly accomplished and threshold verified. Although in my own clinical practice I have found that the most efficacious treatment ranges are below the stimulus detection threshold, and therefore actually subliminal as we understand the term, clinicians should use whatever ranges appear best for their clients. Client improvement is, of course, more important than threshold label. It does appear as though truly subliminal ranges with informed clients are most effective. Clinicians should not be overly concerned about maintaining truly subliminal procedures, but it is imperative that they be precise with regard to presentation procedures so that the ranges relative to specific thresholds can be determined. And, as discussed previously, one can be very precise about an imprecise threshold. In short, one can ask a client if he or she can understand a message or one can precisely determine whether the client can discriminate content without being aware of his or her ability to do so. The clinical research into the efficacy of subliminal treatment procedures is going to depend in great measure on just how diligently clinicians attend to the issue of threshold. To this end, it may be useful to establish a new nomenclature. Rather than refer to all such treatment procedures as subliminal, it may be more appropriate to categorize these treatments as "Out-of-awareness" or perhaps "Below selective attention." However, rather than create other arenas for protracted debate, I have elected to retain the traditional label of subliminal while emphasizing that there are many limens. It is essential, therefore, when reporting one's clinical findings that the reader know to which threshold the message was subliminal.

STIMULUS ENERGY LEVELS

Our data, and the data from other laboratories, indicate that subliminal procedures appear to be effective for influencing a very wide range of human behaviors. We have found that physiological, cognitive, and affective behavior can be influenced by stimuli, the content of which is unavailable to recipients' selective attention.

It is also quite clear that identical stimuli can give rise to quite different effects depending on the physical energy of the stimulus relative to the recipient's physiological receptivity. In fact, some investigators maintained that the acid test of subliminality is that a stimulus must give rise to qualitatively different responses when presented subliminally versus supraliminally (Silverman, 1985). Others, as we have discussed, argued that the influences of subliminal versus supraliminal stimuli are essentially parallel (Brody, 1988; Dixon, 1971). The evidence indicates that differences are often observed, but theoretically there seems to be no compelling reason to maintain that the qualitative difference in response is a necessary condition for subliminality. It seems to me that the issue of qualitative difference in response is more of a practical clinical issue. If supraliminal works as well as subliminal then by all means use supraliminal procedures. They are after all, easier, cheaper, and less ethically troublesome than subliminal presentations.

The issue of qualitative difference in response is not as straightforward as we might imagine. One may, for example, find no qualitative differences at the individual level whereas differences are observed at the group level. A good example of this problem is found when using a lever-pressing research preparation. When one exhorts subjects to "press faster" one often finds that group variance increases. Some subjects comply and attempt to increase their lever pressing rates, others demonstrate reactance (Brehm, 1966) and slow down, whereas still others appear to make such an effort that their speed actually declines (Swingle & Moors, 1966).

When the "press faster" message is presented subliminally, group variance often decreases reflecting increases in the speed of the slower subjects. This effect is also often found when incentives such as money or competition are instrumentally associated with higher lever-pressing rates (Swingle, 1970b).

At the individual level, on the other hand, one may find only one pattern that reflects a difference between subliminal and supraliminal presentations. If a subject wishes to comply with the experimenter's requests than both subliminal and supraliminal presentations are likely to give rise to similar patterns. Similarly, if subjects are very close to their maximum speed, further effort often reduces lever-pressing rates and again similar patterns are observed. Only when the subject is motivated to react against an experimenter's requests would one be likely to find a qualitative difference between subliminal and supraliminal presentations of the "press faster" message.

On the other hand, the evidence clearly indicates that there may indeed be very important qualitative differences in responses as the energy level of the message is varied across the range of subliminal and supraliminal receptivity. As previously discussed, stimuli are more likely to be processed structurally as the energy level of the stimuli approach and penetrate the content discrimination threshold. Somekh and Wilding (1973) and Groeger (1984, 1986a, 1986b) demonstrated that semantic meaning is more likely to be processed when stimulus words are presented below detection thresholds. The same stimulus word is more likely to be processed structurally when presented above detection or above discrimination thresholds. For example, structural processing of the word "harpy" as "happy" or "snug" as "smug" are more likely at above detection threshold energy levels. This discontinuity in the processing of the meaning of a message presented above versus below specific thresholds may be responsible for some paradoxical effects reported in the literature (e.g., Borgeat, Elie, Chaloult, & Chabot, 1985).

It should also be noted that the discontinuity effect may result from a shift in processing systems of the organism as stimuli attract selective attention. The notion of single, dual, or multiple cognitive processing systems was discussed earlier. For our present purposes, it is important to note that there is evidence that indicates the presence of a perceptual "dead zone" in the region just below the content discrimination threshold. As discussed earlier, our research indicates that subliminal messages are ineffective around -5 dB(A). Although there has been considerable debate regarding the effective range for subliminal stimuli, with some researchers advocating energy levels "close" to "awareness" thresholds, the finding of no, or very limited effects, at "near-liminal" ranges is often reported (e.g., Spence, 1983). Hence, the common finding of enhanced physiological response with increased stimulus energy at supraliminal levels does not hold for cognitive and affective responses at subliminal stimulus levels. As discussed previously, there does appear to be a critical effective range with a "dead zone" separating subliminal from supraliminal ranges. As well, there is a physiological lower limit to the subliminal range. Our own research indicates that presentations below -32 dB(A) are simply not physiologically detectable. A study conducted in our laboratories using subliminal messages that were effective at -15 dB(A) found these messages to be absolutely ineffective at -35 dB(A). Presentations were right or left unilateral, or bilateral, and measures included subjective mood ratings, heart rate, blood pressure, frontalis

EMG, and finger temperature. Although effects were found for the presentation of music, no effects were observed for any of the presentation procedures when the message energy level was − 35 dB(A). It should be noted that one of the principal reasons for conducting this study was a report of a commercial application of auditory subliminal messages indicating a presentation level of − 35 dB. Our data indicate no effects at this level. Our data indicate that for auditory presentations, the effective range is from − 10 to − 30 dB(A), with the most effective range being between − 15 and − 25 dB(A) relative to ambient or embedding sound levels.

We have found, however, that there are ranges of effectiveness when group procedures are being used. For example, in several of the studies reported earlier, and in some reported in the present chapter, only subjects seated at certain distances from the sound source demonstrated an effect. Furthermore, for tapes used by individuals at home, clients appear to have a preferred volume level that elicits the desired effects.

For visual procedures, without mask, effects can be demonstrated with as few as four exposures to a 4 msec presentation with a ratio of blank field to stimulus field illumination ranging from 1:1 to 3:1 (see Bornstein & Masling, 1984; Fudin, 1986; Porterfield & Golding, 1985, for details of the nonmasked procedures). The effective range for subliminal presentations is an exposure of less than 12 msec with background illumination at least as bright as the stimulus illumination (a range of 15 fl to 10 fl for the blank and the stimulus field appear effective). The presentation rate of 5 exposures per stimulus with an interstimulus interval of approximately 5 seconds is sufficient to demonstrate behavioral effects (Bornstein, Leone, & Galley, 1987; Seamon, Marsh, & Brody, 1984; Silverman, 1977).

A presentation of 4 msec with a brighter blank-field prestimulus presentation of 4 msec, although sufficient for yielding behavioral effects, will not be above chance for forced recall, recognition, or discrimination judgments (Bornstein, Leone, & Galley, 1987).

For masked visual procedures, verbal messages are presented above the levels that would permit some subjects to recognize letters. Porterfield and Golding (1985) reported that the *recognition* threshold for letters falls in the presentation range of 12 to 80 msec ($M = 31$, $SD = 18$). The discrimination of the stimulus message is blocked by the presentation of a visual pattern. The effective presentation durations for this procedure appear to be 17 msec for the message followed immediately by a 100 msec pattern mask. There are some variations on this procedure including preceding and following a 17 msec message with pattern masks at 50 to 100 msec durations. Again, the pattern masks are generally capitalized letters randomly arranged with respect to order, placement, and orientation which cover the entire visual field subtended by the message stimulus (Cheesman & Merikle, 1986; Lewicki, 1986).

In my opinion, pattern-masked procedures are not appropriate for clinical purposes. Although one can convincingly demonstrate that pattern masks block recognition of the stimulus, one is burdened with the potential influence of the mask itself. Furthermore, the procedure is more cumbersome than unmasked visual presentation and, of course, the behavioral efficacy of the 4 msec unmasked procedure has been well established.

Although both of the preceding visual techniques appear to be effective and both have been shown to be below discrimination thresholds they are nonetheless above the detection threshold for some subjects. Hence, in my judgment, clinical practice clearly favors auditory subliminal procedures. It appears that keeping a subliminal message well below discrimination thresholds affords the most effective behavioral influence. And auditory techniques are the most efficient and reliable procedures for presenting messages in the effective ranges. For reasons already stated, however, visual techniques may prove to be extremely useful in clinical contexts, and for these purposes Silverman's unmasked procedure is recommended.

Finally, it should again be stated that our criterion for considering a treatment procedure useful is simply whether or not the procedure gives rise to clinically meaningful effects. It so happens that with respect to auditory procedures, clinically meaningful effects occur when the stimulus message is subliminal with reference to the detection threshold. The situation is less certain, in my judgment, with regard to visually presented material. The debate regarding whether or not visually presented material is really subliminal rages on and will continue to do so for quite some time. Nonetheless, clinically meaningful effects have been reported with visually presented materials at durations that are below an individual's threshold for content determination. To become enmeshed in efforts to assure that stimuli are subliminal with regard to some arbitrarily established threshold is to miss the point of clinical practice investigation. It would be rather like a peace researcher rejecting a demonstrably effective hostilities reduction procedure because the protagonists fail to accept the conventional definition of conflict resolution. The peace researcher should value peace more than an understanding of why a conflict resolution strategy works. Similarly, clinical practice investigations focus on client improvement first. Concerns regarding the probity, or lack thereof, of particular labels or concepts should be a distant second.

In the following sections, I include treatment procedures that appear to be clinically useful. Those procedures that make use of the visual modality may not be subliminal with regard to the detection threshold but have been included because they offer useful insights for clinical practice treatment and research.

My own research, presented both in the present section as well as elsewhere in this book, makes use of a procedure that is clinically effective *and is subliminal* with regard to the objective detection threshold determined by the method of limits. Furthermore, the stimulus ranges that we have established were derived on the basis of behavioral effectiveness—they are actually below the objective detection threshold. It would be easy to become involved in a quarrel regarding the assertion of subliminality of the auditory messages. After all, if a person responds to the stimulus, how can it be subliminal? The critical element in this debate is the subject's or client's response. If the client's attention is cognitively focused on such properties of the stimulus as discrimination of content, discrimination between different stimuli on the basis of structure, or detection of the presence or absence of a stimulus, a subliminal range of stimulus effectiveness will be determined. The client will not demonstrate processing of the stimulus because he or she has not been required to do so. If, on the other hand, the client is asked to discriminate on the basis of affect, stimulus processing may well be in evidence. There is considerable evidence to indicate that subjects can discriminate stimuli affectively that they cannot discriminate cognitively (Bornstein, Leone, & Galley, 1987; Henley, 1975; Kunst-Wilson & Zajonc, 1980; Zajonc, 1980). The basic design is to present stimuli to subjects at energy levels below their ability to detect when asked to respond with a "present-absent" or "same-different" choice. The subjects are then asked to make an affective judgment of these same stimuli, such as being asked which stimuli they "like" best, or which make them "feel the best," or to aesthetically evaluate some simultaneously presented stimulus.

This basic design has been replicated frequently and appears quite robust. The range of subliminal effectiveness then is between the cognitive and affective response levels. As a result the subject or client is found to respond to stimuli of which he or she claims, and is objectively found, to have no cognitive awareness.

If the situation was as uncomplicated as the preceding, I think the controversy regarding subliminal perception would have been settled long ago. In the final analysis it would seem plausible that rather than temporal primacy of affective versus cognitive processing (see Lazarus, 1984; Zajonc, 1984) being the issue, perhaps primary refers to the stimulus energy levels required for cognitive versus affective processing. Specifically, affect and meaning are processed at lower stimulus energy levels than are the structural and cognitive content properties of stimuli.

Perhaps affective primacy, relative to stimulus energy levels, accounts for some subliminal effects. However, it is also clear that thoughts can be directly influenced by stimuli below the cognitive detection threshold. As discussed elsewhere in this book, our research indicates that categories of judgment, problem solving, and thought concepts can be influenced by auditory stimuli that subjects cannot detect. It is difficult to conceptualize just how affect could be implicated in this process. The evidence suggests that thought processes are influenced by stimuli that are well below the content discrimination threshold. It also appears that priming or preparing the subject for the subliminal intrusion is important for the stimuli to be effective.

It may well be, therefore, that subliminal effects operate somewhat differently in cognitive versus affective domains. Thus, although we can demonstrate cognitive intrusions of subliminal stimuli, the effect may be of trivial clinical importance when compared with procedures designed to implicate affective behavior. As the following sections indicate, clinically useful procedures appear to be largely affective in nature. One might quarrel that the psychodynamic subliminal research indicates an important unconscious cognitive component; nonetheless, major implication of affective domains appears plausible, if not obvious. In short, the jury is not only still out, but will apparently remain out for some time. Clinicians, by carefully constructing treatment contrasts, following methods of the type discussed in the Methodology chapter (chapter 3) of this book, will be able to contribute importantly to our understanding of these intriguing issues.

THE EMBEDDING MEDIUM

Elsewhere in this book, the technical issues associated with the embedding medium were reviewed. Some embedding media are easier to use or are more ecologically valid. Enhancing people's relaxation in a waiting room or while listening to a radio broadcast (Borgeat & Chaloult, 1985) may require that the embedding medium be music. For a time- and space-restricted clinical treatment, on the other hand, white noise may be a more appropriate medium.

Music is itself an effective modifier of affect. Indeed, musical therapy is, in many areas, a highly respected method of clinical assessment and treatment. Hence it is important to determine the mood altering influence of the musical selections used as the embedding medium for subliminal treatments. My own experience in the clinical use of subliminal messages indicates quite clearly that if clients do not like the music selected as the embedding medium, they simply do not listen to the subliminal tapes. In fact, I have found that clinical clients are more likely to use subliminal treatments embedded in white noise as compared to those embedded in music they do not like.

On the other hand, I have found that if one offers the client a choice between musical selections, one can use either the most *or* the least preferred selection as an embedding medium and obtain good compliance with treatment regimen. Of course, I always offer a rationale for using as an embedding medium either the most or least preferred musical selection. Nonetheless, if given a choice, the client's commitment to treatment regimen is enhanced. It is important, as discussed more thoroughly in chapter 3, that one instruct the client to select the musical selection least (or most) liked of the two offered. The process that appears to enhance compliance is the forced choice. Instructing a client to select a musical piece "that you like" will often give rise to the response "I don't like either." The instruction that has, in my experience, worked quite well is simply: "I am going to give you a cassette tape recording with two musical selections, one on each side. Play each side as often as you like until you decide which selection you like least (or best). Based on your decision, I will use one of these selections as an embedding medium for the subliminal treatment . . . that we discussed earlier."

The decision as to whether to use music, white or pink noise, or pure tones as the embedding medium rests largely on the treatment objectives and on the time and environmental constraints associated with the treatment utilization. The synergic effect of the embedding medium on the subliminal treatment is also important. If one were attempting to enhance arousal, for example, one might wish to avoid music that has a relaxing influence although the interactive effects of medium and message have not been explored. It is not inconceivable that "arousing" messages might be more effective in "relaxing" media as compared with media that are themselves arousing.

White noise has an arousing influence at both supraliminal as well as at subliminal levels (Zenhausern & Hansen, 1974). As discussed earlier, we find evidence that white noise, or any added sound energy, presented at levels below detection threshold have the effect of enhancing performance. For clinical purposes, in my experience, white noise is an effective embedding medium for treatments in which relaxation or positive mood induction are not paramount focuses. Such treatments would include aversive conditioning, modification of affective association, modification of cognitions, and modification of unconscious processes. Such treatments are generally applied in an office context although white noise can be used for materials prepared for home use.

Music, on the other hand, appears to be an appropriate embedding medium for mood modification and relaxation induction treatments. Music has been found to be effective in induction of the moods of elation and depression (Pignatiello, Camp, & Rasar, 1986). More specifically, Nielzen and Cesarec (1981) reported that music influences two orthogonal factors associated with subjective mood. They defined the two factors as "Tension-Relaxation" and "Gaiety-Gloom." This finding is quite consistent with the work of Russell (1978) and others that indicates that all emotions or moods include three general orthogonal factors of "Pleasure," "Arousal," and "Dominance," with the major contributions to variance being from "Pleasure" and "Arousal."

Tempo, loudness, and the structural characteristics of music have also been found to have a systematic influence on arousal as well as on subjective mood (Nielzen & Cesarec, 1982; Pearce, 1981; Rieber, 1965; Sundberg, 1982).

Physiological corroboration of the relaxing or arousing effects of music was reported by McFarland (1985). McFarland found that music judged by subjects as evoking negative emotions terminated increasing peripheral blood flow as measured by surface skin temperature, giving rise to continued decreasing blood flow. The opposite effects were found for music judged by subjects as evoking calm, positive emotions. Increased peripheral blood flow as measured by surface skin temperatures is a measure of sympathetic tone and hence an indicator of the state of relaxation of the subject.

It is important to note that the effects were associated with music rated by the subjects as evoking either positive or negative emotions. Wheeler (1985) reported that the subjects' enjoyment of music is an important determinant of the mood altering effectiveness of music. We have also found that subject ratings of the pleasantness and arousing properties of music are important determinants of the effectiveness of music on enhancement of relaxation and positive mood. Positive correlations were found between subject ratings of the pleasantness of music and positive mood changes after exposure to the music ($r(40) = .40, p < .01$). Similar correlations were found between subject ratings of the arousing or relaxing properties of musical selections and their postexposure ratings of subjective arousal and relaxation ($rs(40)$ between .30 and .39, $p < .03$).

A related issue is that of the subliminal stimuli used for control or contrast conditions. Given that it is known that sound energy added to an embedding medium can have an effect on behavior, the problem of the appropriateness of control or contrast conditions presents itself. In general, for nonclinical research, it would seem propitious to include a sound pressure level control condition. This is generally accomplished by including a condition in which white noise is presented, embedded in the medium, at a comparable SPL as the active subliminal message. The difficulty with this procedure, of course, is that one can only approximate the SPL of the active message. Given that the SPL of voice fluctuates, whereas the SPL of white noise is constant, there is no convenient way of preparing an exact SPL control tape of fluctuating white noise. Electronically, one can prepare such a tape by yoking a white noise generator to the subliminal message. Such technology allows one to produce an exact white noise "print" of the message used in the subliminal tape.

In practice, one cannot generally afford either the technology or the time required for such precision. Hence, practitioners generally attempt to keep the verbal message below a specific SPL and prepare a white noise control at the maximum SPL level of the subliminal message.

An alternative procedure, which appeared to offer considerable merit, was that of the use of the active message played backwards during the embedding recording procedure. On the surface this appears to solve the problem of keeping the added SPL of the subliminal sound constant for both the experimental and the control conditions. The only difference between forward and backward presentations of the messages would appear to be that the latter is deprived of meaningful content while maintaining a constant total SPL between the two conditions. Some of our research presented in this book used a "backward control" condition as the control or contrast treatment. Our complacency regarding this procedure was disturbed by the Reverend Gary Greenwald (Tisdall, 1983) and the excellent follow-up research by Vokey and Read (1985). Basically, Greenwald was exhorting parents regarding the evil influences of satanic messages played backwards in recordings of popular rock music. Several legislative efforts to restrict such procedures or at least to warn the consumer of the presence of backward subliminal messages followed the publication of Greenwald's views.

I am not particularly troubled by the possibility of processing backward messages, either subliminally or supraliminally. The work of Vokey and Read (1985) did, however, point out that backward speech may not be neutral. Specifically, the backward message could contain sounds or phrases that may be interpreted as meaningful. Subjects are able to discriminate the gender of the speaker and often conclude that the backward speech is a foreign language. Further, we have found isolated instances in which a backward message containing two or three words seemed to have a distressing influence on subjects.

Although it is interesting to speculate on the unconscious processes that may be implicated in extracting meaning from backward human speech, for our purposes it is only important to keep in mind that a message played backwards may not be cognitively or affectively neutral. As such, it may not be the most appropriate procedure for the preparation of control or contrast treatment materials. White noise or pure tones, although also imperfect, may prove to be a clinically more appropriate contrast to the subliminal message. However, as detailed in the methodology section (chapter 3), once one establishes the clinical effectiveness of a treatment procedure, other treatments can be tested, with the client choice method, using a known treatment as the contrast condition. This procedure is not only methodologically less troublesome but is also ethically more compatible with clinical treatment procedures.

THE SUBLIMINAL PSYCHODYNAMIC
ACTIVATION METHOD (SPA)

One of the most intriguing challenges of subliminal treatment procedures is that of developing theoretically plausible explanations for clinically effective treatments. The situation is not at all simple. How can a message that is below cognitive detection threshold exercise an influence on a person's mood? When the messages are simple and straightforward such as "Relax, be happy" we can speculate that the message directly enters a person's conscious thoughts, conceptualized as self-talk. There may be conditions that are necessary to this process such as a person being in a state of focusing on subjective mood or bodily arousal. But nonetheless such intrusions on the semantic stream of consciousness do not seem implausible. We are, of course, still faced with the problem of the neurophysiology of message reception at energy levels that do not permit cognitive detection.

Such semantic intrusions on stream of consciousness or self-talk are clearly possible as demonstrated by the studies conducted in our laboratories and elsewhere as reviewed earlier in this book. Words presented subliminally are found to emerge in the written output of subjects asked to simply record their thoughts.

A second process that also seems plausible is that a semantic label, presented subliminally, activates an episodic memory of an event of comparable emotional tone. Thus a "Be happy" message might activate a memory of a happy event which, in turn, enhances a person's subjective feelings of happiness. Auditory messages presented below the objective detection threshold might access or implicate both "semantic" and/or "episodic" memory (Tulving, 1972). The question of whether or not accessing semantic memory or intruding on self-talk results in affective change as compared with procedures that access or implicate episodic memory remains a challenging area for clinical research.

Many of the treatment procedures described in this chapter seem most parsimoniously explained as such intrusions into ongoing thought processes or as eliciting stimuli for semantic or episodic memories. Thus, although the auditory messages are outside of awareness, the thought processes affected by the subliminal messages are not, in themselves, unconscious. That is, although subjects cannot discriminate or detect the word "happy" presented subliminally, nonetheless they do have direct access to phenomenal representations of memories activated by the message. The subjects could, if requested, bring the semantic or episodic memories into consciousness and give a verbal report of such memories.

When one works with subliminal procedures, as well as with hypnosis, one begins to appreciate that affect-laden experiential representations exist at levels that vary with regard to a person's ability to selectively access such representations. Such material may be of considerable psychological and emotional importance but may exist in a state or process that would be considered to be sub- or unconscious. This unconscious material, although not directly available to a person's selective attention, influences ongoing cognitive and affective consciousness and in turn ongoing observable behavior.

One important theoretical rationale for the use of subliminal treatment procedures is that the technology permits direct access to the unconscious. Just how this might occur is an issue of considerable debate. As discussed previously, it may be that material presented at levels that escape conscious labelling, or processing of some sort, associates with unconscious material of comparable emotional tone or cognitive or affective meaning. Many psychodynamically oriented therapists who use hypnosis maintain that under certain trance conditions, the therapist can communicate directly with a client's unconscious. Such procedures as ideomotor (Barnett, 1981) or ideodynamic signaling (Rossi & Cheek, 1988) are said to permit communication with the unconscious by avoiding consciousness. Hence, unconscious material becomes available without censoring, scrutiny, or distortion of a client's conscious processes. Similarly, subliminal procedures are believed by some (e.g., Silverman, 1983; Shevrin, 1988) to allow direct access to the unconscious because the messages escape conscious detection and thereby also escape all of the distortions, both conscious and unconscious, that inevitably result when material is consciously processed.

Both conscious and unconscious processes appear to be accessible by subliminal methods. The question remains whether or not such techniques can alter the processes themselves. Although all procedures modify to some extent the processes they interact with, it may be that subliminal techniques simply elicit or add on to experiential conscious or unconscious representations. Subliminal messages may bring memories to consciousness but not alter those memories in any way.

On the other hand, subliminal messages may associate two memories or fantasies and thereby alter the affective or psychological meaning of one or both. Further, messages that are specifically targeted at psychodynamic unconscious conflicts (e.g., Oedipus complex) or unconscious fantasies (e.g., symbiosis) may arouse (i.e., intensify) or calm (i.e., reduce) such unconscious content and thereby actually alter the content.

Although clinical investigators strongly disagree on these issues, it does seem apparent that procedures developed under the aegis of a psychodynamic metaphor do seem to have therapeutic benefit. The most prominent investigator who researched psychodynamic subliminal procedures was Silverman and the procedure is called the Subliminal Psychodynamic Activation method (SPA).

Although the SPA method is included in subsequent sections that deal with specific classes of disorders, an overview of the methods and rationale for this procedure is presented here. A thorough account of the research on SPA and the important critiques of this work may be found in Balay and Shevrin (1988), Fudin (1986), Hardaway (1990), Silverman and Weinberger (1985), Weinberger (1989), and Weinberger and Silverman (1987).

Silverman's methodology was not consistent across the many studies conducted by him and his associates, an often-stated criticism of his work. Generally, however, the SPA procedure involves the tachistoscopic presentation of a short written message such as "Mommy and I are one" or "Go shit" accompanied by an appropriate picture of two people joined at the shoulders or of a person defecating. The picture usually precedes the written message and the stimuli are presented for 4 msec. Each treatment generally involves four presentations of the stimuli. The 4 msec stimuli are preceded and/or followed by a brighter blank field for durations that have varied from 30 msec to 4 msec. Bornstein, Leone, and Galley (1987) reported that subjects are not able to discriminate between message and blank slides at better than chance levels using this procedure.

Silverman maintained that verbal and pictorial messages presented subliminally directly access the unconscious. Subscribing to psychodynamic conceptualizations, Silverman proposed that symptoms related to unconscious fantasies and conflicts could be altered, that is, intensified or reduced, by arousing, calming, or gratifying such unconscious motivations. Silverman's SPA work commenced with an attempt to reduce the symptomatology of schizophrenics (much of the SPA research has been conducted on schizophrenics).

The psychoanalytic view is that behavior in general and pathological behavior in particular is motivated by unconscious ideas and images. The disturbed behavior and distorted thinking of schizophrenics are believed to be determined in part by such unconscious conflict relating to aggressive impulses. In a series of studies (Silverman, 1966; Silverman, Bronstein, & Mendelsohn, 1976; Silverman & Candell, 1970; Silverman, Candell, Pettit, & Blum, 1971; Silverman & Spiro, 1967a, 1967b; Silverman, Spiro, Weisberg, & Candell, 1969) schizophrenic patients were exposed to subliminally presented aggressive stimuli including pictures of a tiger, a charging lion, a menacing man with a knife, and a man stabbing a woman with the verbal message "Destroy Mother" or "Argument." The control or contrast conditions included a picture of a bird or the verbal messages "People talking," "People thinking," or "People are walking."

Silverman and his colleagues reported that the pathological thinking and behavior of schizophrenics are increased by exposure to the aggressive subliminal material, but that such behavior is unaffected by the control stimuli. Pathological thinking was assessed in a variety of ways (another often-cited criticism) including inkblot responses, story recall, and word association. Disturbed behavior was based on the experimenter's observations of inappropriate laughter, odd behavior, twitching, and the like.

Reduction of schizophrenic symptomatology was thought to be related to unconscious symbiotic needs, the desire to merge with another. Silverman (1972), in fact, postulated that much of the benefit of psychotherapy results from the patient's experiencing a merging with the therapist. Generally, however, the notion of symbiosis refers to the universally held unconscious need for oneness with another. More particularly it is the desire to be cared for and protected by the "good mother" of infancy.

Silverman settled on the message "Mommy and I are one," often accompanied by a picture of two people joined at the shoulder, as the symbiotically gratifying stimuli. He did so, apparently, because of anecdotal accounts of schizophrenics improving when they received symbolic gratification of their symbiotic wishes. The phrase "Mommy and I are one" was used by a patient (in treatment with Silverman's wife) when talking about her relationship with her mother.

Again, in a long series of studies, the "Mommy and I are one" message was found to reduce the symptomatology of schizophrenic patients. Silverman (Silverman & Weinberger, 1985) contended that the effect was not as pronounced in female subjects as compared with male subjects. Meta-analyses of a large number of studies (Hardaway, 1990) suggest, however, that females respond as positively as do male subjects. Some studies do indicate, however, that females respond positively to the message "Daddy and I are one" (Jackson, 1983) and "My lover and I are one" (Silverman & Grabowski, 1982).

The effect appears quite specific. Messages such as "Mommy feeds me well," "Mommy is always with me," "I cannot hurt Mommy," "Mommy and I are the same," and "Mommy and I are alike" do not reduce pathology. Further, if "Mommy" was not the term used in childhood by the patient (e.g., "Mama" in the southern United States) the "Mommy and I are one" message does not reduce pathology (Silverman, 1985). However, meta-analyses of a number of studies (Hardaway, 1990) indicate a small but reliable effect of other Mommy and other Oneness messages.

Aside from the methodological criticisms of Silverman's work, many more behaviorally oriented therapists find the results implausible because of the psychodynamic framework. Indeed, Silverman's theoretical explanations for the SPA effects do, at times, seem forced (Balay & Shevrin, 1988; Oliver & Burkham, 1985). Nonetheless, considering the vast number of studies conducted on the psychodynamics of aggression-symbiosis using a technique that is clearly subliminal relative to content discrimination, the "box score" seems to indicate that schizophrenic thinking and behavior can be influenced. Hardaway (1990) concluded that, based on his meta-analysis of SPA studies, the "Mommy and I are one" message produces a modest but robust improvement in adaptive behavior. Further, he maintained that the observed effect sizes appear large when one considers that most subjects have been exposed to the message for a total of only 32 msec or less.

With regard to treatment, Silverman pointed out that a "dose" of 4 presentations of 4 msec has a temporary effect on symptomatology, either positive or negative, lasting for 15 min or less. Longer term improvements in schizophrenic symptomatology and in other disorders as well, require three or more "doses" of the "Mommy and I are one" message per week for a minimum of 6 weeks. Dose–response relationship has not been researched, however. Further, it seems plausible that "overdose" is possible given that some differentiation between self and object-representations would seem to be necessary for healthy ego functioning (Hardaway, 1990). It is possible that a curvilinear relationship between dose level and positive outcome will be found. Beneficial effects of the message may be positively associated with exposure up to a point after which further exposure gives rise to negative effects.

The "Mommy and I are one" message appears to evoke memories with positive emotional tone. This enhanced emotional mood has a stabilizing influence that in turn may facilitate learning and therapy or reduce the disabling effects of anxiety (Hardaway, 1990). It is also important to note that positive effects are apparent only when the message is subliminal. Supraliminal presentations of "Mommy and I are one" give rise to no positive effects (Silverman & Grabowski, 1982) or negative effects, such as increased anxiety state (Garske, 1984).

The most striking SPA research was the series of studies designed to demonstrate specificity effects of particular symptom exacerbating subliminal content. Derived from psychoanalytic notions, Silverman hypothesized that anal conflicts are implicated in stuttering, and that homosexual arousal is motivated in part by incestuous fantasies. Again, all of these conflicts are unconscious and if activated should, according to Silverman, give rise to exacerbation of the related behavior. More importantly, Silverman postulated that the effect would be specific to the symptomatology implicated in the unconscious conflict. Thus, subliminal incestuous content should not have any affect on stuttering nor should anal content affect homosexual arousal.

To test these notions, several studies were conducted using emotionally laden messages designed to activate or arouse the unconscious conflicts considered relevant according to psychoanalytic theory (Silverman, 1976; Silverman, Bronstein, & Mendelsohn, 1976; Silverman, Klinger, Lustbader, Farrell, & Martin, 1972; Silverman, Kwawer, Wolitzky, & Coron, 1973).

The anal conflict message was "Go shit" accompanied by a picture of either a dog or a person defecating. The message designed to activate incestuous fantasies was "Fuck Mommy" with a picture of a man and a woman in a sexually suggestive pose.

Speech disruptions during a paraphrasing task, responses to an inkblot, and stories told in response to TAT cards were used as measures of stuttering (not all measures were used in each study). Homosexual arousal was assessed from subjects' ratings of the sexual attractiveness of photographs of males and of females which provided a sexual orientation index.

The basic findings of these studies were that subliminal content only had an effect on the relevant symptomatology. Message content designed to exacerbate anal conflict had no effect on homosexual orientation but did increase speech disruptions of stutterers. Similarly, messages designed to activate incestuous fantasies increased homosexual orientation of male homosexuals but did not affect the speech behavior of stutterers. Although there are questions about Silverman's methodology (Balay & Shevrin, 1988), the results of these studies are provocative and have focused attention on the issue of the specificity of subliminal messages used in clinical treatment.

SUBLIMINAL TREATMENT PROCEDURES
FOR THE MODIFICATION OF AFFECT AND AROUSAL

It should be stressed again that subliminal treatments are not "stand-alone" procedures. As with many other clinical methods, such as biofeedback, relaxation training, and hypnosis, the procedures must be integrated within a broader treatment regimen. Subliminal procedures can be a clinically useful adjunct to virtually any treatment orientation. In the present section we review the studies that focus on the modification of subjective mood and arousal. Although perhaps of greatest interest for the treatment of affective and anxiety disorders, such procedures seem to be widely applicable in any situation in which it appears desirable to alter either or both axes of pleasure and arousal that are common to all emotional states. It should be noted that although we tend to focus on enhancing subjective happiness and calmness, there are many situations in which clinicians may deem it therapeutically beneficial to enhance arousal or sadness.

We know from the research previously discussed, that subliminal messages that stress happiness or sadness do influence the traits attributed to stimulus persons. In addition, such messages have been found to influence the emotional tone of fictional stories written by subjects. Furthermore, self ratings of mood and anxiety have likewise been found to be affected by subliminal messages.

In the present section we review research that indicates effective modification of subjective emotional states such as happiness and depression. In addition, we review research focused on the effects of subliminal messages on self-rated arousal, state anxiety, and phobias. It should be noted that some of these studies are primarily relevant to affective disorders whereas others are relevant primarily to anxiety disorders. However, for the purposes of this section, we structure the review in terms of subliminal procedures that impact on one or both of the axes of affective (hedonic) tone and arousal (sympathetic activation) of the clients' subjective emotional state.

We know from some of the earlier work on perceptual defense (Lazarus & McCleary, 1951) that stimuli associated with unpleasant emotional content or states are processed differently than emotionally neutral stimuli. Differences in processing can be demonstrated when the stimuli are at energy levels that are in ranges that we would call subliminal, as well as when the stimuli are presented supraliminally.

Several recent studies have demonstrated that in addition to differences in processing time or in energy levels required for recognition, emotionally laden subliminal stimuli can influence the arousal state of the perceiver. Robles, Smith, Carver, and Wellens (1987), for example, had subjects view, for 2 minutes, computer generated graphics in which subliminal images were imbedded. The images were presented 20 times for about 17 msec, which is above the lower range for the recognition threshold for letters (Porterfield & Golding, 1985). The images presented were a humorous cartoon, a threatening "horror movie" image, and a featureless control image. Subjects' scores on a State-Trait anxiety questionnaire, completed immediately following the 2-minute presentation, indicated an effect of the subliminals on state anxiety but not on trait anxiety. Subjects in the humorous image group had the lowest average state anxiety score, whereas those in the threatening image group had the highest average state anxiety score. The neutral group was found to be between the above two groups with respect to average state anxiety scores, as would be expected. The fact that this procedure impacted on state anxiety but not on trait anxiety is consistent with the nature of the manipulation. We would not expect any alteration in trait anxiety associated with humorous or frightening pictures at either a subliminal or a supraliminal level. Of particular interest is the discovery that a humorous cartoon figure can reduce state anxiety when the image is presented at levels in the subliminal range.

Kemp-Wheeler and Hill (1987) matched undergraduate subjects for State-Trait anxiety and presented half with 20 emotional words and half with 20 neutral words. Stimuli were presented "10% below detection threshold." Ratings of a number of variables associated with anxiety were taken before and after the presentations. The results indicated that sweating and self-rated anxiety increased in the group exposed to the emotional words and decreased in the neutral group. Shaking and self-rated muscle tension increased in both conditions but significantly more so in the group exposed to the emotional words.

The above studies are in the tradition of Lazarus and McCleary (1951) in the sense that subliminal stimuli designed to alter general hedonic tone are found to influence indicators and self-ratings of state anxiety. These effects would not be unexpected if the stimuli were supraliminal. If one looks at an amusing picture, one is likely to feel subjectively less anxious. However, it is important to note that subjects in these studies are kept uninformed as to the type of stimuli to which they are being exposed. As well, they have no expectation regarding the expected influence of the treatment. When clients are told what to expect, the effects can be dramatically different from those found in laboratory or uninformed client research procedures.

Consider the interesting study by Olson (1988). Subjects were asked to read a speech in front of a camera—an anxiety producing task. Among other conditions, Olson included a sham subliminal procedure. Subjects were exposed to white noise and were told that subliminal messages in the white noise would "unpleasantly arouse" them while reading the speech. There were no subliminal messages in the white noise, of course, but nonetheless subjects in this condition reduced speech dysfluencies during their speeches relative to subjects who were not exposed to white noise but who were given accurate information about how they would feel. Olson interpreted his results within the framework of attribution theory as evidence that neutral labels for arousal can reduce emotionality.

Several studies from the SPA researchers also indicate that state anxiety can be influenced subliminally. Clark and Procidano (1987) found that neither the "Mommy and I are one" subliminal message nor social support from the experimenter (verbal reward and encouragement) were effective for improving task performance of "highly" test-anxious subjects. However, generally, the results of several studies (Fulford, 1980; Garske, 1984; Packer, 1984) indicate effects that appear to be related to reduced state anxiety when SPA procedures are used. Silverman and Grabowski (1982) reported that although the "Mommy and I are one" message reduced anxiety in males, the message "My lover and I are one" was effective for reducing anxiety in females.

Bryant-Tuckett and Silverman (1984) and Cook (1985) reported that the "Mommy and I are one" message increased grades and other school-rated variables for populations as varied as graduate students in statistics classes and emotionally disturbed 11- to 19-year-old residents of a treatment school. If Silverman is correct, the effect of the "Mommy and I are one" message is that of satisfying the unconscious need for symbiosis with the attendant enhancement of subjective quiescence. As we have already discussed, considerable controversy surrounds this contention.

Phobia, being a heightened anxiety condition, is likewise a target for subliminal treatment research. Later in this chapter, a treatment procedure is reviewed, which was found to be very effective for treating appetitive behavior disorders. Related to that procedure is a similar method for dealing with a phobic reaction to nonallergenic foods.

As one might imagine, the SPA researchers have applied the symbiosis model to the treatment of simple phobias. Only two are reviewed here because they offer interesting results other than superiority of the symbiotic "Mommy and I are one" subliminal message for treating phobias. Silverman, Frank, and Dachinger (1974) developed an interesting procedure that incorporates conventional systematic desensitization procedures, the treatment of choice for phobia. Insect phobic clients created hierarchies of situations involving insects on the basis of subjective distress. Proceeding as usual with the desensitizing procedure, subjects were instructed to look into a tachistoscope whenever their imagined situation evoked Subjective Distress (SUDS) above a specific criterion. When the subjects looked into the tachistoscope, two 4 msec exposures of the "Mommy and I are one" or the control messages were presented. Subjects who received the symbiotic message showed greater reduction in phobic behavior and subjective anxiety as compared with subjects in the control condition. This treatment preparation would appear to be a very useful method for using subliminal messages to enhance systematic desensitization procedures. I think it is particularly appropriate that clients can exercise a choice with regard to exposing themselves to the subliminal messages. One might also improve this procedure by offering the client the choice between two different subliminal messages with the instruction to select that which most effectively reduces his or her SUDS. Biofeedback instrumentation could also be usefully integrated into this treatment preparation. We discuss the effects of subliminal messages on physiological changes later in this chapter.

A study by Emmelkamp and Straatman (1976) points out the importance of ecologically valid treatment research procedures. As discussed at length elsewhere in this book, clients informed about subliminal treatments and what to expect may respond dramatically differently from those not so informed. Many investigators have shown that clients who expect to improve are more likely to improve. In addition, the mystery surrounding subliminal procedures in all likelihood enhances the expectation effect.

Emmelkamp and Straatman presented snake-phobic subjects with either the symbiotic message "Mommy and I are one" or "The snake and I are one." The subjects were given either research instructions (avoiding expectations) or therapeutic instructions that encouraged positive treatment expectations. Results indicated that therapeutic instructions led to greater reduction in fear than research instructions. The "snake and I are one" message with therapeutic instruction was the only condition that gave rise to significant reduction in fear as measured both behaviorally and with self-report. The authors suggested that the snake message may have been more relevant to the client as compared with the mommy message. However, the authors further pointed out that, after the experiment, 2 of their 20 subjects were able to reproduce the stimulus "exactly." This suggests that the messages may have been, in whole or in part, supraliminal. Hence, coupled with the therapeutic instruction, subjects consciously perceiving the word "snake" may have demonstrated improvement as a result of therapeutic expectations rather than as a result of some nonconscious process.

A series of studies using films was designed to determine the effects of subliminal and supraliminal exposure of phobic scenes on the behavior of agoraphobics (Lee & Tyrer, 1980; Lee, Tyrer, & Horn, 1983; Tyrer, Lee, & Horn, 1978). Agoraphobic patients viewed a film twice a week for 3 weeks. Patients in the control condition viewed a film of a potter working at his wheel. Patients in the various experimental conditions viewed a film containing a range of anxiety-provoking agoraphobic scenes. The illumination of the film relative to ambient varied from supraliminal to below content discrimination threshold. The researchers included several conditions including constant supraliminal, constant subliminal, and two fading conditions. The two fading conditions included one moving from subliminal to supraliminal and one moving from supraliminal to subliminal. Subliminal presentations were found to be superior to supraliminal presentations and fading from supraliminal to subliminal was reported to be more effective in reducing symptomatology as compared with constant subliminal presentations. The improvements were maintained at a 12-week follow-up. With a group of severely agoraphobic patients who had failed to respond to other treatments, the fading from subliminal to supraliminal was found to be superior to the other conditions. Although some of the commercially available subliminal treatment packages present the messages supraliminally prior to the subliminal presentation, the therapeutic efficacy of fading procedures remains an area for interesting research.

The effects of subliminal messages on mood have not had the research attention that one might expect. Of course the SPA researchers have reported the effectiveness of symbiotic messages on depression. Thornton (1987), for example, reported that changes in depression as measured with the Beck Depression Inventory (Beck, 1970) indicated that the "Mommy and I are one" message decreased depression for males. Thornton further reported that for females, the message "Daddy and I are one" had the effect of decreasing depression.

Dauber (1984) reported a finding that again points out that subliminal message content may have to be quite subject specific to give rise to behavioral effects, a point also made by Balay and Shevrin (1988). Dauber reported that the message "Leaving Mom is wrong" increased depression for depressed (i.e., Beck score greater than 10) undergraduate females. Dauber further pointed out that the message was particularly effective for those subjects who scored high on introjected depression, commonly understood to be guilt related.

We have completed a number of studies both in the laboratory and under clinical conditions to determine the effect of messages that were designed to enhance subjective feelings of well-being. Borgeat, Chabot, and Chaloult (1981) conducted a study in which subjects were exposed to auditory subliminal messages, embedded in music, that were designed to either enhance arousal or to enhance feelings of relaxation. Using a mood adjective checklist, these investigators found that the arousal items were differentially effected in the direction advocated by the subliminal message.

Using a similar procedure, we prepared 15-minute per side audio cassettes containing music with subliminal messages, music with the subliminal message recorded backwards, music with a white noise subliminal stimulus, and white noise with subliminal messages. The music was commercially available network instrumental selections, five in all. They were selected by the present author on the basis of being pleasant and uplifting. The selections were arranged so that the tempo of each selection became more lively as the tape played.

For the first study, the message contained 32 statements including: "feel loved, be loved, feel good, feel happy, feel calm, feel content, you can feel comfortable, feel kind, feel relaxed, feel beautiful, feel nice, be cheerful, like yourself, be friendly, be peaceful, be calm, be relaxed, you will feel good, the world is good, the world is warm, the world is beautiful, the world is wonderful, feel healthy, be healthy, feel strong, be strong, you are content, you are happy, you are relaxed, you are healthy, you are strong.''

The message was recorded at -15 dB(A) relative to the music (i.e., the maximum subliminal sound level was 15 dB below the music) and the message repeated every minute. Each cassette contained the identical musical selections (i.e., identical on both sides). One side contained the subliminal message described earlier, whereas the second side contained the same subliminal message but recorded in reverse in the music. Although this procedure appears to have merit for controlling the sound pressure level of the active versus the contrast treatments, it may not be a completely neutral control, as we discussed earlier.

One cassette tape was given to each of 22 undergraduate subjects who volunteered to participate. They were told that both sides of the tape recording contained subliminal messages embedded in the music. They were also informed that the messages were designed to make them "feel better, happier and more relaxed." The purpose of the study, they were told, was to determine which message (i.e., which side of the tape) was best for enhancing a sense of well-being. The subjects were asked to listen to the tape a total of six times, three times on each side. They were further instructed to alternate between the sides (i.e., Side 1, then Side 2, or the reverse). The starting side of the tape was counterbalanced so that one half of the subjects started on Side 1, whereas the second half started on Side 2.

Subjects were asked to fill out a brief questionnaire before and after listening to the entire side of the tape. In addition, they were instructed on how to take their pulse and were also asked to record their heart rate in beats per minute before and after listening to the tape.

Each questionnaire contained eight 99-point bipolar adjective scales (e.g., *up-down, happy-sad*) and a line to record heart rate. Only the two scales for pleasure (i.e., *happy-sad*) and arousal (i.e., *anxious-calm*), and the scale *rested-fatigued,* were scored for analysis. The other items were included principally for distraction purposes.

The differences between the before and after ratings for the three exposures were averaged for the subliminal and the contrast sides of the tape. The data for the pleasure factor indicate that subjects rated themselves as happier after listening to the subliminal message relative to their ratings after listening to the contrast side ($M = 2.28$ and -1.51; $SD =$ 6.6 and 7.1 for the subliminal and the control conditions, respectively; $t(21) = 1.70$; $p < .06$). The number of improvements per subject for each side of the tape (i.e., the frequency of after ratings being "happier" than before ratings) indicates greater effectiveness for the treatment condition

(M = 1.73 and 1.18 for the subliminal and the control conditions, respectively ($t(21)$ = 2.24, p < .025). Further, relative to the music-only condition, subjects experienced, on average, a 7.5% greater improvement in "happiness" when listening to music with the embedded subliminal message. Finally, the magnitude of the increase in happy mood was related to the level of self-rated sadness before listening to the subliminal message. The point biserial correlation between initial ratings on the happy–sad scale and positive (i.e., happier) change in the after rating was $r_{pb}(20)$ = − .60, p < .05. The correlation for the music-only side of the tape was $r_{pb}(20)$ = − .16, NS. Thus, the data indicate that the increase in subjective happiness was greater when subjects were listening to music with the embedded subliminal message as compared to when they were listening only to the music. Furthermore, subjects were more likely to indicate a positive change in self-rated happiness when listening to the subliminal message. Finally, sadder subjects were more likely to show larger improvements in self-rated happiness when listening to the subliminal message. No such relationship was found when subjects were listening to music alone.

The data from the arousal factor (i.e., anxious–calm) similarly indicated that the subliminal message was more effective in reducing anxiety as compared with music alone. The average difference between the before and after ratings on the anxious–calm scale was 5.5 for the subliminal side and 2.4 for the contrast side ($t(21)$ = 1.14, p = .13). The effect was more pronounced when the median change was determined; 8.0 versus 2.9 for the subliminal and contrast conditions respectively ($t(21)$ = 2.02, p < .03).

The self-ratings of *rested–fatigued* likewise indicated a superiority of the subliminal treatment. The average change in the rating of rested was 3.62 for the subliminal message side and − .40 for the music alone side ($t(21)$ = 1.80, p = .042).

A similar study was conducted with 25 female undergraduate students. Each student was given a tape with white noise recorded on both sides. One group, consisting of 7 subjects, received a tape containing only white noise. A second group of 8 subjects received a tape with the words "happy" and "calm" repeated at one second intervals at − 15 dB(A) in a male voice. A third group of 10 subjects received a tape similar in all respects to that given to the second group except that the subliminal words were presented by a female voice. Subjects were asked to call into a telephone answering machine immediately after listening to the tape and give, numerically, their self-reports on several mood dimensions. Three such telephone calls were made by each subject. Even with such brief exposure, the subjects exposed to the subliminal message reported being less sad (M = 1.62, 1.48 and 1.39 for the control, male voice and female voice, respectively) and less excited (M = 2.05, 2.00 and 1.68). Although not statistically significant, these data were consistent with the finding of superiority of the subliminal message relative to contrast conditions and superiority of female voice relative to the male voice.

The tapes used in the study reported earlier—the tape containing 32 statements embedded in music—were submitted to clinical test. Each tape contained one side with music into which was embedded the subliminal message described earlier. On the flip side of each tape, the same music was recorded within which the subliminal message was recorded in reverse. The subliminal material was recorded at − 15 dB(A) and the entire recorded section on each side of the tape lasted for 12 minutes.

The master tape was prepared in the author's voice under studio conditions. An electronic process maintained the subliminal sound at a minimum of − 15 dB(A) with the message faded out during low volume passages of the music. The master tape was then reproduced under studio conditions. Twenty-six copies were prepared with five-letter codes identifying the content of each side of the tape.

One tape was given to each of 26 consecutive clients seen by the author in his private psychotherapy practice. A tape was given to each client on the second visit without regard to the client's diagnosis or presenting complaint(s). Several clients seen for only one visit or consultation were not included in this clinical trial. Further, the subliminal tape was provided without charge and was in addition to other treatment procedures. The subliminal treatment was not in substitute for nor did it compromise any other treatment provided in office or home contexts.

The technical issues and theoretical rationale of subliminal procedures were explained to each client. Further, they were told that each side of the tape contained subliminal messages and that their task was to select the side of the tape (i.e., the subliminal message) that impacted most beneficially on their feelings of well-being. They were told that the subliminal message contained many positive statements about their feelings of happiness, peacefulness, physical health, and contentment.

Following the forced-choice research procedure detailed in the methodology section of this book, the clients were told to play each side of the tape, alternately as often as they wanted and in any context. They could play the tape when they were resting, walking, doing work about the house, and so on. They were instructed to focus their attention on their feelings while playing the tape and to eventually determine which side of the tape made them *feel* best. Each client was told that he or she would not be able to notice any cognitive differences between the sides (i.e., they would sound the same), so that the only way the sides could be discriminated would be on the basis of feelings. At this point the therapist elaborated on the importance of focusing on feelings, and explained that the purpose of the treatment was to find the subliminal message that was most effective in enhancing well-being for that particular client. The positive feelings could be those of happiness, physical well-being, contentment, relaxation, belonging, or any subjective feeling of greater well-being.

Clients were instructed to continue to play the tape until they decided which side made them *feel* the best and then to use that side of the tape exclusively. In addition to the subliminal tape, each client received instructions and materials for the treatment of his or her complaint as usually applied in the author's practice. Such procedures included various forms of relaxation exercises, biofeedback, logging of behavior, monitoring self-talk, self-hypnosis, autogenic exercises, recording of physiological data, thought change or control exercises, recording of appetitive behavior, social skills exercises, and so on.

Of the 26 consecutive clients, 2 returned the tape at the following visit stating that they could not listen to the tapes because they strongly disliked the music. Two additional clients were added to the trial bringing the total N back to 26. Of the 26 clients tested, 22 selected the side containing the active subliminal message as the treatment that gave them the most positive feelings of well-being ($Z = 3.33$, $p < .01$). Clients used the subliminal treatment for a variety of purposes. Many found the treatment very helpful for inducing sleep or as a method for relaxing. Several clients reported that they used the subliminal tape as a substitute for anxiolytic medications or more generally as a method for calming themselves during times of distress.

The four clients who did not select the subliminal treatment side of the tape are of particular interest. Three of the four clients selected the contrast side (i.e., the side with the subliminal message played in reverse), and one client stated that he found no differences between the two sides of the tape. Of the three who selected the backward subliminal sound, all were males and all had the presenting complaint of depression. Initially it appeared as though the backward subliminal message might have an arousing effect on depressed clients, which gave them a sense of improved well-being. This assumption was based in part on the work of Zenhausern and Hansen (1974) described earlier in which subliminal noise increased arousal as reflected in enhanced performance. In addition, our own research has indicated that backward subliminal messages appear to arouse or distress some subjects. Hence, it seemed plausible that the backward subliminal message was therapeutically useful for dysphoric clients, presumably because of some arousing or activating property of the content-free subliminal sound.

Although plausible, this reasoning appears to be wrong. When dealing with clients, particularly those who present with depression, I have found that it is often very useful to obtain an indication of their compliance with treatment regimen. One method that I have found to be a most useful indicator is to request that clients measure and record, in a small notebook, their heart rate, subjective mood, and the type of activity they are involved in, about 15 times per day for a 1-week period. In my experience, clients who respond well to home treatment procedures are those who comply with the monitoring task as evidenced by the entries in their notebooks. Every one of the three clients who selected the contrast side of the tape gave evidence of noncompliance. Not one of these three clients had more than 2 entries per day and all had more blank pages than pages with any entries at all. Hence, the most plausible explanation of the relationship of the presenting complaint of depression to the selection of the backward subliminal message is that the clients did not comply with the task instructions and when asked by the therapist to make a decision some depressed clients simply gave an answer so as not to appear uncooperative, and some of those choices were for the nonactive side of the tape.

All clients are followed up 6 months after treatment termination. At that time a questionnaire is mailed to the client. Among other items, the questionnaire asks the client to indicate which of the home treatment materials he or she uses at present with an indication as to frequency of use. Given that clients have different types and numbers of home treatment regimens, the use questions are open-ended. A client might have been given, for example, only a progressive muscular relaxation exercise in addition to the subliminal tape, whereas another client might have been instructed on or provided materials for 5 or more home treatment procedures.

The follow-up forms from the 22 clients who selected the active subliminal treatment side of the tape indicated continued use of the tape. Further, the subliminal tape was often selected as the most frequently or second most frequently used home treatment procedure.

Two year follow-up of a client treated for symptoms associated with systemic lupus erythematosus (SLE), reported in the following case study, suggests that in addition to benefit attributable directly to the subliminal message itself, the subliminal treatment may acquire generalized conditioned effects as a function of being associated with other effective treatment procedures. Although this client was exposed to a wide variety of treatment procedures, after 7 months and again after 20 months he reported using the subliminal tape as the primary home treatment procedure to sustain the gains he made during his active treatment.

Treatment of Symptoms Associated with Systemic Lupus Erythematosus: A Case Study

This case illustrates the use of biofeedback, relaxation, hypnosis, auditory subliminal messages, and guided imagery in conjunctive treatment of a 35-year-old white male client referred with the diagnosis of SLE. A chronic inflammatory connective tissue disease which is most frequently discovered in the third and fourth decades of life and which is five to ten times more frequent in females, SLE can affect the skin, joints, kidneys, nervous system, serous membranes, and often other organs of the body (Schur, 1979).

The client was very obviously anxious and short of breath during the first session. His major complaints were shortness of breath, pain and numbness in his right foot and ankle, in his right cheek, and in his right rib cage. The client was most fearful of surgical intervention. In particular, he felt that he was very likely to lose his right foot because of circulatory insufficiency. Preliminary physiological measures indicated major temperature disparities between areas of pain and/or numbness and the contralateral location. The temperature difference between the right and left foot was over 11°F as measured on the distal phalanx of the third toe. The right cheek was 1.5°F lower than the left cheek and the painful area in the right rib cage was 1°F lower than the contralateral area. The rationales of the various treatments were explained to the client and target objectives of reducing heart rate (HR) and decreasing the disparity in temperature between the areas of pain and the contralateral areas were agreed upon.

The client was being taken off indomethacin, which he did not find helpful, and was started on systemic corticosteroid therapy of 60 mg of prednisone per day which was gradually tapered to a lower maintenance dosage (see Fig. 4.1).

The treatment regimen for the client included home practice of

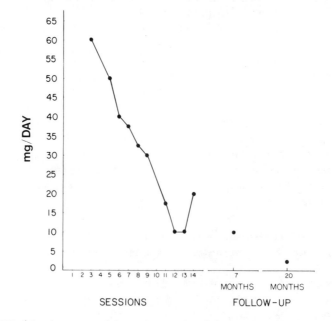

FIG. 4.1.   Average prednisone dosage taken daily as reported by the client.

Progressive Muscular Relaxation (Jacobson, 1929) and, later, Cognitive Muscular Reduction (CMR). The latter procedure involves having the client imagine each muscle group being more tense than it is, and then imagine the group relaxed. Peper (1976) reported that such imaging can increase electromyographic activity in a resting muscle (forearm) from 3 to 6 times the relaxed levels. The important aspect of CMR is that it is designed to be used in vivo after preliminary training. Both relaxation procedures are guided by audio tape recordings.

In addition to the relaxation exercises, the client was given the subliminal tape described previously. He was instructed on the choice procedure and the following week he stated that he found that Side A (the active subliminal message) made him feel best. A motivated client, he reported using the relaxation tape twice a day and the subliminal tape three or four times per day, often after his relaxation exercise.

During the early sessions, the client's potential control over biological processes was emphasized. Biofeedback sessions with HR and peripheral temperature of the finger and the toe of his nonproblematic (left) foot indicated good progress in lowering HR and raising peripheral temperature. Biofeedback training lasted approximately 20 minutes and commenced after the session had been in progress for at least 30 minutes to allow for adaptation (Yates, 1980).

The main thrust of the remaining sessions was that of guided imagery focusing on warming (Taub, 1977) and enhancing peripheral blood flow to target areas. Starting with Session 7, foot warming imagery with feedback of toe temperature from both the problematic (right) and nonproblematic (left) foot was included during each session. A summary of the toe temperature data is shown in Fig. 4.2. As the data indicate, the client was markedly successful in reducing the temperature disparity between his two feet.

Session 11 is of particular interest. The client was most agitated when he arrived due to uncertainties regarding employment, renewed fear of possible surgical intervention, and a general feeling of heightened anxiety. The physiological measures obtained at the beginning of the session, as shown in Fig. 4.2, were a dramatic demonstration to the client of the direct effects of his psychological state on his physical state. Relaxation, foot warming imaging, and biofeedback of HR and temperature resulted in reduced HR and increased peripheral blood flow, but as the data also indicate, the temperature recovery of the nonproblematic foot was superior to that of the problematic foot (i.e., at the end of the session, a disparity of over 5°F was still in evidence). Malmo (1975) reported that individuals with anxiety or psychosomatic symptoms take longer than control subjects to recover to prestress levels once stimulated. The present data suggest slower recovery of symptomatic areas relative to contralateral areas of the body in individuals with complaints exacerbated by anxiety.

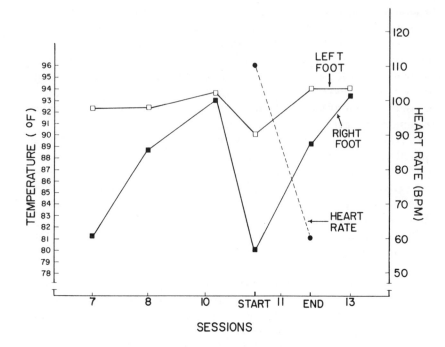

FIG. 4.2.   Toe temperature of the right and left feet over five sessions. Temperatures shown are maxima attained during the session with the exception
of Session 11 where "start" temperatures were the measurements obtained
at the start of the session. Heart rates during Session 11 are the modal rates
of five consecutive beats taken simultaneously with the temperature data.

The interesting aspect of this case for our present purpose is that significant gains made by the client appear to be sustained by continued use
of the subliminal home treatment. Although he had a number of relaxation
and self-regulation procedures for home use, he reported at both 7- and
20-month follow-ups that he used the subliminal treatment as the principal
method for sustaining treatment gains. As stated earlier, this client reported that he used the subliminal tape in conjunction with various other
relaxation procedures. It is possible, therefore, that the subliminal message
or the embedding music or both became associated with the relaxed state
and hence was capable of eliciting the relaxation response.

Treatment of Obsessive–Compulsive Disorder:
A Case Study

One of the most interesting potential applications of subliminal procedures is for the treatment of obsessive–compulsive disorder (OCD). It is
difficult to conceptualize the devastating nature of this emotional disorder
in the absence of direct clinical experience. In its extreme forms, the

disorder may be so debilitating that the patient has unbearable generalized anxiety, recurrent panic attacks, debilitating avoidance, and major depression all occurring simultaneously (Barlow, 1988). Severe washers, caught in their ritual because of unrelenting fears of contamination, may shower or wash almost continuously or scrub their hands raw from the excessive scrubbing with increasingly strong detergents. Because of the severity and debilitating nature of the extreme forms of this disorder, patients must frequently be treated on an in-patient basis.

In its milder forms, treated in private practice context, individuals may appear calm and relaxed and may be able to keep their obsessive-compulsive behavior a secret, even from those individuals sharing the same living environment. In my experience, they usually present for treatment because the disorder becomes somewhat more severe as a result of increased stress levels in other areas of their lives. The following case represents just such a situation. The client was a 28-year-old male who presented with a 13-year history of moderate compulsive rituals. As is often the case, this individual had a strict religious background and the disorder-precipitating event was sexual. Over the course of some 13 years he had experienced several periods when the disorder was quite severe and several occasions of a few months' duration when he reported that he was "virtually" symptom free. He was seeking treatment at this time because the disorder was again becoming severe. He anticipated moving into a shared living accommodation in the near future, and he was concerned that his rituals would not be able to be kept secret. He was experiencing a closing in of his environment due to contamination in that, because of using and touching things, he was contaminating elements and objects in his environment more rapidly than the could decontaminate them. Decontamination was accomplished by washing or wiping articles. The severity of his hand washing ritual varied from day to day. On "good" days, he would wash his hands from three to five times for durations of between 5 and 10 minutes each. On "bad" days he felt severely stressed and preoccupied with contamination and would often get caught in rituals that lasted 20 to 40 minutes or more. This could occur on five or more occasions per day.

Treatment of choice for obsessive-compulsive disorder is "exposure and response prevention" (Meyer & Levy, 1973). This treatment procedure involves gradually exposing clients in a systematic manner to objects or situations that evoke the ritualistic response but under conditions in which the ritual is prevented. Foa, Grayson, Steketee, Doppett, Turner, & Latimer (1983) reviewed the results from a number of controlled studies and reported that 51% of clients treated by exposure and response prevention were either symptom free or much improved at the end of the treatment. Of the remaining 49% of clients, 39% reported moderate improvement and 10% failed to benefit from therapy.

The procedure that I use for treatment of obsessive–compulsive disorder follows the exposure and response-prevention method but is integrated within a biofeedback and self-regulation model. In-office treatment procedures are similar to systematic desensitization procedures with the exception that physiological indicators of distress are used in addition to and preferentially to Subjective Units of Distress (SUDS). This procedure involves obtaining a biofeedback stress profile on the client to determine which physiological system(s) reacts most rapidly and/or most strongly to stressors. The client's HR, blood pressure, electromyographic response, dermatological response, and peripheral blood flow are measured during exposure to various stressors. After a baseline measurement period, the client is asked to do a variety of cognitive tasks, to imagine pleasant and unpleasant events, and to look at, approach and/or touch phobic objects and/or objects perceived as contaminated. The physiological responses associated with each of these conditions determines home treatment and office treatment protocols.

It was determined that hand temperature responded rapidly to stressors and the magnitude of the response was large. Specifically, from a baseline of 85.3°F, a cognitive stressor (counting backwards) gave rise to temperature decline within 5 seconds. After 2 minutes of counting backwards, the client's finger temperature declined to 76.6°F. Further, it was found that the client's HR was labile, responding rapidly and arhythmically to exposure to objects perceived as contaminated. Specifically, the client's HR varied from 50 Beats Per Minute (BPM) up to 114 (BPM) when the proximity of the object perceived as contaminated was varied.

Treatment consisted of thermal biofeedback and home thermal autogenetic exercises in which the client learned how to increase hand temperature. In the home environment, the client was instructed to increase hand temperature before any hand-washing activity and further to desensitize himself to "contaminated" objects by increasing hand temperature over the criterion value of 93°F and in that state of "comfort and relaxation" to approach, touch, and handle objects provided that he felt that he could do so without precipitating a ritual. Office procedures involved a similar procedure of approaching, touching, and handling contaminated objects in response to changes in the client's HR. Thus when the client's HR was below 60 BPM, he was asked to approach, touch, and handle contaminated objects. When the heart rate exceeded 60 BPM, he did not approach the contaminated objects but rather used a relaxation procedure to again bring the HR below criterion. This procedure is similar to that reported by Shahar and Marks (1980) in which tachycardia associated with exposure to stimuli that evoked rituals was extinguished by in vivo exposure.

A procedure that has proven to be most useful in such desensitization by exposure procedures is the paradoxical use of a physiological response.

It was found that initially during the heart rate guided approach procedure, the client's HR was very erratic and a lot of time was required for the client to be able to bring his heart rate under the 60 BPM criterion. The paradoxical procedure involving having the client approach a contaminated object (i.e., hold his hand over the object) when the heart rate monitor indicated that his pulse rate exceeded a higher criterion value (e.g., 85 BPM) and to withdraw his hand anytime the heart rate monitor indicated a reading below 85 BPM. This procedure was found to give rise to rather rapid stabilization of heart rate. The criterion for approach was then consistently dropped by 5 BPM until the criterion value of 60 BPM had been reached. At that point the procedure was changed so that the client approached, touched, and handled the contaminated objects when his heart rate was below 60 BPM but would stop the approach, touching, or handling if his heart rate went above 60 BPM. This procedure proved to be very efficient and at each office session two or three contaminated objects were touched and handled within approximately 15 minutes of treatment time. Using this procedure, a watch that the client had been unable to touch or wear for several months was "decontaminated" in less than 5 minutes and the client put the watch on and continued to wear it without distress.

The subliminal procedures were used adjunctively during later sessions to enhance the efficacy of the previously described procedure. The central theme with this client was that he felt guilty, impure, and unclean. The nature of subliminal treatment procedures were explained to the client and he was told that the procedure would be a strong complement to the exposure procedures described earlier. He was told that subliminal messages are useful because they can effect important changes in the processes that are maintaining his obsessive–compulsive behaviors because they enter below levels of consciousness. He was further told that the effect of the subliminal messages would be to increase his sense of well-being, reduce his feelings of stress, and increase the efficiency with which he could desensitize himself to objects in his environment, and would strongly reduce the compulsion to engage in ritualistic behavior.

The subliminal treatment consisted of a 5-minute presentation during two office visits. The subliminal messages were presented after the exposure procedure described earlier. The messages were as follows: "I am a good person, I am a kind person, I am a clean person, I am a pure person, I am at peace, I am not guilty, I am not to blame, it is not my fault, my hands feel good, I do not need to wash my hands, you are a good person, you are a kind person, you are a clean person, you are a pure person, you are at peace, you are not to blame, you are not guilty, your hands feel good, you do no need to wash your hands, Mommy and

I are one." The client was not told the content of the subliminal messages. After presentation of the subliminal messages, the client was asked to describe his experience. On the first occasion, he indicated "it felt like praying and I felt clean and pure and cleansed." At the end of the second presentation on the following visit, he indicated that he started to make statements to himself while the subliminal message was being presented. Those statements were "I am pure, I am innocent, I am not to blame, I am good." The transfer of content from unconscious to conscious, which appears to have occurred with this client, is consistent with work done in our laboratories by Hutchinson as described previously.

This client made excellent progress such that after the sessions in which subliminal procedures were used, his daily log revealed that his hand washing was below 42 seconds in duration and did not occur at inappropriate times. More specifically, the client reported that hand washing felt "almost normal" in that it was much less likely to be experienced as an anxiety-reducing procedure.

Given the manner in which treatment was presented, it is not possible to determine the exact effect of the subliminal treatment procedure on the client's symptomatology. The client was treated with biofeedback, various relaxation and self-regulation procedures, exposure with response prevention, and hypnosis, as well as two brief subliminal treatments. The purpose of the subliminal treatments was, of course, to modify the feelings of guilt, self-loathing, uncleanliness, impurity, and the like. Based on the client's report of his subjective experience during the subliminal exposure, it appears as though the subliminal message may have contributed to that therapeutic goal. Without knowledge of the contents of the subliminal message, the client reported that he felt "clean, pure, and cleansed." Furthermore, after the second exposure he reported self-statements that were directly related to the statements contained in the subliminal message. The extent to which these self-stated feelings in turn contributed to improvement in the client's condition cannot be determined.

The client experienced an increase in his symptomatology that resulted from a change in his living environment and increased work stress. An endless loop tape recording was prepared that contained the previously described subliminal message embedded at -15 dB(A) in white noise. The client uses the tape in response to increased stress in conjunction with his hand-warming procedure. At the time of this writing he reports a regaining of his improvements. He finds that the subliminal tape is extremely effective and, because he can use it in a Walkman cassette player, the treatment can be applied anywhere.

A variation on the choice procedure described earlier is to instruct the client to experiment with sound level to determine the volume that is most effective. This client reported that when the tape was played at very low volume the subliminal message had a strong positive effect which was not apparent at higher volume levels. There are many possible explanations for this effect other than that of a critical subliminal range. We often find, however, a critical distance from the sound source for subliminal effects in our group studies, reported earlier. Thus, even though the subliminal sound is always -15 dB(A) relative to the embedding medium, it is possible that there is a critical SPL range for the processing of auditory subliminal messages. Two other clients were asked to experiment with the sound level of their subliminal tapes and both reported noticeable effective volume ranges. Research addressed to this issue is in progress, but in the interim all clients are advised to determine their critical effective volume for subliminal effects.

Treatment of Obsessive Rumination: A Case Study

A slightly modified version of the subliminal message used in the treatment of obsessive-compulsive disorder was used to modify obsessive rumination. The client, a 36-year-old male, suffered severe neck and head injury with accompanying anoxia resulting in paralysis and impaired cognitive functioning.

The obsessive rumination consisted of incessant repetition of the statement "Oh Lord, I've been wrong." This behavior was giving rise to "burnout" of the caregivers and strain on family relations.

Although one can never be certain about the cause of such behaviors, it appears as though the client was exposed to continuous fundamentalist religious messages when in coma for 10 weeks while at a rehabilitation center. Furthermore, after recovery from coma, the client shared a room with a fundamentalist Christian who continuously listened to fundamentalist radio programs. Because the client sustained the injuries in work-related violence, it is also possible that self-blaming processes (Kushner, 1981) contributed to the obsessive behavior.

The client had been in weekly therapy sessions for several years during which many approaches to eliminating or modifying the obsessive behavior were attempted. During this time the client apparently acquired an understanding of the inappropriateness of the statement in certain social contexts. It was reported that the client often initiated the repetitious statement but terminated it prior to completion.

In consultation with the client's guardian and his primary therapist, it was agreed to attempt to provide some relief with the use of auditory subliminal messages. The message was similar to that used in the treatment of the obsessive-compulsive client described in the previous case study. The only difference in the message was that all references to the hands and to washing were deleted. Given the client's cognitive impairment and the nature of his distress, the primary therapist and the client's guardian recommended that the client be kept uninformed about the presence of subliminal messages. The message was embedded in white noise with no peaks above -17 dB(A). The tape was played continuously in the morning when the client was awake.

Data were collected by health care providers during a specific 2-hour period each day. Every "Oh Lord, I've been wrong" statement was recorded. During a 12-day baseline period, the client repeated the statement an average of 9 times during each 2-hour period (range 5 to 15). After treatment commenced the average rate of "wrong" statements dropped to 4.9 during the first 10 days (range 2 to 15), 5.7 during the second 10-day period (range 1 to 10), 5.5 during the third 10-day period (range 3 to 9), and 3.1 during the last 5-day period (range 2 to 4) for which data are available. It is also interesting to note that the average frequency of "wrong" statements recorded during a 10-day period when new staff were in attendance, but before subliminal treatment had commenced, was 6.1 (range 3 to 12). This appears to substantiate the belief that the client was less likely to verbalize the statement when in the presence of people with whom he was less familiar.

SUBLIMINAL TREATMENT PROCEDURES FOR THE MODIFICATION OF APPETITIVE BEHAVIORS

Effective procedures for assisting in the control of the nature and/or amount of substances that clients put in their mouths are a useful adjunct to many treatment programs. Anxious or depressed individuals often have appetitive behavior difficulties that become nonrecursively related to the presenting complaint. Depressed individuals may eat more (or less) than required, and their weight change and/or nutritional state in turn exacerbates their depression. Anxious clients, likewise, may smoke heavily which, because of well-known health implications, contributes to their level of anxiety. Similarly psychologically distressed clients may be "self-medicating" by excessive use of alcohol which in turn contributes to intrapersonal and interpersonal factors that enhance their distress.

If the sales figures for some of the companies marketing subliminal tapes for weight control, smoking cessation, and the moderating of alcohol use are any indication, the public need for assistance in appetitive behavior control is very great indeed.

In the present section, subliminal procedures found to modify various appetitive behaviors are reviewed. Such behaviors include eating, smoking, drinking, and the use of alcohol and illicit drugs. Ethical drug dependency and sexual behavior, although arguably appetitive in nature, will not be included in this section. It is important to realize that subliminal treatment procedures are not stand-alone therapies. As some of the case studies indicate, clients with appetitive behavior disorders often have other complaints that require attention. One often finds that a particular appetitive disorder is only a part, and often a small part, of the symptom complex. This does not mean that giving relief to a problematic behavior could not contribute substantially to a client's well-being. Depressed individuals who also have an eating disorder can find significant benefit from relief from a factor that is exacerbating their affective state.

There appear to be several distinct traditions in the use of subliminal procedures for treating appetitive disorders. As one might expect, the Subliminal Psychodynamic Activation method (SPA) has been used to modify appetitive behaviors. The rationale again is that the message "Mommy and I are one" gratifies the unconscious desire for symbiosis with another person, in particular with the nurturing good mother of childhood.

A related procedure is what might be called subliminal persuasive communications. Statements designed to persuade clients to change their appetitive behaviors are presented in contexts in which priming has occurred and in which the clients have been told what changes in behavior to expect. Becker, Corrigan, Elder, Tallant, & Goldstein (1965) described a procedure in which a supraliminal message is presented simultaneously with a subliminal message. The subliminal message influences the subject's attitude toward the supraliminal message. As described in greater detail later in this section, the author has treated several clients with straight-forward subliminal persuasive messages. There are important distinctions between SPA and the persuasive communication procedures. In SPA, the symbiotic gratification afforded by the "Mommy and I are one" message is believed to ameliorate the need for gratification derived from appetitive behavior. The person presumably experiences a reduction in need or cravings with the attendant increase in the person's ability to resist appetitive gratification.

Persuasive messages, on the other hand, are rational at conscious levels and would generally be considered by the client to be consistent with his or her own beliefs. Thus the message, "I am the custodian of my body—smoking tobacco poisons my body" is one with which many people would agree. Such persuasive messages usually also include statements designed to directly alter the appetite associated with the behavior. Statements such as "I am not hungry—I must eat only to nourish my body" are designed to alter both the appetite as well as the meaning of the appetitive behavior. SPA procedures, on the other hand, probably would not seem rational to a person if the messages were presented at a supraliminal level. The relation between "Mommy and I are one" and reduced appetite would likely escape most clients in treatment for obesity. However, whether or not this is the case, the point I wish to emphasize is that subliminal messages designed to modify appetitive behavior may be rational at a conscious level or may be rational only in the context of a psychodynamic tradition.

A third tradition is that of modifying the attractiveness of a substance by repetitive subliminal exposure. As discussed in detail earlier in this book, the attractiveness of stimuli can be enhanced by mere exposure at either a subliminal or at a supraliminal level.

The fourth tradition is based on the notion of classical conditioning, as it is generally understood. That is, two stimuli that are contiguously experienced evoke responses that become modified by the stimuli pairing. Thus, an object paired with electric shock may, after several paired presentations, acquire the capacity to evoke fear when presented alone without any electric shock. The early research on the use of disuifiram (Antabus) with alcoholics was based on just such a model. Alcoholics who had ingested Antabus would become nauseous after drinking alcohol. The experience of nausea after drinking alcohol, it was thought, should reduce the alcoholic's interest in alcohol in that the sight, smell, taste, or even the thoughts of these properties of alcohol would elicit a feeling of nausea. There are many variations on this model as well as many theoretical conceptualizations of the therapeutic applications of the classical conditioning model. Systematic desensitization, for example, is based on the notion that pairing a stimulus with an incompatible response will modify the higher probability response to that stimulus. Thus, if a feared object is gradually brought physically closer to a client who is trained to maintain a relaxed state, the usual fear response to the object will be reduced. Similarly, a child learns to enjoy novel tasting foods by experiencing them not only when hungry but also when tasting them under positive psychosocial conditions. Because stimuli and messages are processed outside of a person's selective attention, subliminal procedures offer intriguing possibilities for conditioning of appetitive behaviors.

As discussed previously, we know that subliminal messages can alter subjective ratings of hunger and thirst as well as the attractiveness of visual stimuli. Swingle (1979) and Bornstein, Leone, and Galley (1987) reported that subjects' ratings of the attractiveness of pictorial stimuli can be increased or reduced with subliminal procedures. Subjective ratings can be modified by mere subliminal exposure of the target stimulus. Further, pairing the supraliminal pictorial target stimulus with subliminal messages can increase or decrease subjects' ratings of the attractiveness of the target stimulus.

Byrne (1959) reported that subliminal presentation of the word "beef" did not alter subject's preference for a beef sandwich but did increase self-rated hunger. Similarly, Hawkins (1970) reported that the subliminal presentation of the word "Coke" increased self-rated thirst but did not alter subject's specific choice of soft drink.

These studies suggest that subliminal messages affect general motivational states but are less likely to alter appetitive preferences. There are, however, many interesting questions raised by these studies. Although these studies suggest a general motivational effect, we do not know how a subject's existing motivational state or existing food preferences are implicated in the subjective response to subliminally presented food-related stimuli. People who like beef, for example, may experience greater hunger and an increased likelihood to select a beef sandwich when exposed to the subliminal presentation of the word "beef." People who are less fond of beef but are hungry may be more inclined to select a beef sandwich, whereas less hungry subjects may respond with increased subjective hunger but no change in preference.

Subliminal Treatment of Food Phobia: A Case Study

This client was referred by her primary psychotherapist, for "behavioral treatment of a food phobia." The client, a 39-year-old female, stated that she had an "irrational fear of eating fish, shellfish, and nuts." She reported that she had no adverse physical reactions to such foods, but nevertheless, she would experience severe anxiety when she learned that she had unknowingly ingested a food from one of these groups. She stated that she was becoming "obsessed" with her concerns about poisoning or harming her body by eating such foods to the extent that her behavior was causing her social concern. At social functions she would refuse to eat anything that contained the "phobic" foods. In restaurants she felt that she "obsessed" in her inquiring about the presence of the phobic food groups in anything that she might eat.

The client was somewhat overweight and claimed that she tended to overeat and her motivation to deal with her food phobia was so that she could eat less fattening but highly nutritious fish dishes. An intelligent woman who worked in a health profession, the client emphasized that there was no allergic or other physical condition that was associated with her eating any of the three phobic foods. Although she had a number of other complaints for which she was in treatment with her primary therapist, her motivation for eliminating the food phobias was essentially social. She wanted to be able to behave in social eating situations in a manner which she considered to be more rational. Furthermore, she was prompted to seek the referral for treatment at that time because of a major upcoming family reunion in which the principal social event was to be a fish fry.

Barlow (1988) pointed out that very few individuals with simple phobia come for treatment. When they do come for treatment, the individuals usually present with a variety of additional anxiety or affective complaints. In this particular case the client's other complaints were being dealt with by the referring therapist and my subliminal treatment was targeted solely on the food phobias.

An essential part of any treatment of phobia is that of in vivo exposure structured in such a manner that the client experiences ''success'' (i.e., reduced anxiety when exposed to the anxiety producing object or situation). Systematic desensitization of anxiety producing visualizations of phobic objects is followed by graduated exposure to the objects in vivo. Similarly, when other procedures are used, such as affective anchoring in the neurolinguistic programming tradition or various hypnotic techniques, graduated in vivo exposure to the phobic object or situation is planned. The greater sense of control, or reduced anxiety, that the client experiences when gradually increasing actual exposure to the phobic object or situation is strongly therapeutic and decreases the anxiety experienced by the client. The first in vivo exposure is, of course, critical. Should the client experience a level of anxiety that forces an escape response, the phobic reaction will be exacerbated. Hence, graduated exposure is important to structure, with the client, prior to commencing subliminal treatment. Repeated and more intense or closer exposures will result in decreases in the anxiety level produced by the phobic objects or situations.

In the present case, first in vivo exposure to the three foods was to be in a situation that the client considered highly conducive to a relaxed state. Although she considered preparing these foods at home for her first exposure she decided instead to go to a favorite restaurant with her husband. She knew the menu in this restaurant and planned to order and eat a small quantity of each food.

Since ridding herself of her phobia toward the eating of fish was her stated priority, the subliminal message placed maximum emphasis on fish. Shellfish received second most emphasis with least emphasis on nuts.

In this case, and in the other case studies of the treatment of appetitive behavior complaints that are presented later in this chapter, subliminal treatment consists of two phases. The first phase involves the presentation of a message designed to enhance the view of custodianship over one's body. The messages vary slightly depending on the nature of the substance that is the focus of treatment. The elements of the message that are common to all treatments are: ''My body is my friend. I am the protector of my body. My body is the place where I live.'' For food related treatments additional statements might include: "I must eat to keep my body functioning." "Too much food or the wrong foods poison or harm my body." "I am not hungry." "I must eat only to keep my body healthy." "I will eat slowly." "I will eat less." "I feel content and satisfied." The Phase 1 message is presented repeatedly for 5 minutes.

An interesting phenomenon occurred with some regularity when this message was presented. Of the 5 clients described in this section, 4 experienced a strong emotional response to the custodianship message. Specifically they started to cry quite uncontrollably. Although each client was in very good spirits at the end of the treatment, the four who broke down during Phase 1 reported a rather confusing emotional reaction. Some reported flashbacks of food-related situations associated with their mothers, feelings of love, warmth, and security of a childhood home, warm social gatherings of friends, and in one case a feeling that she was worthy of self-care. My more analytically oriented colleagues have counselled me that the meaning of this is obvious. Essentially they maintain that the message gives permission for the client to love and care for themselves, and that the experience of self-love floods the client with emotion. Given that the message is subliminal, it cannot be blocked, distorted, or discounted by the client's negative self-image. I might add that although no measures were obtained, all of these clients with appetitive behavior complaints made statements reflecting self-criticism and low self-esteem.

The message presented during Phase 2 is specific to the substance and the nature of the disorder. For the food phobic client, the Phase 2 message consisted of these statements: "Fish is good for me," "Fish tastes good," "I like fish," "Fish is good for my body," "My body likes fish." Seven such statements referred to fish, four such statements referred to shellfish, and three statements referred to nuts.

The second phase message was presented for 5 minutes at -15 dB(A) relative to room ambient. Although the client knew the intention of the treatment (i.e., to eliminate her avoidance of fish, shellfish, and nuts), she was not aware of the specific content of the tapes nor the stronger emphasis on fish relative to shellfish and nuts.

The client was asked to report on her success in eating small amounts of the three foods the morning after her dining at the restaurant. The following day she left the message: "Fish, OK no problem; shellfish, fair, experienced tight throat; nuts, chickened out."

The case study demonstrates effects consistent with the varied emphasis, but alternative explanations for the beneficial effects cannot be excluded. However, the procedure warrants study, for it certainly appears to be a cost-effective adjunct to therapy for the purpose of symptom control and modification. Total active treatment time in this case was under 15 minutes, although intake, client priming, and preparation required the remainder of the clinical hour. The benefits of the treatment are undoubtedly related to carefully planned successful exposure to the avoided object.

Food aversions of the type presented in this case are quite common and robust (Garb & Stunkard, 1974; Logue, 1985, 1986) but generally do not represent a clinical problem. People can normally avoid foods that they find aversive without any nutritional or social difficulties. In this case, the client felt that her aversions were becoming problematic because she was behaving rather frantically in her efforts to avoid consumption of such foods. Also, as previously mentioned, a forthcoming family reunion was going to focus on a feast with the featured food being one for which she had an aversion.

Although the client in this case study did not recall any event that would have given rise to a food aversion, many food aversions are acquired through conditioned taste avoidance learning, such as when a food is associated with gastrointestinal illness. Aversions acquired in other ways (such as culturally or when a food is associated with an unpleasant experience or when the person cannot account for the aversion) do not appear to be functionally different from conditioned taste aversions (De Silva & Rachman, 1987). Further, although some widespread food aversions may be problematic such as with cancer patients or anorexics (Bernstein & Borson, 1986; Bernstein & Webster, 1980), limited food aversions are rarely of clinical importance. However, as De Silva (1988) pointed out, many people might seek help for such aversions if clinically efficacious treatments were offered. It does appear as though subliminal procedures may be quite effective for modification of such aversions.

More generally, however, people seek help for quite the opposite appetitive behavior problem. Namely, they wish to limit or avoid consumption of substances that are detrimental to health or their feelings of well-being. People may wish to limit the quantities of certain foods because of weight problems. They may, on the other hand, wish to totally eliminate certain foods from their diet because of allergic reactions. Still others wish to stop exposing themselves to substances to which they feel "addicted" or for which they feel strong cravings but which are allergenic to their bodies. As discussed later in this section, I recently treated two clients referred with the diagnosis of hyperallergic syndrome who binged on foods to which they appeared to be allergic.

Certain foods have been shown to have an effect on both the pleasure and the arousal axes of mood through their effects on receptor sites and neurotransmitters (Snyder, 1984; Wurtman, Hefti, & Melamed, 1981). The effects of carbohydrate rich meals (Spring, Maller, Wurtman, Digman, & Cozolino, 1983), refined sucrose (Wright, Jacisin, Radin, & Bell, 1978), and caffeine (Gilliland & Bullock, 1984; Greden, Fontaine, Lubetsky, & Chamberlain, 1978) on arousal, anxiety, and depression have been demonstrated. Krietsch, Christensen, and White (1988), for example, found that individuals who were responsive to caffeine- and refined-sucrose-free diets presented with fatigue, moodiness, nervousness, and depression. Although fading techniques can be used to reduce consumption of these foods by dietary responders (James, Stirling, & Hampton, 1985), subliminal techniques appear to contribute to some clients' ability to abstain from or limit intake of problematic foods.

Silverman and his associates have studied the effects of the symbiotic message "Mommy and I are one" on various appetitive behavior disorders. Silverman, Martin, Ungaro, and Mendelsohn (1978), for example, had obese clients imagine situations in which they were tempted to overeat. During this visualization, half of the clients received two 4-msec exposures to the "Mommy and I are one" message. The second half of the clients were exposed to the usual control message "People are walking" for the same duration. Both groups of clients were then instructed to visualize the flash of the tachistoscope whenever they were tempted to overeat. In two separate studies, follow-up at 4 and 24 weeks indicated that experimental subjects were more likely to be losing weight or to be keeping off the weight they had lost. Control clients, on the other hand, were continuing to gain weight or had gained back the weight they had lost.

An interesting aspect of this procedure is that clients were instructed to visualize the flash of the tachistoscope whenever they felt the temptation to overeat. Assuming that the message does have the effect of reducing generalized anxiety, as Silverman has suggested, then the visualized flash may have acquired anxiety reducing properties. If clients are led to believe that such visualizations will strongly help them reduce their anxiety and the related urge to overeat, the effect could be similar to affect anchoring procedures used in certain forms of hypnotic treatments and neurolinguistic programming. In the latter treatment procedures, positive anxiety-reducing affect is associated with images or motor responses that clients can evoke during situations of increased anxiety or temptation. Silverman's procedure could well function in much the same manner in which affect associated with the tachistoscope flash experienced during treatment can be evoked at a later time when the client visualizes the flash.

The "Mommy and I are one" message has also been applied to the treatment of other appetitive behaviors. Using a procedure similar to that described earlier, Palmatier and Bornstein (1980) asked smokers to imagine situations in which they felt a strong urge to smoke. During the visualization, experimental group subjects were exposed to the "Mommy and I are one" message, whereas control group subjects were exposed to the "People are walking" message. The procedure involved 4 presentations per session and all subjects received 12 sessions over a 3-week period. At the end of a 4-week follow-up, 67% of the experimental group subjects were abstaining as compared to 13% of the control group subjects. After 12 weeks, however, there were no statistically significant differences between the groups. Thus, it appears as though subliminal treatment was effective but treatment effects decayed over time, suggesting that booster sessions might be required to sustain treatment gains.

Alcohol and drug use was likewise the focus of research using the Silverman procedure. Schurtman, Palmatier, and Martin (1982) studied 72 alcoholics, half of whom were exposed to the "Mommy and I are one" message, and the remaining half of whom were exposed to the "People are walking" control message. Six sessions were given over a 2-week period with 4 exposures per session. Results after 3-month follow-up indicated that experimental group alcoholics were more involved in treatment, had reduced anxiety and depression, enhanced self-concept, and reduced alcohol consumption.

Thornton, Igleheart, and Silverman (1987) tested the symbiotic message procedure on male heroin addicts who were receiving methadone treatment. After 24 sessions, addicts exposed to the "Mommy and I are one" message reported reduced heroin and other illicit drug use as compared with the control group addicts.

As discussed in detail earlier in this guide, Silverman argued that the message "Mommy and I are one" influences appetitive behavior by reducing generalized anxiety and/or by gratifying symbiotic needs. This in turn reduces the role of appetitive substances for ameliorating anxiety or symbiotic needs.

The subliminal procedure that we have been testing for assisting clients to avoid substances is based on the principle of conditioned aversion. Foods paired with nausea may become aversive (Bernstein & Webster, 1980; Logue, 1986) although despite the robustness of taste aversion learning, some remit with time (Gustavson & Gustavson, 1985). Similarly, alcoholics have been treated with a taste aversion paradigm where alcohol consumption is paired with disuifiram (Antabus) which, with alcohol, creates strong nausea. However, alcohol aversion developed in this fashion may not last long (Nathan, 1985). Further, the pairing of nauseating odors with audiovisual stimuli of inappropriate sexual objects and behavior has been shown to reduce deviant sexual arousal (Earls & Castonguay, 1989; Laws, Meyer, & Holman, 1978).

It is known that food aversions can be acquired without the subject's awareness (Logue, 1986). It is tempting to hypothesize that aversions that are acquired outside of a person's awareness are less likely to remit than those acquired under conditions known to the person. However, there appears to be little difference between aversions acquired with and those acquired without awareness of the conditions associated with the learned aversion (De Silva & Rachman, 1987). Furthermore, subjects who reported knowledge of the aversion conditioning responded equally well to treatment as those who reported lack of awareness of aversion conditioning (De Silva, 1988).

On the other hand, treatments designed to enhance flavor aversions may be more robust if acquired under conditions not available to a client's selective attention. When an alcoholic takes an alcoholic beverage laced with Antabus, the flavor aversion resulting from the association with strong nausea might well be more robust if the alcoholic was unaware of the presence of the Antabus. Similarly, smokers given electric shocks while smoking may find any negative affect conditioned to smoking to be short-lived because attributions to voluntary causal conditions are obvious.

However, in practice, I have found that evoking fear-inducing images during hypnosis, with full recollection by the client, has been an effective treatment for some clients desirous of acquiring aversion to cigarettes. Given that they have full recollection of the hypnotic experience, the aversion, if any, was acquired under conditions of awareness.

The procedure that I use for subliminal aversive conditioning is based on an olfactory aversion procedure that I have found useful for assisting clients who wish to limit intake of a specific food. The procedure is quite simple to apply and, on the basis of client testimonials at least, appears to have the desired effects. One such case was a 44-year-old overweight female who asked to be helped to avoid yielding to the temptation of eating Danish pastries during her two daily coffee breaks. This client, who was in treatment for other complaints, felt that she could keep to her diet and lose weight if only she could "pass up" the Danish sold by the vendor who came by at each coffee break. The client was instructed to place about 1 ounce of chopped beef in a plastic vial that was supplied to her, and leave the closed vial unrefrigerated for 5 days. After the five day "ripening" procedure she was to carry the vial with her to work. At the next opportunity, she was instructed to buy a Danish pastry and take it to the place where she usually had her coffee break. She was further told not to take any other food or beverage with her to her coffee break location. The client was instructed to smell the Danish, break off a small piece and then take a very small taste at the same time that she popped the top off of the vial and smelled the rancid meat.

This single trial procedure appeared to be effective for the client. Several months after the aversion trial she reported that "I simply do not think about Danish pastries anymore." I have used this procedure on several occasions for similar types of client requests. Interestingly, one client reported the development of the aversion from the description alone. That is, she did not have to actually go through the trial and smell the rancid meat. Apparently, her imaging of the situation during my description was adequate to give rise to the aversion.

The procedure for subliminal aversive conditioning involves the presentation of two messages, each for about 15 minutes. The first message, as described previously, stresses the concept of custodianship of the body and that food serves the purpose of providing fuel and nutrients for the body. For clients with food allergies, additional statements are included in the messages such as "The wrong foods can harm my body." For clients with a general overeating problem additional statements such as "Too much food can harm my body" and "I feel content" are added. For specific substance aversions such as nicotine or alcohol statements such as "cigarettes (or alcohol) poison my body," "cigarettes (alcohol) taste bad," "I will not smoke," are included in the custodianship message.

The second subliminal message is a tape of aversive or nauseating sounds.[1] These sounds include retching, vomiting, spitting, clearing the throat, clearing the nose, heavily labored breathing, and the statement "I feel sick" stated under actual conditions of nausea. Both messages are imbedded in white noise at -15 dB(A) relative to the imbedding noise.

During the presentation of the first message the client is relaxing in a recliner chair. After 15 minutes the second message is presented. During the presentation of the second message the client is instructed to look at pictures of the target food(s), touch and manipulate the foods, and then to smell and finally taste the foods. The client is instructed to stop the process if he or she feels too uncomfortable to continue.

---

[1]The aversive nature of the aversive sounds subliminal message was determined in two short experiments. The first was conducted in a class context with students enrolled in a special topics course on subliminal perception. Students in this course are involved in a number of in-class demonstrations, some designed by classmates, designed to test various subliminal effects. The students, therefore, were well informed regarding subliminal messages and had experience with subliminal exposure.

The students were told that six subliminal messages would be played for 3 minutes each. They were further told that three of the presentations would be white noise only whereas the other three would be white noise with the imbedded aversive sounds. The students were told the exact nature of the subliminal message. Their task was to focus on their feelings and record, during each presentation, whether or not that tape contained the aversive subliminal sounds. The results indicated that for the control white-noise only tapes, the responses were at chance levels (i.e., 52% yes, 48% no, NS). For the aversive tapes the response distribution was 67% yes and 33% no ($p < .10$).

The second study (conducted with the assistance of Matthew Simpson) was a flavor aversion preparation in which subjects tasted a novel flavor either when exposed to the aversive subliminal sounds or to white noise alone. Two groups of 5 subjects each were asked to taste and rate, for color, aroma, and flavor, two novel beverages. The beverages were actually the same and were composed of approximately equal amounts of apple juice, cranberry juice, and fruit punch to which approximately 3% white vinegar (5% acetic acid) was added. The added acetic acid was approximately .14% by volume.

Subliminal Flavor Aversion Conditioning: Three Case Studies

The following cases demonstrate the use of auditory subliminal procedures for assisting clients in abstaining from or limiting the intake of food. In two cases the clients had difficulty avoiding foods to which they were allergic. In the third case, although not allergic, the client would binge on specific foods when she felt anxious or depressed. Furthermore, she felt as though she was generally overeating and wanted to lose about 25 pounds.

Case Study 1

The first case is that of a 36-year-old female referred by a clinical ecologist with the diagnosis of hyperallergic syndrome. The client had a long history of severe allergies to many foods as well as to many common environmental elements. She reported that she rarely tasted her food and her sense of smell was virtually absent. According to both the client and her referring physician, the overriding problem with her dealing with the hyperallergic condition was to stick to her very restrictive diet. She would abstain from wheat products, chocolate, and sweet baked goods (all of which gave rise to very severe reactions when consumed) for periods of 2 to 4 weeks. Inevitably after this period of abstention, she would binge on one or all of these foods. She described her bingeing in terms that strongly suggest addiction in that once she started eating she could not stop until she ate all that was available (e.g., a full box of

---

The subjects were asked to observe, smell, and taste the first beverage and then rate that beverage. They were then told to drink a small amount of water to "cleanse the palate" and to wait 5 min before the second tasting. During the 5-minute pause, half of the subjects were exposed to the subliminal message at -15 dB(A) whereas control group subjects were exposed to white noise at the same SPL.

After rating the second beverage, subjects were asked to complete another questionnaire that stated "Tasting novel foods and liquids occasionally gives rise to feelings of discomfort. Please rate the extent of discomfort, if any, that you feel at this time." Two statements followed, the first: "At this time, I feel nauseous" and the second: "At this time, I am experiencing an unpleasant aftertaste." Each statement was rated on a 0-to-6 scale where a rating of 3 or higher indicated an affirmative reply.

The flavor ratings indicate the aversive effect in that four of the five subjects in the subliminal condition rated the second beverage less favorably than the first. Control subjects, on the other hand, all rated the second beverage as more flavorful ($p < .03$). Ratings on the post-experimental questionnaire also indicate a subliminal treatment effect. Three of the five treatment group subjects responded affirmatively to the statement regarding feelings of nausea whereas none of the control group subjects responded affirmatively ($p = .03$). Similarly, four of the five treatment group subjects responded affirmatively to the unpleasant aftertaste question as compared to two of the five control group subjects ($p = .19$).

saltine crackers or until she became very ill. Her discomfort, including swollen face and body, gastrointestinal upset, shortness of breath, and fatigue, would continue for several days following her binge.

The client felt that wheat products, in particular, crackers, cookies, and bread, were her most serious problem. She was asked to bring some magazine pictures of these items as well as small portions of the actual foods to the treatment session. The client was seated in a recliner chair for the first subliminal message which was presented via headsets. She was instructed to simply relax during the presentation of the first message.

During the presentation of this message the client became very emotionally upset. She had images of warmth and love associated with food, which she found quite startling. Following the first message she sat up and proceeded with the second phase of the treatment. During this phase she looked at the pictures, and then handled and tasted each food (she was not able to smell the food because of her condition). During this phase she reported physical symptoms associated with gastrointestinal upset which she said often occurred after eating large quantities of the wheat products. The symptoms she experienced during treatment, burping in particular, occurred very shortly after the aversive sound tape was begun.

The client reported an immediate strong reduction in her craving for the treated foods. After 6 months she reported that her ability to resist such foods was excellent and that she was regaining her sense of smell.

Case Study 2

The second client, a 42-year-old female also referred by a clinical ecologist with the diagnosis of hyperallergic syndrome, likewise had a craving for wheat products. Like the first client, she was sensitive to wheat although her allergic reaction was far less severe. She expressed an interest in reducing her intake of pasta, bread, and a particular type of cracker with melted cheese that her family enjoyed. Her major complaint was that she could not seem to limit her intake of these foods to sensible portions, and hence she was about 15 pounds overweight. She claimed that she would have at least three portions of pasta at a meal and would snack "uncontrollably" on bread and the crackers with melted cheese.

The treatment of this client was similar to that described in the first case. The client was exposed to the custodianship message for 12 minutes, during which she likewise became quite emotional. The aversive message was then presented while the client looked at pictures of the target foods and then handled, smelled, and tasted a small portion of each of the three target foods that she had brought with her. It should be noted that the custodianship message for this client also contained statements designed to limit food intake such as "I am not hungry," "I must eat only to keep my body healthy," and "I will eat slowly," "I will eat less."

During the aversive message the client experienced some gastric activity that she described as mild upset but not nausea. At a 2-month follow-up, the client had lost weight and reported that she felt full after a limited portion of pasta, bread had "no taste," and she could limit her intake of the cracker with cheese.

Case Study 3

The final case is a 35-year-old female who stated that she was about 25 pounds overweight mainly because of "uncontrollable" binges of eating chocolate candies, cookies, or other sweet pastries. She was under treatment for other complaints but asked for help to limit her cravings for sweets. The subliminal messages for this client were identical to those used for the previously described client. However, in the present case, a cassette tape was prepared for the client's home use. Because of the aversive message, the client contracted to use the tape only twice while handling, smelling, and tasting the target foods. Further, she agreed to use the tape only when alone. The taped messages were 14 min each and embedded in white noise at -15 dB(A). The client did not report any emotional reaction to the custodianship message nor did she report any feelings of nausea or stomach upset. Eight weeks after the two home treatments, the client had lost 9 pounds and reported no cravings or binge eating of chocolates or cookies.

Although these cases are uncontrolled clinical trials, the consistency of the results suggests that the procedure may have clinical efficacy. The laboratory-based experimental data likewise indicate that subliminal aversive conditioning is a plausible treatment procedure.

Subliminal Aversion Conditioning
for Smoking Cessation: A Case Study

One final case illustrates the use of the subliminal aversive conditioning model for smoking cessation. It has become obvious that people who wish to give up smoking are well aware of the very serious health hazards associated with smoking. Although motivated to quit, studies have indicated relapse rates of 80% or more for even the best abstinence-based smoking intervention programs (Glasgow, Morray, & Lichtenstein, 1989). The major problem with smoking cessation programs is that of large attrition rates; furthermore, those who do withdraw are more likely to be heavier smokers than those who complete treatment.

The present case was a 38-year-old female with a 22-year smoking history. She had attempted to quit on several occasions and recently had a close friend die of lung cancer as a result of heavy smoking. She was motivated to request subliminal treatment because her friend had been successfully treated for binge eating with subliminal procedures. Although she had a 22-year smoking history, the client was generally capable of limiting her smoking to 6 to 8 cigarettes per day.

The custodianship of the body message for smoking included additional statements such as "Smoking is silly," "Smoking poisons my body," and "I feel sick when I smoke." The procedure, as in the other cases described, involved exposing the client to the custodianship of the body message for 14 min. Following the custodianship message, the aversive message was presented while the client looked at pictures of people smoking, and then handled, smelled, and finally smoked a cigarette until she wished to stop.

This client also experienced an emotional reaction to the custodianship message, which she described as a feeling of "grieving." During the aversive message she stated that she felt extremely hot and started to perspire heavily. At this writing, 4 weeks after treatment, the client reports that she has been successful in abstaining. Also, she finds that, generally, she has no interest in cigarettes although she has experienced a few urges to smoke. However, she reports that such urges are short-lived and that generally she finds that she just does not think about cigarettes.

Although this procedure appears to have promise, it is clear that careful study will be needed to determine dosage and booster sessions required to sustain cessation. Given that this client had strong positive expectations regarding the efficacy of subliminal treatment her ability to abstain could be unrelated to the subliminal procedure.

The fact that this client reported experiences similar to those of the previously described clients does lead one to hypothesize that the subliminal messages were having the desired effects. Given the large relapse rate for smoking cessation programs, it may be necessary to provide clients with abbreviated treatment messages that they can use whenever they experience a craving for a cigarette. With heavy smokers, it is possible that many pairings of the aversive message with smoking will be required to establish sufficient conditioned aversion to reduce or limit the craving. After all, heavy smokers with years of experience have had hundreds of thousands of smoking trials. It is probably unrealistic to expect a conditioned aversion established in a single or even a few sessions to remain robust against such a strong habit.

We are presently examining a chronic pairing model in which, after initial sessions of hypnosis and subliminal treatment as described earlier, the smoker pairs the aversive message with every cigarette smoked in vivo until aversion is established. The smoker is provided with an endless loop tape with the subliminal aversive message to be played on a Walkman cassette tape player on every occasion when a cigarette is either desired or smoked. Pilot work suggests that this procedure may be effective for reducing smoking rate. It may well be that this procedure will not result in complete abstinence but rather clinically significant reductions in smoking for heavily addicted smokers (Lubin et al., 1984).

One such client, presently in treatment, is a 46-year-old male with a 25-year smoking history. The client stated that since the age of 21 he had smoked between 30 and 60 cigarettes per day. His average at time of treatment was reported to be just over 50 per day. The client had a family history of severe lung and heart disease associated with smoking and was very highly motivated to stop or limit his smoking. He had made many attempts to quit and had been under psychiatric treatment for over a year in which the focus was smoking cessation. The psychiatrist referred the client for additional treatment for the smoking problem.

This client received a hypnotic session in which health, well-being, and custodianship of the body were emphasized. During hypnosis, cigarettes were paired with aversive images. During the second session the client received the two-phase subliminal treatment described earlier. He was also provided with the endless loop cassette of the aversive subliminal message to be played anytime he craved or actually smoked a cigarette.

At this writing the client has reduced his cigarette intake to between 8 and 12 per day with occasional problem days of 12 to 14 cigarettes. After the hypnotic and the subliminal sessions the client reported that he abstained from cigarettes for 17 and 25 hours, respectively. He reported that the first cigarette that he smoked following the in-office subliminal aversion treatment gave rise to immediate nausea and then vomiting. Furthermore, he reported that the tape always gives rise to a feeling of nausea when played while smoking. This procedure appears promising for obtaining clinically meaningful reductions in smoking. Whether or not this subliminal treatment procedure will be found to assist heavily addicted smokers to achieve complete abstinence remains to be determined.

THE EFFECTS OF SUBLIMINAL MESSAGES ON DREAMS AND IMAGES

As discussed earlier in this book, subliminally presented messages intrude upon cognitive processes. Several studies in our laboratories have demonstrated that subliminally presented words were recovered in free association in which subjects were asked to simply jot down every concept that crossed their minds and in short stories that they were asked to write. Furthermore, as we discussed earlier, Groeger (1986a, 1986b) demonstrated that words that are presented below detection thresholds are more likely to have a semantic intrusion on cognitive processes. Words that are presented above detection but below recognition thresholds, on the other hand, are more likely to intrude phonologically upon cognitive processes.

An issue of clinical interest is that of the potential for subliminal messages to intrude on dream processes. In the early 1900s Poetzl (Erdelyi, 1972) demonstrated that a visual image presented subliminally could influence dream content. Poetzl maintained that subliminally presented visual images would intrude upon dream content whereas supraliminally presented consciously perceived images would not be utilized in dreams. The Poetzl phenomenon has been replicated by several investigators under a variety of different conditions. Fisher (1988), for example, reported that subliminally presented visual stimuli do influence dreams and images but he found, contrary to Poetzl's observation, that supraliminal stimuli were also utilized in dreams. However, for therapeutic purposes, it appears as though significant recovery of primary process aspects of the stimulus material and much, presumably unconscious, unreported content appears to be recovered in dream content stimulated by the subliminal presentations. Kaser (1986) used an auditory procedure in which a sung message was speeded up until it could not be consciously understood. It was then mixed with music. A group of subjects who listened to the music with the mixed-in, speeded-up message were compared with a group of control subjects who listened to the music alone. Drawings of visual images after listening to the tape and of any dreams that subjects had the night following the tape presentations were rated by an art therapist. Kaser reported that there were significant differences between the drawings of the experimental and the control group subjects in that the drawings of the experimental group subjects reflected content of the subliminal message.

It is interesting to note that dream content can also be influenced by presenting auditory messages to subjects during Rapid Eye Movement (REM) periods of sleep. De Koninck and Koulack (1975) conducted an interesting study in which subjects viewed a stressful film before going to sleep and again in the morning. Half of the subjects were presented with part of the soundtrack from the film during REM periods of sleep. These messages would have been supraliminal for an awake subject. The results indicated that there were more incorporations of content from the film into dreams of those subjects in the film plus sound condition as compared with dreams of subjects in the film only condition. It was also found that subjects with more incorporation of film elements in their dreams tended to exhibit more emotionality during the second film presentation.

There are several very interesting and potentially clinical useful possibilities associated with the subliminal manipulation of dream content. Although the studies described previously hint at the potential for such subliminal procedures, considerable research will be required before we can conclude that such procedures have clinical efficacy. In the first instance, it appears as though subliminally presented messages may access material that is not directly or easily available to a person. Shevrin (1986) found that much information that was not reported by a person and which was presumably unconscious was recovered in dreams that had been stimulated by subliminal images. This of course could be quite useful for assisting clients in the uncovery process. Often hypnosis and/or dream analysis is used to help clients recover memories of earlier traumatic events. Content recovered during hypnosis can often initiate dreams that provide additional information regarding the traumatic event (Barnett, 1981). Furthermore, during hypnosis, clients can be given the suggestion that they will have a significant dream that will be recalled and reported at the next session (Wolberg, 1964). It is not unlikely that subliminal presentations of messages with content prepared to stimulate recall of a particular event, might initiate dream activity that accesses significant content.

There are a number of very practical issues that warrant serious investigation. First, it appears as though dream content can be influenced by either subliminal messages presented to subjects in the awake state or by supraliminal messages presented at sub-waking threshold levels to a sleeping subject. An issue of some importance of course is the determination of which procedure is likely to be most effective in stimulating the recovery of content not easily available to a client. If material presented to a sleeping subject must be presented during specific stages of sleep, the clinical practicality of this procedure would be limited. Subliminal presentations, particularly if the modality can be auditory, would be a much more clinically useful procedure.

The second issue of importance is the relative efficacy of material that is presented auditorily versus material that is presented visually at sub-detection levels. The little available research relevant to this issue seems to indicate that both auditory and visual modalities may be used to stimulate dream content, but no data are available as to the relative efficacy of subliminal presentations in either modality.

THE EFFECTS OF SUBLIMINAL MESSAGES ON PHYSIOLOGICAL PROCESSES

Exciting potential uses of subliminal technology include physiological diagnostics and modification of autonomic functioning, both of which were suggested by the early work of Lazarus and McCleary (1951). As discussed previously, these investigators reported that subliminally presented stimuli of different affective tone could be autonomically discriminated as measured by changes in Skin Conductance Level (SCL). Changes in cortical or autonomic functioning as measured by evoked cortical potentials, SCL, HR, or peripheral blood flow might be found to be sensitive to psychologically or psychodynamically meaningful material. Hence therapeutically useful information not directly or easily available to a person might be revealed using such a subliminal preparation. This, of course, is a direct analog to the polygraph when used as "lie detectors" for supraliminal material. Whether subliminal presentation of content will reveal information not available to supraliminal presentation is, of course, the question of particular importance.

The second potential application is that of modifying autonomic functioning or enhancing other clinical procedures, such as biofeedback, that are designed to assist clients to control specific autonomically related systems. This is a complicated issue and one that will require considerable study. For example, regularization of the vascular system by means of biofeedback training of vasodilation and vasoconstriction is a treatment of choice for certain forms of migraine headache. As Shellenberger and Green (1986) pointed out, however, the critical feature of thermal biofeedback for peripheral bloodflow training as a treatment for migraine is that of mastery. Clients who master vasomodulation are those who experience symptom relief. Although this seems patently obvious, it is remarkable that many researchers and clinicians do not seem to comprehend the concept. It is not warm hands that is fundamental to symptom remission, but rather it is the mastery of vasoregulation that is central to the successful treatment of migraine headache.

With this in mind, the issue of the beneficial effects of subliminal techniques for enhancement of biofeedback or other treatments can be defined in clinically meaningful researchable terms. As is discussed later in this section, subliminal effects on physiological responses can be demonstrated. Whether such enhancement implies greater mastery on the part of the client or whether enhanced levels give rise to greater improvement in the target symptom remains to be determined. For example, if the subliminal message "My hands are warm" gives rise to increased hand temperature, the effect of this on mastery of vasodilation is uncertain. Further, it is possible that such subliminal enhancement of biofeedback treatment effects could be detrimental to treatment goals because the client's mastery of the physiological process is affected in some manner. By analogy, putting gloves on a client attempting to learn handwarming would certainly increase hand temperature but would not be indicative of mastery of vasodilation.

In the present section we review some of the recent work regarding psychophysiological changes associated with the presentation of stimuli at levels that are within subliminal ranges. The section is divided into two parts. The first part reviews some of the work that has been done on brainstem and cortical evoked potentials (i.e., the central nervous system) which appears to have promise both as a diagnostic procedure as well as a research preparation for studying unconscious processes. The second part of this section reviews work that indicates subliminal influence on the autonomic nervous system as reflected by physiological activity in modalities commonly used in biofeedback treatment. The second part of this section reviews work that indicates subliminal influence on the autonomic nervous system as reflected by physiological activity in modalities commonly used in biofeedback treatment.

Central Nervous System Activity

That information is processed outside of selective attention has been established by investigators studying evoked potentials during sleep. Of particular interest was Berger's (1963) finding that the auditory presentation of a subject's own name can evoke a cortical response during sleep without the subject reporting awareness or memory of the stimulus presentation. Other researchers (Amadeo & Shagass, 1973; Campbell & Bartoli, 1986; Linden, Campbell, Hamel, & Picton, 1985; Mendel & Kupperman, 1974) reported data that indicate that auditory stimuli presented during sleep give rise to evoked potentials. There is some debate as to whether the evoked potentials differ between wakefulness and sleep and among the different stages of sleep, but nonetheless the data do indicate, not surprisingly, that brainstem and cortical activity are influenced by auditory stimuli outside of selective attention. Furthermore, as Berger (1963) indicated, this cortical activity is further affected by the meaningfulness of the stimuli even though the messages are presented outside of subject's selective attention. Sleeping subjects have been found to overtly (e.g., microswitch pressing) or covertly (e.g., heart rate variation, EEG changes) respond to stimuli of emotive significance of either an intrinsic (e.g., familiar) or extrinsic (e.g., associated with punishment) nature (Granda & Hammack, 1961; Williams, Murlock, & Murlock, 1966; Zung & Wilson, 1961).

However, responsiveness to messages presented during sleep is not limited to material with particular emotive significance (Shanon, 1979). Subjects will microswitch press in response to specific words, identified prior to sleep, when the words are presented during sleep (Shanon, 1979). In addition, subjects' recall and recognition of words is facilitated by repetition of the words during sleep (Tilley, 1979).

There is a tendency to have great confidence in physiological measures as providing the definitive test that stimuli presented outside of selective attention are, in fact, processed. After all, subjects cannot reliably detect the presence or absence of a stimulus above chance levels, but physiological responses do discriminate stimulus presentation; we have greater confidence in the physiological indications that subliminal effects are real than in subjective reports. The research in the area of event-related potentials (ERP) during sleep as described previously is consistent with research reported in the area of sleep assisted instruction (SAI). As Aarons (1976) reported, learning of material presented during sleep can be demonstrated. Although the signals used in SAI research would be above detection or discrimination threshold in awake subjects, detection of some part of the material can be demonstrated under conditions in which the subject is not selectively attending to the content. Research in SAI has further suggested that the minimum number of repetitions for learning appears to be 8 (Tani & Yoshii, 1970) and that the fundamental condition for SAI improvement is that the repetition of the material be in the same sequence (Bliznichenka, cited in Aarons, 1976).

One of the problems associated with the work that has been conducted on ERP associated with subliminal stimuli is lack of consistency in the definition of the dependent variable. Several researchers have worked with specific components of the ERP, such as the N100, the early negative component that appears at about 100 msec after stimulus presentation. Another is the P300, which is the positive component prominent in selective attention paradigms that occurs at about 300 msec.

Another procedure that has been used is the transinformation method of ERP data reduction. This procedure involves summing the peak or maximum amplitude potential in the "early" (i.e., 0 to 400 msec) and "late" (i.e., 404 to 700 msec) portions of the ERP. Not surprisingly, a number of individuals reported positive findings with regard to ERP associated with subliminal messages and a number of researchers reported negative results. Also, there is controversy about the appropriateness of some of the data reduction procedures that were used to define the ERP (Marcel, 1988; Schwartz & Rem, 1975). One very interesting study that was conducted from the perspective of signal detection theory analyzed ERP associated with weak sensory signals (Parasuraman & Beatty, 1980). Subjects listening to 60 dB wide band noise were exposed to embedded 50 msec pure tones. Subsequent to the presentation, subjects were asked to give one of four responses consisting of detection or no detection of signal and whether they were sure or unsure of whether or not they had detected a tone. Thus there were four conditions associated with presentation or nonpresentation of the tone: "yes, sure," "no, sure," "yes, unsure," and "no, unsure." For our purposes, the interesting results of this study indicated that the N100 varied only with detection of the tone whereas the P300 varied with both detection and recognition (i.e., which tone has been presented). The P300 had greater amplitude for recognized versus unrecognized targets. Furthermore, the difference in amplitude between the P300 for targets more likely to be confused were smaller than for those targets less likely to be confused. Finally, the N100 amplitude was highest for confident detection and the amplitude associated with the N100 decreased with less confidence and was lowest for no detection. This indicates that the N100 appears to be sensitive not only to detection but also to the subject's confidence associated with his or her detection response. The previous study made use of stimuli that might be considered to be very close to threshold.

Other researchers likewise reported that the N100 and the P300 components of the ERP are affected by stimuli that are below recognition threshold (Hillyard, Squires, Bauer, & Lindsay, 1971; Libet, Alberts, Wright, & Feinstein, 1967). It appears that these components vary in accordance with the a posteriori likelihood ratio that a signal had been presented. Thus there does seem to be a relationship between detection and ERP components. Signal likelihood and the subject's confidence in response accuracy are likewise implicated in amplitude differences in these ERP components.

The studies reported earlier were conducted in the context of signal detection theory in which subjects were required to discriminate signal plus noise from noise alone. A number of researchers have shown that there are differences in the ERP associated with differences in the connotative or affective meaning of words presented supraliminally. Begleiter, Porjesz, and Garozzo (1979) and Chapman, McCrary, Chapman, and Martin (1980) reported that pleasant and unpleasant words give rise to differences in the ERP. Further, the ERP has been found to be sensitive to verb-noun differences (Brown & Lehmann, 1979) as well as to antonym-homonym differences (Kutas, Lindawood, & Hillyard, 1983).

The P300 component has been found to be affected by meaningful subliminal stimuli as well. Kostandov and Arzumanov (1986), for example, reported that the P300 amplitude is greater in response to subliminal emotional words as compared to subliminal neutral words. Further, this effect was similar as recorded over both cerebral hemispheres. Of particular interest was the finding that subliminally presented words that evoked an "unaccountable emotion" gave rise to greater right hemispheric P300 amplitude. The authors suggested that the right hemisphere may play a predominant role in the cortical organization of unconscious affective processes.

In a later study, these same authors (Kostandov & Arzumanov, 1989) reported that the P300 shows greater amplitude to subliminally presented emotional words relative to neutral words. They also reported an intriguing subliminal conditioning effect. Visually presented verbal stimuli that could not be recognized by the subject were paired so that a word with emotional meaning followed, "reinforced," a neutral word. The neutral word then was found to evoke increased P300 amplitude. The authors reported that the connections were very stable and inert and would not extinguish in spite of many trials in the absence of the emotional word. They also pointed out that this subliminal conditioning effect may explain the "longstanding observation of psychiatrists on the rigidity of emotional feelings and neurotic reactions, when the subject is unaware of their reason" (p. 272).

When diazepam (10 mg intramuscular) was administered, subliminal conditioning did not occur. However, diazepam did not suppress the effect if conditioning had occurred prior to the drug administration. These findings were interpreted to mean that emotional subliminal stimuli implicate the limbic system where emotional reactions are integrated. Should such procedures access the limbic hypothalamic system the implications for mind/body healing are indeed very far reaching. As Rossi (1986) pointed out, procedures such as hypnosis that access the limbic hypothalamic system implicate, in turn, the autonomic nervous system, the immune system, the endocrine system, and the enteric system.

Differences in the topography of the ERP fields with respect to the P300 component specific to subliminal material was suggested by Brandeis and Lehmann (1986). These authors reported that the P300 component of the ERP showed topographical differences in response to the noun and verb meaning of supraliminally present homophone words. Further subliminal presentation of information likewise influences the topographical configuration of the P300 component.

Genkina and Shostakovich (1986) studied the P300 component of the ERP of alcoholics and nonalcoholics in response to the subliminally presented word "vodka" as compared with neutral words. Greater amplitude of the P300 component of the ERP was found for alcoholics in response to the word "vodka" relative to the neutral words. No such difference in amplitude was found for the control subjects.

In a series of studies Shevrin and his colleagues (Shevrin & Fritzler, 1968; Shevrin, Smith, & Fritzler, 1971; Shevrin, Smith, & Hoobler, 1970) showed that the P300 discriminates between subliminally presented stimuli of different content. Schwartz and Rem (1975) reported a failure to replicate this ERP discrimination effect when the stimuli were presented above detection but below discrimination thresholds. Shevrin and his associates presented the subliminal stimuli at 1 msec duration whereas Schwartz and Rem (1975) presented stimuli at 3 msec duration. Hence it appears as though the P300 component of the ERP is sensitive to differences in meaning and affect of subliminally presented messages. Furthermore, it appears as though such differences are also sensitive to or are related to the confidence a subject reports regarding response accuracy. In addition, it again appears that stimuli below detection threshold give rise to qualitatively different cortical responses as compared with stimuli presented in other threshold ranges. Finally, given the effects of weak but detectable stimuli on the N100 and the P300 components of the ERP, the use of the backward masking procedure for research and clinical treatment is contraindicated. As discussed earlier in this chapter, backward masking does interfere with stimulus detection and discrimination. However, because of the effects of the mask itself on cognitive processes, the backward masking preparation is not recommended for either research or clinical purposes (see Henley, 1984).

Another approach to studying cortical activity associated with unconscious processes and subliminally presented messages is the transinformation method of data reduction of the ERP (Shevrin, 1988). Essentially this method involves cumulating the largest or peak amplitude wave in the "early" (i.e., 100 to 400 msec) and the "late" (i.e., 404 to 740 msec) ranges. Shevrin was particularly interested in the possibility that subliminally presented words associated with unconscious conflict would give rise to different ERP patterns as compared with other words having pleasant or unpleasant meaning. Hence, if words related to the unconscious conflict underlying a patient's consciously experienced symptom would give rise to distinctive ERP patterns, then researchers would have a method for investigating the dynamic unconscious.

It does appear as though evoked cortical potentials are differentially affected by supraliminal and subliminal messages. Conscious processing is reflected primarily by increased cortical activity in the left hemisphere (Gazzaniga & LeDoux, 1978). Unconscious processing, on the other hand, appears to be associated with increases in cortical activity in the right hemisphere (Shevrin & Dickman, 1980; Weimer, 1977). It is interesting that both affective and cognitive supraliminal information that is processed unconsciously is related to increased evoked cortical activity in the right hemisphere. Furthermore, both affective and cognitive subliminal material that is processed unconsciously is reflected in increased evoked cortical activity in the left hemisphere (Branscombe, 1988). As Branscombe suggested, perhaps the distinction between left and right hemisphere processing is not so much that of emotional versus cognitive processing but rather reflects differences in levels of consciousness associated with the information processing.

It should be noted that the relationship between brain potentials and auditorily presented subliminal meaningful messages may be nonrecursive. Budzynsky (1976) described a preparation for presenting meaningful material under conditions of "twilight" states of consciousness. The procedure involves monitoring the theta component of the brain wave spectrum and harnessing the message delivery to states of theta predominance. Hence in predominant theta state the client receives the auditory message which terminates anytime the client's EEG pattern becomes nontheta dominant. Phenomenologically, the theta state reflects absence of selective attention. When the client does selectively attend, beta predominates and the message terminates. The experience is rather like being in a crowded room and being passively aware of conversations among people around one but not attending to the content of the conversations.

Boddy (1981, 1986, 1989) found that ERP amplitude will distinguish between different classes of words within a latency range of 150–250 msec. This latency is at least 300 msec faster than digital response of word recognition. Boddy stated that the ERP latency is in the range of the zone of preconsciousness (Libet et al., 1967), inferring that the ERP is reflecting preconscious attainment of meaning. Roth and Boddy (in press) reported that verbal stimuli presented repeatedly at subliminal exposures until they are identified elicit ERPs that show progressive changes over the prerecognition trials. They stated that successive subliminal stimulus exposure progressively increments a trace until the threshold for emergence into consciousness is passed. Boddy (1989) further stated that the evidence suggests subconscious attainment of word meaning on individual trials rather than accumulation of word fragments. Thus, the evidence indicates that meaning is attained from stimuli that do not have a phenomenal representation.

Autonomic Nervous System Activity

A number of investigators have reported that subliminal messages influence the autonomic nervous system as reflected in changes in HR, electrodermal (EDR), and electromyographic (EMG) responses. In some of these studies one (or more) of these responses was monitored in nonfeedback mode to determine the influence of subliminal messages on passive subjects (e.g., Borgeat & Goulet, 1983). Other investigators, on the other hand, studied the effect of subliminal messages on biofeedback training (e.g., Cohn, DeSimone, Frank, & Silverman, 1979).

Consistent with the earlier work that indicated that visually presented subliminal stimuli differentially affected EDR (Dixon, 1958; Lazarus & McCleary, 1951; O'Grady, 1977), several investigators reported similar effects for auditory subliminal stimuli. Corteen and Dunn (1974), using a shadowing procedure, found greater EDR to shock-associated words as compared to nonshock-associated words. Borgeat and his associates (Borgeat et al., 1985; Borgeat & Pannetier, 1982; Corbisiero & Borgeat, 1980) reported influences of auditory stimuli on EDR and HR that are differentially associated with message content. Although greater EDR and

HR to emotionally laden words would be expected both subliminally and supraliminally, it appears as though a paradoxical effect may occur at stimulus intensities that are below discrimination *but above* detection threshold (Borgeat et al., 1985). In this range the EDR and HR were found to be more pronounced in response to neutral words relative to emotional (sexual) words. This finding seems to corroborate findings in our work that indicate, in agreement with Dixon (1971), that effective subliminal stimulus ranges are below detection threshold. The paradoxical effects found in the detectable stimulus range could well be attributed to partial cues, structural as opposed to semantic processing, or, perhaps, could reflect a process similar to perceptual defense, an explanation offered by Borgeat and his colleagues (1985).

In a subsequent study Borgeat, Boissonneault, and Chaloult (1989) alternately exposed subjects to activating or neutral subliminal messages and then to a stressing task (mental calculations). The activating messages were words suggesting wakefulness, readiness for action, alertness, and concentration. The words were embedded in white noise at an intensity range of -10 to -20 dB relative to the white noise. As the authors stated, this range is above detection threshold, but subjects were reported to be unable to recognize the meaning or content of the messages.

The results indicate that the messages gave rise to increases in HR during the stressing task. This increase in HR persisted for about 8 minutes after the termination of the stressing task. No effects were found for either skin conductance responses or skin conductance levels.

A pilot study, conducted with the assistance of Matthew Simpson, exposed 10 subjects to either white noise or white noise plus the autogenic phrase "My hands and arms are heavy and warm" while finger temperature was being monitored. The messages were maintained at a range that was at least -15 dB(A) relative to the white noise. Following the 20-minute session subjects completed a post-experimental questionnaire that asked them to give several subjective ratings including how warm they felt. Only data from subjects whose initial baseline finger temperature was below 89°F were retained for analysis.

The results indicated that subjects exposed to the subliminal message had greater increments in finger temperature, relative to controls (M = 8.3°F versus 4.1°F, $p = .086$). Further, subjects exposed to the subliminal message rated themselves as feeling warmer than did the subjects exposed only to the white noise (M = 73.5 versus 53.2, on a 100 point scale, $p = .086$).

This pilot study suggests issues that warrant systematic investigation. The subliminal message used in the study was a combination of the first two formulas of the six standard autogenic training exercises (Luthe, 1973). Increases in subjective sensations of warmth and increases in peripheral blood flow are associated with the autogenic exercises "My arm is heavy" and "My arm is warm" (Luthe, 1973; Schultz & Luthe, 1969; Tebecis et al., 1976/1977). However, such training generally requires daily practice for 2 to 6 weeks for each exercise.

Should subliminal procedures be found to influence peripheral blood flow, as suggested by this pilot study, this may indicate a more efficient method for influencing specific physiological systems. Further study is required to determine if peripheral blood flow changes are due to general enhanced relaxation or to specific influences on the vascular system. In addition, the beneficial effects, if any, of such subliminal enhancement of peripheral blood flow remains to be determined.

The effects of auditory subliminal messages on EMG responses were investigated by Silverman and his colleagues (Cohn et al., 1979) and by Borgeat and his colleagues (Borgeat et al., 1985; Borgeat & Goulet, 1983). Silverman studied the potential facilitative effect of the symbiotic message "Mommy and I are one" on EMG biofeedback training. Subjects, matched for initial state-trait anxiety level, sex, and initial EMG baseline received 6 EMG training sessions. One half of the subjects received the message "Mommy and I are one," whereas the control subjects received the "People are walking" message. Results indicate superior EMG learning, as reflected in lower levels relative to baseline, for subjects exposed to the symbiotic message. It appears, therefore, that subliminal messages do affect sympathetic arousal as well as cortical evoked potentials. There are several issues of importance that will require investigation.

The first issue is that of determining the processes involved in the relaxing effects of subliminal messages. The research by Cohn and colleagues (1979), which indicated that the message "Mommy and I are one" enhanced EMG biofeedback learning, suggests that the process is not direct. As we discussed earlier in this book, Silverman argued that the beneficial effects of the "Mommy and I are one" symbiotic message are attributable to enhanced quiescence of unconscious conflicts. This quiescence in turn gives rise to several benefits, one of which apparently is enhanced relaxation as reflected in greater EMG reductions relative to baseline.

Subliminal messages may also operate in the direct fashion in which statements such as "You are relaxed, you feel happy, calm, peaceful, rested" and the like had the direct effect of enhancing clients' feelings of well-being and relaxation, which would in turn be reflected in reduced sympathetic arousal.

It is also possible that statements designed to directly influence particular physiological systems may give rise to changes in that system. Autogenic statements such as "My hands and arms are heavy and warm" can be used by clients to enhance vasodilation as well as to increase feelings of relaxation. Should subliminal autogenic messages influence physiological response, it will be important to determine the extent to which such subliminal messages have a specific or general effect. In biofeedback training, for example, the client should be taught to reduce muscle tension or increase surface temperature at various sites to facilitate a generalized state of reduced muscle tension or enhanced peripheral blood flow. Similarly, with subliminal messages, one wonders whether the statement "My hands and arms are heavy and warm" or "My forehead is relaxed" presented subliminally will have a very specific effect on those areas or whether it will generalize to other areas in the body as well.

As discussed previously, it remains to be determined if physiological system enhancements are related to symptom improvement. If it is found that statements such as "My hands are heavy and warm" give rise to enhanced finger temperature, does this in turn give rise to improvement in client complaint such as migraine headache. It is entirely possible that such procedures may in fact reduce mastery of vasodilation and in turn reduce the effectiveness of thermal biofeedback for the treatment of migraine headache. This, of course, remains to be determined.

Research indicates that some types of disorders (e.g., tension headache) often respond equally well to EMG biofeedback and to progressive muscular relaxation. Presumably, this is due to the fact that both procedures teach muscular relaxation. Both of these are active treatment procedures in which the client masters a skill. The question of the comparative efficacy of subliminal relaxation messages versus progressive muscular relaxation was investigated by Borgeat (1985). Borgeat compared subliminal relaxation messages with Progressive Muscular Relaxation (PMR) on passive EMG levels (i.e., not in biofeedback mode). He reported no difference between these two relaxation procedures, although PMR did appear to be superior on EMG performance of more anxious subjects (as measured on the IPAT Anxiety Scale).

There are a number of issues involved with the question of the relative efficacy of subliminal versus supraliminal relaxation procedures. One of the benefits of biofeedback training, for example, is that mastery of a skill such as muscle tension reduction provides clients with a sense of empowerment and feelings that they can exercise control or at least influence their general state of health and well-being. Similarly, a technique such as progressive muscular relaxation can have many side benefits above and beyond the general enhanced relaxation in the sense that clients feel that they are doing something for themselves in an effort to improve their conditions. Progressive muscular relaxation, for example, has been shown to be effective for the treatment of depression presumably just because it creates the feeling that one is actively doing something to deal with a psychological problem (McLean & Carr, 1989). Hence, one of the potential dangers of subliminal treatment procedures is that it could encourage passivity in the client. If the client conceptualizes the subliminal message in a manner comparable to the way clients often conceptualize medication, then of course some of the advantages of cognitive behavioral approaches to client treatment could be compromised. However, in my experience the use of client choice procedures as described in the methodology section of this book not only minimizes this risk but seems to actually enhance client involvement in treatment procedures.

The obvious questions that require further research involve the determination of whether subliminal procedures are superior to supraliminal relaxation procedures, or perhaps better for certain types of client complaints. Also, it is entirely possible that the combination of supraliminal relaxation procedures in combination with subliminal relaxation messages might be superior to either or may in fact be synergic. It is possible that client success with a particular relaxation procedure might be enhanced by the application of a subliminal relaxation segment before, during, or after the supraliminally presented relaxation exercise.

It is also possible that a conditioned relaxation effect may occur. Subliminal messages may be associated with relaxation induced by supraliminally presented instructions. The client who was treated for symptoms associated with systemic lupus erythematosus, described earlier, reported that he often played the subliminal tape after he had completed one of the relaxation protocols, such as progressive muscular relaxation or cognitive tension reduction. He also reported that he often played the subliminal tape concurrently with other relaxation procedures such as hand warming, relaxation by recall, and so on. As was reported in the case study, this client reported that he found the subliminal tape to be the most useful home treatment for maintaining the gains he made in treatment.

In summary, it appears as though subliminal treatment procedures may prove to be very useful for enhancing relaxation, reducing sympathetic tone, and perhaps for directly modifying physiological processes and cortical activity. Whether these procedures will prove to have therapeutic merit remains to be determined.

CONCLUDING REMARKS

There are, of course, some contraindications for subliminal treatment. As with hypnosis and biofeedback, subliminal treatment with clients who are likely to be negatively affected by issues associated with control should be guarded. Similarly, clients with psychotic tendencies are at risk for negative reaction to subliminal messages.

As discussed in the previous chapter, particular care should be taken by the clinician to avoid enhancing client passivity. Clients may be inclined to view subliminal treatment as a relief-providing procedure that releases them from responsibility for active involvement with their treatment.

A contract should always be struck between the clinician and the client, which establishes the conditions and terms for the use of any subliminal materials designed for home use. Although useful for the client, the effects of some of the subliminal messages on persons not under treatment are unknown.

As with some relaxation procedures, subliminal procedures may trigger enhanced anxiety in some clients. This may result from changes in plasma CO_2 brought on by relaxation in clients with panic disorder. On the other hand, clients are often distressed by unfamiliar feelings associated with states of relaxation not previously experienced. Clients should be screened for relaxation-induced anxiety prior to recommending subliminal procedures.

Client improvement is the goal of all treatment. We must exercise care that our treatment procedures do not negatively interact. If our therapeutic goal is to teach the client a skill, subliminal enhancement of the response in question may compromise skill mastery.

A fascinating potential application of the subliminal technology is in psychoneuroimmunology. It has become clear that cognitive-emotional states are implicated in immunosuppression and enhancement. Stress-inducing events can have an immunosuppressive effect (Hall & Goldstein, 1984). Daily relaxation exercises have been found to affect both the humoral and the cellular divisions of the immune system (Green, Green, & Santoro, 1988). Black (1963) reported that hypnosis can give rise to augmentation in immune-responsiveness. Furthermore, classically conditioned immunosuppression and enhancement have been demonstrated in animals (Spector, 1986). In addition, changes in the immune system and prognosis of cancer patients have been found to be associated with relaxation and guided imagery (Gruber, Hall, Hersh, & Dubois, 1988; Simonton, Matthews-Simonton, & Sparks, 1980).

There are several important issues associated with the use of subliminal messages for the modification of immune system functioning. The data seem to indicate that one can influence the immune system with cognitive manipulations at various levels of abstraction. Guided imagery or hypnosis can be direct in the sense that specific system changes are suggested. On the other hand, metaphorical images (such as big fish devouring little fish) appear likewise to enhance immune system functioning. General suggestions regarding health and well-being appear also to enhance treatment prognosis.

We are presently studying the effects of subliminal messages on clients' reactivity to allergic substances. This work is in the preliminary stages and extreme caution is being exercised to avoid any generalized immuno-suppressive response. Essentially, messages designed to enhance response discrimination are being incorporated into messages focused on general feelings of health, strength, and well-being.

Subliminal treatment self-help tapes are big business. As such, commercial exploiters of this technology are understandably reluctant to reveal their techniques. Although some of my clients use these commercially available products, I have never systematically tested the clinical efficacy of such tapes. If a client tells me that he or she finds these products helpful, my response is "great." In fact, however, I have no idea whether or not any of these products have any therapeutic benefit. Merikle (1990), however, spectographically analyzed subliminal tapes from four commercial suppliers and concluded that none contained identifiable speech within the background sound. He also conducted forced-choice detection trials and found that listeners could not distinguish between "signal" and "placebo" tapes. He concluded that the products tested did not contain any embedded subliminal messages that could conceivably influence behavior.

On the other hand, serious researchers have reported subliminal effects which seem promising for clinical application. I have attempted in this book to review the research that seems relevant to such application. The procedures for auditory and visual subliminal treatment have been described and some of the important theoretical issues have been discussed. After reading this book, it will be obvious to the reader that the major work lies ahead of us. The technology looks promising and the possibilities for therapeutic use are exciting

References

Aarons, L. (1976). Sleep-assisted instruction. *Psychological Bulletin, 83*, 1-40.

Amadeo, M., & Shagass, C. (1973). Brief latency click-evoked potentials during waking and sleep in man. *Psychophysiology, 10*, 244-250.

Balay, J., & Shevrin, H. (1988). The subliminal psychodynamic activation method: A critical review. *American Psychologist, 43*, 161-174.

Barlow, D. H. (1988). *Anxiety and its disorders: The nature and treatment of anxiety and panic.* New York: Guilford Press.

Barnett, E. A. (1981). *Analytical hypnotherapy: Principles and practice.* Kingston, Ontario: Junica.

Beck, A. T. (1970). *Depression: Causes and treatment.* Philadelphia: University of Pennsylvania Press.

Becker, H. C., Corrigan, R. E., Elder, S. T., Tallant, J. D., & Goldstein, M. (1965). Subliminal communication: Biological engineering considerations. *Digest of the Sixth International Conference on Medical Electronics and Biological Engineering* (pp. 452-453).

Beecher, H. (1959). *Measurement of subjective responses: Quantitative effect of drugs.* New York: Oxford University Press.

Begleiter, H., Porjesz, B., & Garozzo, R. (1979). Visual evoked potentials and affective ratings of semantic stimuli. In H. Begleiter (Ed.), *Evoked brain potentials and behavior* (pp. 127-142). New York: Plenum Press.

Beiman, I., Israel, E., & Johnson, S. A. (1978). During training and posttraining effects of live and taped extended progressive relaxation, self relaxation, and electromyogram biofeedback. *Journal of Consulting and Clinical Psychology, 46*(2), 314-321.

Beisser, A. (1961). Psychodynamic observations of a sport. *Psychoanalytic Review, 48*, 69-76.

Berger, R. J. (1963). Experimental modification of dream content by meaningful verbal stimuli. *British Journal of Psychiatry, 109*, 722-740.

Bernstein, D. A., & Borkovec, T. D. (1975). *Progressive relaxation training.* Chicago: Research Press.

Bernstein, I. L., & Borson, S. (1986). Learned food aversion: A component of anorexia syndromes. *Psychological Review, 93*, 462-472.

Bernstein, I. L., & Webster, M. M. (1980). Learned taste aversions in humans. *Physiology and Behavior, 25,* 363-366.

Black, S. (1963). Inhibition of immediate-type hypersensitivity response by direct suggestion under hypnosis. *British Medical Journal, 1,* 925-926.

Blanchard, E. B., & Haynes, M. R. (1975). Biofeedback treatment of a case of Raynaud's disease. *Journal of Behavior Therapy and Experimental Psychiatry, 6,* 230-234.

Boddy, J. (1981). Evoked potentials and the dynamics of language processing. *Biological Psychology, 12,* 125-140.

Boddy, J. (1986). Event-related potentials in chronometric analysis of primed word recognition at different stimulus onset asynchronies. *Psychophysiology, 23,* 232-245.

Boddy, J. (1989). The benefits of physiological psychology. *British Journal of Psychology, 80,* 479-498.

Borgeat, F. (1985). Psychophysiological effects of two different relaxation procedures: Progressive relaxation and subliminal relaxation. *Psychiatric Journal of the University of Ottawa, 8,* 181-185.

Borgeat, F., Boissonneault, J., & Chaloult, L. (1989). Psychophysiological responses to subliminal auditory suggestions for activation. *Perceptual and Motor Skills, 69,* 947-953.

Borgeat, F., Chabot, R., & Chaloult, L. (1981). Perception subliminale et niveaux d'activation [Subliminal perception and levels of activation]. *Canadian Journal of Psychiatry, 26,* 255-259.

Borgeat, F., & Chaloult, L. (1985). A relaxation experiment using radio broadcasts. *Canada's Mental Health, 33,* 11-13.

Borgeat, F., Elie, R., Chaloult, L., & Chabot, R. (1985). Psychophysiological responses to masked auditory stimuli. *Canadian Journal of Psychiatry, 30,* 22-27.

Borgeat, F., & Goulet, J. (1983). Psychophysiological changes following auditory subliminal suggestions for activation and deactivation. *Perceptual and Motor Skills, 56,* 759-766.

Borgeat, F., & Pannetier, M. F. (1982). Intérêt des réponses électrodermales cumulées dans la perception subliminale auditive. Une étude préliminaire [The relevance of cumulated electrodermal responses in auditory subliminal perceptions: A preliminary study]. *L'Encéphale, 8,* 487-499.

Borkovec, T. D., & Sides, J. (1978). Critical procedural variables related to the physiological effects of progressive relaxation: A review. *Behaviour Therapy, 17,* 119-125.

Bornstein, R. F. (1989). Subliminal techniques as propaganda tools: Review and critique. *The Journal of Mind and Behavior, 10,* 231-262.

Bornstein, R. F., Leone, D. R., & Galley, D. J. (1987). The generalizability of subliminal mere exposure effects: Influence of stimuli perceived without awareness on social behavior. *Journal of Personality and Social Psychology, 53,* 1070-1079.

Bornstein, R. F., & Masling, J. M. (1984). Subliminal psychodynamic stimulation: Implications for psychoanalytic theory and therapy. *International Forum for Psychoanalysis, 1,* 187-204.

Bower, G. H. (1981). Mood and memory. *American Psychologist, 36,* 129-148.

Bower, G. H., Gilligan, S. G., & Monteiro, K. P. (1981). Selectivity in learning caused by affective states. *Journal of Experimental Psychology, 103,* 751-757.

Bowers, K. S. (1975). The psychology of subtle control: An attributional analysis of behavioural persistence. *Canadian Journal of Behavioral Science, 7,* 78-95.

Bowers, K. S. (1984). On being unconsciously influenced and informed. In K. S. Bowers & D. Meichenbaum (Eds.), *The unconscious reconsidered* (pp. 227-272). New York: Wiley.

Bowers, K. S. (1987). Revisioning the unconscious. *Canadian Psychology, 28,* 93-104.

Brandeis, D., & Lehmann, D. (1986). Event-related potentials of the brain and cognitive processes: Approaches and applications. *Neuropsychologia, 24,* 151-168.

Branscombe, N. R. (1988). Conscious and unconscious processing of affective and cognitive information. In K. Fiedler & J. Forgas (Eds.), *Affect, cognition, and social behavior* (pp. 3-24). Toronto: C. J. Hogrefe.

Brehm, J. W. (1966). *A theory of psychological reactance.* New York: Academic Press.

Brody, N. (1988). *Personality.* New York: Academic Press.

Brown, W. S., & Lehmann, D. (1979). Linguistic meaning-related differences in ERP scalp topography. In D. Lehmann & E. Callaway (Eds.), *Human evoked potentials* (pp. 31-42). New York: Plenum Press.

Bruner, J. S., & Postman, L. (1947). Emotional selectivity in perception and reaction. *Journal of Personality, 16,* 69-77.

Bryant-Tuckett, R., & Silverman, L. H. (1984). Effects of the subliminal stimulation of symbiotic fantasies on the academic performance of emotionally handicapped students. *Journal of Counselling Psychology, 31,* 295-305.

Bryden, M. P. (1971). Attentional strategies and short-term memory in dichotic listening. *Cognitive Psychology, 2,* 99-116.

Budzynski, T. H. (1976). Biofeedback and the twilight states of consciousness. In G. E. Schwartz & D. Shapiro (Eds.), *Consciousness and self-regulation* (pp. 361-385). New York: Plenum Press.

Byrne, D. (1959). The effect of a subliminal food stimulus on verbal responses. *Journal of Applied Psychology, 43,* 249-251.

Campbell, K. B., & Bartoli, E. A. (1986). Human auditory evoked potentials during natural sleep: The early components. *Electroencephalography and Clinical Neurophysiology, 65,* 142-149.

Carroll, J. B., Daview, P., & Richman, B. (1971). *The American Heritage word frequency book.* New York: Houghton Mifflin.

Chapman, R. M., McCrary, J. W., Chapman, J. A., & Martin, J. K. (1980). Behavior and neural analysis of connotative meaning: Word classes and rating scales. *Behavior and Language, 11,* 319-339.

Cheesman, J., & Merikle, P. M. (1986). Distinguishing conscious from unconscious perceptual processes. *Canadian Journal of Psychology, 40,* 343-367.

Clark, D. M., & Teasdale, J. D. (1985). Constraints on the effects of mood on memory. *Journal of Personality and Social Psychology, 48,* 1595-1608.

Clark, M. M., & Procidano, M. E. (1987). Comparison of the effectiveness of subliminal stimulation and social support on anxiety reduction. *Social Behavior and Personality, 15,* 177-183.

Cohn, L., De Simone, J., Frank, B., & Silverman, L. (1979). The effect of subliminal psychodynamic stimulation on EMG biofeedback training. *Biofeedback and Self-Regulation, 4,* 245.

Cook, H. (1985). Effects of subliminal symbiotic gratification and the magic of believing on achievement. *Psychoanalytic Psychology, 2,* 365-371.

Corbisiero, R., & Borgeat, F. (1980). *Etude de la relation des perceptions subliminales et des paramètres psychophysiologiques [Study of the relation between subliminal perception and psychophysiological parameters].* Report to the Faculty of Medicine, University of Montreal.

Corteen, R. S., & Dunn, D. (1974). Shock-associated words in a non-attended message: A test for momentary awareness. *Journal of Experimental Psychology, 102*(6), 1143-1144.

Corteen, R. S., & Wood, B. (1972). Autonomic responses to shock-associated words in an unattended channel. *Journal of Experimental Psychology, 94,* 308-313.

Cousins, N. (1957, Oct. 5). Smudging the subconscious. *Saturday Review, 40,* 20.

Cousins, N. (1979). *Anatomy of an illness as perceived by the patient.* New York: Norton.

Dauber, R. B. (1984). Subliminal psychodynamic activation in depression: On the role of autonomy issues in depressed college women. *Journal of Abnormal Psychology, 93,* 9-18.

De Koninck, J. M., & Koulack, D. (1975). Dream content and adaptation to a stressful situation. *Journal of Abnormal Psychology, 84*, 250-260.

De Silva, P. (1988). The modification of human food aversions: A preliminary study. *Journal of Behavior Therapy and Experimental Psychiatry, 19*, 217-220.

De Silva, P., & Rachman, S. (1987). Human food aversions: Nature and acquisition. *Behavior Research and Therapy, 27*, 457-468.

Dixon, N. F. (1958). The effect of subliminal perception upon autonomic and verbal behaviour. *Journal of Abnormal Social Psychology, 57*, 29-36.

Dixon, N. F. (1971). *Subliminal perception: The nature of a controversy.* New York: McGraw-Hill.

Dixon, N. F. (1981). *Preconscious processing.* New York: Wiley.

Dixon, N. F. (1987). Subliminal perception. In R. L. Gregory (Ed.), *The Oxford companion to the mind* (pp. 752-755). New York: Oxford University Press.

Dixon, N. F., & Henley, S. H. (1984). Extraction of information from continuously mashed successive stimuli: An exploratory study. *Current Psychological Research and Reviews, 3*, 38-44.

Earls, C. M., & Castonguay, L. G. (1989). The evaluation of olfactory aversion for a bisexual pedophile with a single-case multiple baseline design. *Behavior Therapy, 20*, 137-146.

Emmelkamp, P. M. G., & Straatman, H. (1976). A psychoanalytic reinterpretation of the effectiveness of systematic desensitization: Fact or fiction? *Behavior Research and Therapy, 14*, 245-249.

Erdelyi, M. H. (1972). Role of fantasy in the Poetzl (emergence) phenomenon. *Journal of Personality and Social Psychology, 24*, 186-190.

Eriksen, C. W. (1954). The case for perceptual defense. *Psychological Review, 61*, 175-182.

Evans, F. (1985). Expectancy, therapeutic instructions, and the placebo response. In L. White, B. Tursky, & G. Swartz (Eds.), *Placebo: Theory, research and mechanism* (pp. 215-228). New York: Guilford Press.

Fake pills part of test, pregnancies result. (1977, Oct. 1). *Hamilton Spectator*, p. 4.

Ferguson, G. A. (1981). *Statistical analysis in psychology and education.* New York: McGraw-Hill.

Fisher, C. (1988). Further observations on the Poetzl phenomenon: The effects of subliminal visual stimulation on dreams, images and hallucinations. *Psychoanalysis and Contemporary thought, 11*, 3-56.

Fisher, S. (1975). Effects of messages reported to be out of awareness upon the body boundary. *Journal of Nervous and Mental Disease, 161*, 90-99.

Fisher, S. (1976). Conditions affecting boundary response to messages out of awareness. *Journal of Nervous and Mental Disease, 162*, 313-322.

Fisher, S., & Greenberg, R. P. (1972). Selective effects upon women of exciting and calm music. *Perceptual and Motor Skills, 34*, 987-990.

Foa, E. B., Grayson, J. B., Steketee, G., Doppelt, H. G., Turner, R. M., & Latimer, P. L. (1983). Success and failure in the behavioral treatment of obsessive-compulsives. *Journal of Consulting and Clinical Psychology, 51*, 287-297.

Fowler, C. A., Wolford, G., Slade, R., & Tassinary, L. (1981). Lexical awareness with and without awareness. *Journal of Experimental Psychology: General, 110*, 341-362.

Freedman, R. R., Ianni, P., & Wenig, P. (1985). Behavioral treatment of Raynaud's disease: Long-term follow-up. *Journal of Consulting and Clinical Psychology, 53*, 136.

Fudin, R. (1986). Subliminal psychodynamic activation: Mommy and I are not yet one. *Perceptual and Motor Skills, 63*, 1159-1179.

Fudin, R. (1987). Subliminal psychodynamic activation: Note on illumination and the bleaching hypothesis. *Perceptual and Motor Skills, 64*, 1223-1230.

Fulford, P. F. (1980). *The effect of subliminal merging stimuli on test anxiety.* Unpublished doctoral dissertation, St. John's University.

Garb, J. L., & Stunkard, A. J. (1974). Taste aversions in man. *American Journal of Psychiatry, 131,* 1204-1207.

Garske, J. (1984, August). *Effects of subliminal activation on affective states.* Paper presented at the meeting of the American Psychological Association, Toronto.

Gazzaniga, M. S., & LeDoux, J. E. (1978). *The integrated mind.* New York: Plenum.

Genkina, O. A., & Shostakovich, G. S. (1986). Conditioning of patients with chronic alcoholism by means of a subthreshold motivationally significant word. *Soviet Neurology and Psychiatry, 19,* 87-100.

Gilligan, S. G., & Bower, G. H. (1984). Cognitive consequences of emotional arousal. In C. Izard, J. Kagen, & R. Zajonc (Eds.), *Emotions, cognition and behavior* (pp. 547-588). New York: Cambridge University Press.

Gilliland, K., & Bullock, W. (1984). Caffeine: A potential drug of abuse. *Addictive Behavior, 11,* 53-72.

Glasgow, R. E., Morray, K., & Lichtenstein, E. (1989). Controlled smoking versus abstinence as a treatment goal: The hopes and fears may be unfounded. *Behavior Therapy, 20,* 77-91.

Goldiamond, I. (1958). Indicators of perception. I, subliminal perception, unconscious perception: An analysis of psychophysical indicator methodology. *Psychological Bulletin, 55,* 373-411.

Granda, A. M., & Hammack, J. T. (1961). Operant behavior during sleep. *Science, 133,* 1485-1486.

Greden, J. F., Fontaine, P., Lubetsky, M., & Chamberlain, K. (1978). Anxiety and depression associated with caffeinism among psychiatric inpatients. *American Journal of Psychiatry, 135,* 963-966.

Green, M. L., Green, R. G., & Santoro, W. (1988). Daily relaxation modifies serum and salivary immunoglobins and psychophysiologic symptom severity. *Biofeedback and Self-Regulation, 13,* 187-199.

Groeger, J. A. (1984). Evidence of unconscious semantic processing from a forced error situation. *British Journal of Psychology, 25,* 305-314.

Groeger, J. A. (1986a). Preconscious influences on word substitutions. *Irish Journal of Psychology, 7,* 88-97.

Groeger, J. A. (1986b). Predominant and non-predominant analysis: Effects of level of presentation. *British Journal of Psychology, 77,* 109-116.

Gruber, B. L., Hall, N. R., Hersh, S. P., & Dubois, P. (1988). Immune system and psychological changes in metastatic cancer patients using relaxation and guided imagery: A pilot study. *Scandinavian Journal of Behaviour Therapy, 17,* 25-46.

Guglielmi, R. S., Roberts, A. H., & Patterson, R. (1982). Skin temperature biofeedback for Raynaud's disease: A double-blind study. *Biofeedback and Self-Regulation, 7,* 79-120.

Gustavson, C. G., & Gustavson, J. C. (1985). Predation control using conditioned food aversion methodology: Theory, practice and implications. *Annals of the New York Academy of Sciences, 443,* 348-356.

Hall, N. R., & Goldstein, A. L. (1984). Endocrine regulation of host immunity: The role of steroids and thymosin. In R. L. Fenichel & M. A. Chirigos (Eds.), *Immunology modulation agents and their mechanism* (pp. 533-563). New York: Marcel Dekker.

Hamberger, L. K., & Schuldt, W. J. (1986). Live and taped relaxation instructions: Effects of procedural variables. *Biofeedback and Self-Regulation, 11*(1), 31-45.

Hardaway, R. A. (1990). Subliminally activated symbiotic fantasies: Facts and artifacts. *Psychological Bulletin, 107,* 177-195.

Hawkins, D. (1970). The effects of subliminal stimulation on drive level and brand preference. *Journal of Marketing Research, 8,* 322-326.

162

Heilbrun, K. S. (1980). Silverman's psychodynamic activation: A failure to replicate. *Journal of Abnormal Psychology, 89*, 560-566.

Heisenberg, W. (1971). *Physics and beyond: Encounters and conversations.* London: Allen & Linisin.

Henley, S. (1975). Cross-modal effects of subliminal verbal stimuli. *Scandinavian Journal of Psychology, 16*, 30-36.

Henley, S. H. (1984). Unconscious perception revisited: A comment on Merikle's (1982) paper. *Bulletin of the Psychodynamic Society, 22*, 121-124.

Hillyard, S. A., Squires, K. C., Bauer, J. W., & Lindsay, P. H. (1971). Evoked potential correlates signal detection. *Science, 172*, 1357-1360.

Holender, D. (1986). Semantic activation without conscious identification in dichotic listening, parafoveal vision, and visual masking: A survey and appraisal. *Behavior and Brain Sciences, 9*, 1-66.

Holroyd, K. A., Andrasik, F., & Noble, J. (1980). A comparison of EMG biofeedback and a credible pseudotherapy in treating tension headache. *Journal of Behavioral Medicine, 3*, 29-39.

Isen, A., & Shalker, T. (1982). The effect of feeling state on evaluation of positive, neutral, and negative stimuli: When you accentuate the positive, do you eliminate the negative. *Social Psychology Quarterly, 45*, 58-63.

Jackson, J. (1983). The effects of subliminally activated fantasies of merger with each parent on the pathology of male and female schizophrenics. *Journal of Nervous and Mental Disease, 171*, 280-289.

Jacobson, A. M., Hackett, T. P., Surman, O. S., & Silverberg, E. (1973). Raynaud's phenomena: Treatment with hypnotic and operant techniques. *Journal of the American Medical Association, 225*, 739-740.

Jacobson, E. (1929). *Progressive relaxation.* Chicago: University of Chicago Press.

James, J. E., Stirling, K. P., & Hampton, A. M. (1985). Caffeine fading: Behavioral treatment of caffeine abuse. *Behavior Therapy, 16*, 15-27.

Jaynes, J. (1976). *The origin of consciousness in the breakdown of the bicameral mind.* Boston: Houghton Mifflin.

Kaplan. R. (1976). *The symbiotic fantasy as a therapeutic agent: An experimental comparison of the effects of three symbiotic elements on manifest pathology in schizophrenics.* Unpublished doctoral dissertation, New York University.

Kaser, V. A. (1986). The effects of an auditory subliminal message upon the production of images and dreams. *The Journal of Nervous and Mental Disease, 174*, 397-407.

Keefe, F., Surwit, R. S., & Pilon, R. N. (1980). Biofeedback, autogenic training and progressive relaxation in the treatment of Raynaud's disease: A comparative study. *Journal of Applied Behavior Analysis, 13*, 3-11.

Kemp-Wheeler, S. M., & Hill, A. B. (1987). Anxiety responses to subliminal experience of mild stress. *British Journal of Psychology, 78*, 365-374.

Kostandov, E. A., & Arzumanov, Y. L. (1986). The influence of subliminal emotional words on functional hemispheric asymmetry. *International Journal of Psychophysiology, 4*, 143-147.

Kostandov, E. A., & Arzumanov, Y. L. (1989). Neural mechanisms of subliminal perception and unaccountable emotions. *International Journal of Psychophysiology, 7*, 271-272.

Krietsch, K., Christensen, L., & White, B. (1988). Prevalence, presenting symptoms, and psychological characteristics of individual experiencing a diet-related mood-disturbance. *Behavior Therapy, 19*, 593-604.

Kunst-Wilson, W. R., & Zajonc, R. B. (1980). Affective discrimination of stimuli that cannot be recognized. *Science, 207*, 557-558.

Kushner, H. S. (1981). *When bad things happen to good people.* New York: Schocken.

Kutas, M., Lindawood, T. E., & Hillyard, S. E. (1983). Word expectancy and event-related brain potentials during sentence processing. In S. Kornblum & J. Requin (Eds.), *Preparatory Processes*. Hillsdale, NJ Lawrence Erlbaum Associates.

Laws, D. R., Meyer, J., & Holman, M. (1978). Reduction of sadistic sexual arousal of olfactory aversion: A case study. *Behavior Research and Therapy, 16*, 281-285.

Lazarus, R. S. (1984). On the primacy of cognition. *American Psychologist, 39*, 124-129.

Lazarus, R., & McCleary, R. A. (1951). Autonomic discrimination without awareness: A study of subception. *Psychological Review, 58*, 113-122.

Lee, I., & Tyrer, P. (1980). Responses of chronic agoraphobic to subliminal and supraliminal phobic motion pictures. *Journal of Nervous and Mental Disease, 168*, 34-40.

Lee, I., Tyrer, P., & Horn, S. (1983). A comparison of subliminal, supraliminal and faded phobic cine-films in the treatment of agoraphobia. *British Journal of Psychiatry, 143*, 356-361.

Lewicki, P. (1986). *Nonconscious social information processing*. New York: Academic Press.

Lewis, J. L. (1970). Semantic processing of unattended messages using dichotic listening. *Journal of Experimental Psychology, 85*, 225-228.

Libet, B., Alberts, W. W., Wright, E. W., & Feinstein, B. (1967). Responses of human somatosensory cortex to stimuli below the threshold of unconscious sensation. *Science, 158*, 1597-1600.

Linden, R. D., Campbell, K. B., Hamel, G., & Picton, T. W. (1985). Human auditory study state evoked potentials during sleep. *Ear and Hearing, 6*, 167-174.

Logue, A. W. (1985). Conditioned food aversion learning in humans. *Annals of the New York Academy of Sciences, 443*, 316-329.

Logue, A. W. (1986). *The psychology of eating and drinking*, New York: Freeman.

Lubin, J. H., Blot, W. G., Berrino, F., Flamant, R., Gillis, C. R., Kunze, M., Schmahl, D., & Visco, G. (1984). Modifying risk of developing lung cancer by changing habits of cigarette smoking. *British Medical Journal, 288*, 1953-1956.

Luthe, W. (1973). *Autogenic therapy: Treatment with autogenic neutralization*. New York: Grune & Stratton.

MacKay, D. G. (1973). Aspects of the theory of comprehension memory and attention. *Quarterly Journal of Experimental Psychology, 25*, 22-40.

Malmo, R. B. (1975). *On emotions, needs, and our archaic brain*. New York: Holt, Rinehart & Winston.

Marcel, A. J. (1983a). Conscious and unconscious perception: An approach to the relations between phenomenal experience and perceptual processes. *Cognitive Psychology, 15*, 238-300.

Marcel, A. J. (1983b). Conscious and unconscious perception: Experiments on visual masking and word recognition. *Cognitive Psychology, 15*, 197-237.

Marcel, A. J. (1988). Electrophysiology and meaning in cognitive science and dynamic psychology—comments on "Unconscious conflict: A convergent psychodynamic and electrophysiological approach." In M. Horowitz (Ed.), *Psychodynamics and cognition* (pp. 169-190). Chicago: University of Chicago Press.

Marini, J., Sheard, M., Bridges, C., & Wagner, E. (1976). An evaluation of the double-blind design in a study comparing lithium carbonate with placebo. *Acta Psychiatrica Scandinavica, 53*, 343-354.

Martin, M. (1978). Retention of attended and unattended auditorily and visually presented material. *Quarterly Journal of Experimental Psychology, 30*, 187-200.

Marx, M. H. (1982). Effects of frequency of prior incidental occurrence and recall of target words on anagram solution. *Bulletin of the Psychonomic Society, 19*, 253-255.

McFarland, R. A. (1985). Relationship of skin temperature changes to emotions accompanying music. *Biofeedback and Self-Regulation, 10*, 255-267.

McLean, P. D., & Carr, S. (1989). The psychological treatment of unipolar depression: Progress and limitations. *Canadian Journal of Behavioural Science, 21*, 452-469.

Mendel, M. I., & Kupperman, G. L. (1974). Early components of the averaged electroencephalic response to constant level clicks during rapid eye movement sleep. *Audiology, 13*, 23-32.

Merikle, P. M. (1990 August). Subliminal auditory messages: An evaluation. Paper presented at the meeting of the American Psychological Association, Boston.

Meyer, V., & Levy, R. (1973). Modification of behavior in obsessive-compulsive disorders. In H. E. Adams & P. Vnikel (Eds.), *Issues and trends in behavior therapy* (pp. 77-138). Springfield, IL: Charles C. Thormes.

Moore, T. E. (1982). Subliminal advertising: What you see is what you get. *Journal of Marketing, 46*, 38-47.

Moore, T. E. (Ed.). (1988). Subliminal influences in marketing [Special issue]. *Psychology and Marketing, 5*, 291-372.

Moore, T. E. (1989). Subliminal psychodynamic activation and the establishment of thresholds. *American Psychologist*, 1420-1421.

Mooreland, R. L., & Zajonc, R. B. (1979). Exposure effects may not depend on stimulus recognition. *Journal of Personality and Social Psychology, 37*, 1085-1089.

Morris, J., & Beck, A. (1974). The efficacy of antidepressant drugs: A review of research (1958 to 1972). *Archives of General Psychiatry, 30*, 667-674.

Natale, M., & Hantas, M. (1982). Effect of temporary mood states on selective memory about the self. *Journal of Personality and Social Psychology, 42*, 1244-1253.

Nathan, P. E. (1985). Aversion therapy in the treatment of alcoholism: Success and failure. *Annals of the New York Academy of Sciences, 443*, 356-364.

Nation (1957, Oct. 5). Diddling the subconscious, *185*, 206-207.

Neisser, U. (1963). The multiplicity of thought. *British Journal of Psychology, 54*, 1-14.

Neuberg, S. L. (1988). Behavioral implications of information presented outside of conscious awareness: The effect of subliminal presentation of trait information on behavior in the Prisoner's Dilemma Game. *Social Cognition, 6*, 207-230.

Nielzen, S., & Cesarec, Z. (1981). On the perception of emotional meaning in music. *Psychology of Music, 9*, 17-31.

Nielzen, S., & Cesarec, Z. (1982). Emotional experience of music structure. *Psychology of Music, 10*, 7-17.

Nisbett, R., & Wilson, T. (1977). Telling more than we can know: Verbal reports on mental processes. *Psychological Review, 89*, 231-259.

O'Grady, M. (1977). Effect of subliminal pictorial stimulation on skin resistance. *Perceptual and Motor Skills, 44*, 1051-1056.

Oliver, J. M., & Burkham, R. (1985). Comments on three recent subliminal psychodynamic activation investigations: Reply to Silverman. *Journal of Abnormal Psychology, 94*, 644.

Olson, J. M. (1988). Misattribution, preparatory information, and speech anxiety. *Journal of Personality and Social Psychology, 54*, 758-767.

Packer, S. (1984). *The effect of subliminally stimulating fantasies aimed at gratifying symbiotic and sanctioning aggressive striving on assertiveness difficulties in women.* Unpublished doctoral dissertation, New York University.

Palmatier, J., & Bornstein, P. (1980). The effects of subliminal stimulation of symbiotic merging fantasies on behavioral treatment of smokers. *Journal of Nervous and Mental Disease, 168*, 715-720.

Parasuraman, R., & Beatty, J. (1980). Brain events underlying detection and recognition of weak sensory signals. *Science, 210*, 80-83.

Patterson, D. R., Questad, K. A., & de Lateur, B. J. (1989). Hypnotherapy as an adjunct to narcotic analgesia for the treatment of pain for burn debridement. *American Journal of Clinical Hypnosis, 31*, 156-163.

Pearce, K. A. (1981). Effects of different kinds of music on physical strength. *Perceptual and Motor Skills, 53*, 351-352.

Peper, E. (1976). The possible uses of biofeedback. *Journal of Biofeedback, 3*, 13-19.

Pignatiello, M. F., Camp, C. J., & Rasar, L. A. (1986). Musical mood induction: An alternative to the Velten Technique. *Journal of Abnormal Psychology, 75*, 81-86.

Porterfield, A. L., & Golding, S. L. (1985). Failure to find an effect of subliminal psychodynamic activation upon cognitive measures of pathology in schizophrenia. *Journal of Abnormal Psychology, 94*, 630-639.

Posner, M., Klein, R., Summers, J., & Buggie, S. (1973). On the selection of signals. *Memory and Cognition, 1*, 2-12.

Posner, M. (1982). Cumulative development of attentional theory. *American Psychologist, 37*, 168-179.

Postman, L., Bruner, J. S., & McGinnies, E. (1948). Personal values as selective factors in perception. *Journal of Abnormal Psychology, 43*, 142-154.

Prioleau, L., Murdock, M., & Brody, N. (1983). An analysis of psychotherapy versus placebo studies. *Behavioral and Brain Sciences, 2*, 275-285.

Rieber, M. (1965). The effect of music on the activity level of children. *Psychonomic Science, 3*, 325-326.

Robles, R., Smith, R., Carver, C. S., & Wellens, A. R. (1987). Influence of subliminal visual images on the experience of anxiety. *Personality and Social Psychology Bulletin, 13*, 399-410.

Rorschach, H. (1942). *Psychodiagnostics*. New York: Grune & Stratton.

Rose, G. D., & Carlson, J. G. (1987). The behavioral treatment of Raynaud's disease: A review. *Biofeedback and Self-Regulation, 12*, 257-273.

Rossi, E. L. (1986). *The psychobiology of mind-body healing*. New York: Norton.

Rossi, E. L., & Cheek, D. B. (1988). *Mind-body therapy*. New York: Norton.

Roth, N., & Boddy, J. (in press). Event-related potentials and the recognition of subliminally exposed words after repeated presentation. *Journal of Psychophysiology*.

Russell, J. A. (1978). Evidence of convergent validity on the dimensions of affect. *Journal of Personality and Social Psychology, 36*, 1152-1168.

Schultz, J. H., & Luthe, W. (1969). *Autogenic therapy: Methods*. New York: Grune & Stratton.

Schur, P. H. (1979). Systemic lupis erythematosus. In P. B. Beeson, W. McDermott, & J. B. Wyngaarden (Eds.), *Textbook of Medicine* (pp. 174-180). Philadelphia: Saunders.

Schurtman, R., Palmatier, J. R., & Martin, E. S. (1982). On the activation of symbiotic gratification fantasies as an aid in the treatment of alcoholics. *International Journal of the Addictions, 17*, 1157-1174.

Schwartz, M., & Rem, M. A. (1975). Does the average evoked response encode subliminal perception? *Psychophysiology, 12*, 390-394.

Seamon, J. G., Marsh, R. L., & Brody, N. (1984). Critical importance of exposure duration for affective discrimination of stimuli that are not recognized. *Journal of Experimental Psychology: Learning, Memory and Cognition, 10*, 465-469.

Seidenstadt, R. M. (1982). Category label and list-item priming in anagram solving. *Psychological Reports, 51*, 207-211.

Shahar, A., & Marks, I. (1980). Habituation during exposure treatment of compulsive rituals. *Behavior Therapy, 11*, 397-401.

Shanon, B. (1979). Semantic processing during sleep. *Bulletin of the Psychonomic Society, 14*, 382-384.

Sheffler, C. C., & Brody, N. (1989 April). The influence of subliminal stimuli on dyadic interaction. Paper presented at the Eastern Psychological Association meetings, Boston.

Shellenberger, R., & Green, J. A. (1986). *From the ghost in the box to successful biofeedback training*. Greeley, CO: Health Psychology Publications.

Shevrin, H. (1986). Subliminal perception and dreaming. *Journal of Mind and Behavior,* 7, 379-395.

Shevrin, H. (1988). Unconscious conflict: A convergent psychodynamic and electrophysiological approach. In M. Horowitz (Ed.), *Psychodynamics and cognition* (pp. 117-167). Chicago: University of Chicago Press.

Shevrin, H., & Dickman, S. (1980). The psychological unconscious: A necessary assumption for all psychological theory? *American Psychologist, 35,* 421-434.

Shevrin, H., & Fritzler, D. (1968). Visual evoked response correlates of unconscious mental processes. *Science, 161,* 295-298.

Shevrin, H., Smith, W. H., & Fritzler, D. (1971). Average evoked response and verbal correlates of unconscious mental processes. *Psychophysiology, 8,* 149-162.

Shevrin, H., Smith, W. H., & Hoobler, R. (1970). Direct measurement of unconscious processes: Average evoked response and free association correlates of subliminal stimuli. *Proceedings of the 78th Annual Convention, American Psychological Association* (pp. 543-544). Washington, DC: American Psychological Association.

Silverman, L. H. (1966). A technique for the study of psychodynamic relationships. *Journal of Consulting Psychology, 30,* 103-111.

Silverman, L. H. (1972). Psychoanalytic considerations and experiential psychotherapy. *Psychotherapy: Theory, Research and Practice, 9,* 2-8.

Silverman, L. H. (1976). Psychoanalytic theory: The reports of my death are greatly exaggerated. *American Psychologist, 31,* 621-637.

Silverman, L. H. (1977). *Ethical considerations and guidelines in the use of subliminal psychodynamic activation.* Unpublished manuscript, Research Center for Mental Health, New York University.

Silverman, L. H. (1978). Unconscious symbiotic fantasy: A ubiquitous therapeutic agent. *International Journal of Psychoanalytic Psychotherapy, 7,* 562-585.

Silverman, L. H. (1983). The subliminal psychodynamic activation method: Overview and comprehensive listing of studies. In J. Masling (Ed.), *Empirical studies of psychoanalytic theories* (Vol. 1, pp. 69-100). Hillsdale, NJ: Lawrence Erlbaum Associates.

Silverman, L. H. (1985). Comments on three recent subliminal psychodynamic activation investigations. *Journal of Abnormal Psychology, 94,* 640-643.

Silverman, L. H., Bronstein, A., & Mendelsohn, E. (1976). The further use of the subliminal psychodynamic activation method for the experimental study of the clinical theory of psychoanalysis: On the specificity of the relationship between symptoms and unconscious conflicts. *Psychotherapy: Theory, Research and Practice, 13,* 2-16.

Silverman, L. H. & Candell, P. (1970). On the relationship between aggressive activation, symbiotic merging, intactness of body boundaries, and manifest pathology in schizophrenics. *Journal of Nervous and Mental Disease, 150,* 387-399.

Silverman, L. H., Candell, P., Pettit, T. F., & Blum, E. (1971). Further data on effects of aggressive activation and symbiotic merging on ego functioning of schizophrenics. *Perceptual and Motor Skills, 32,* 93-94.

Silverman, L. H., Frank, S. G., & Dachinger, P. (1974). A psychoanalytic reinterpretation of the effectiveness of systematic desensitization: Experimental data bearing on the role of merging fantasies. *Journal of Abnormal Psychology, 83,* 131-138.

Silverman, L. H., & Grabowski, R. (1982). *The effects of activating oneness fantasies on the anxiety level of male and female college students.* Unpublished manuscript, Research Center for Mental Health, New York University.

Silverman, L. H., Klinger, H., Lustbader, L., Farrell, J., & Martin, A. D. (1972). The effects of subliminal drive stimulation on the speech of stutterers. *Journal of Nervous and Mental Disease, 155,* 14-21.

Silverman, L. H., Kwawer, J. S., Wolitzky, C., & Coron, M. (1973). An experimental study of aspects of the psychoanalytic theory of male homosexuality. *Journal of Abnormal Psychology, 82,* 178-188.

Silverman, L. H., Martin, A., Ungaro, R., & Mendelsohn, E. (1978). Effect of subliminal stimulation of symbiotic fantasies on behavior modification treatment of obesity. *Journal of Consulting Psychology, 46,* 432-441.

Silverman, L. H., & Spiro, R. H. (1967a). Some comments and data on the partial cue controversy and other matters relevant to investigations of subliminal phenomena. *Perceptual and Motor Skills, 25,* 325-338.

Silverman, L. H., & Spiro, R. H. (1967b). Further investigation of the effects of subliminal aggressive stimulation on the ego functioning of schizophrenics. *Journal of Consulting Psychology, 31,* 225-232.

Silverman, L. H., Spiro, R. H., Weisberg, J. S., & Candell, P. (1969). The effects of aggressive activation and the need to merge on pathological thinking in schizophrenia. *Journal of Nervous and Mental Disease, 148,* 39-51.

Silverman, L. H., & Weinberger, J. (1985). Mommy and I are one: Implications for psychotherapy. *American Psychologist, 40,* 1296-1308.

Simonton, O. C., Matthews-Simonton, S., & Sparks, T. F. (1980). Psychological intervention in the treatment of cancer. *Psychosomatics, 21,* 226-233.

Smith, M. L., Glass, G. V., & Miller, F. I. (1980). *The benefits of psychotherapy.* Baltimore, MD: Johns Hopkins University Press.

Snyder, S. H. (1984). Adenosine as a mediator of the behavioral effect of xanthines. In P. B. Dews (Ed.), *Caffeine: Perspectives from recent research* (pp. 129-141). New York: Springer Verlag.

Somekh, D. E., & Wilding, J. M. (1973). Perception without awareness in a dichotic viewing situation. *British Journal of Psychology, 64,* 339-349.

Spector, N. H. (1986). Old and new strategies in the conditioning of immune responses. *Proceedings of the Second International Workshop on Neuroimmunomodulation.* Dubrovnik, Yugoslavia: New York Academy of Sciences.

Spence, D. P. (1983). Subliminal effects on lexical decision time. *Archiv fur Psychologie, 135,* 67-72.

Spring, B., Maller, O., Wurtman, J., Digman, L., & Cozolino, L. (1983). Effects of protein and carbohydrate meals on mood and performance: Interactions with sex and age. *Journal of Psychiatric Research, 17,* 155-167.

Sundberg, J. (1982). Speech, song, and emotions. In M. Clynes (Ed.), *Music, mind, and brain* (pp. 137-149). New York: Plenum Press.

Swingle, P. G. (1970a). Exploitative behavior in non-zero sum games. *Journal of Personality and Social Psychology, 16,* 121-132.

Swingle, P. G. (1970b). Motivational properties of performance feedback. *Psychonomic Science, 8,* 73-75.

Swingle, P. G. (1979). Damned if we do—Damned if we don't. In L. H. Strickland (Ed.), *Soviet and Western Perspectives in Social Psychology* (pp. 181-200). New York: Pergamon.

Swingle, P. G. (1984). Temporal measures of vocalization: Some methodological considerations. *Journal of Personality and Social Psychology, 47,* 1263-1280.

Swingle, P. G. (1989). The resolution of conflict. *Canadian Psychology, 30,* 650-661.

Swingle, P. G., & Hope, G. H. (1987). Interpersonal influence on temporal measures of vocalization in an interview situation. *Language & Speech, 30,* 159-167.

Swingle, P. G., & Moors, D. (1966). The effects of performance feedback social and monetary incentives upon human lever pressing rate. *Psychonomic Science, 4,* 209-210.

Tani, K., & Yoshii, N. (1970). Efficiency of verbal learning during sleep as related to EEF pattern. *Brain Research, 17,* 277-285.

Taub, E. (1977). Self-regulation of human tissue temperature. In G. E. Swartz & J. Beatty (Eds.), *Biofeedback: Theory and research*. New York: Academic Press.

Tebecis, A. K., Ohno, Y., Matsubara, H., Sugano, H., Takeya, T., Ikemi, Y., & Takasaki, M. (1976/1977). A longitudinal study of some physiological parameters and autogenic training. *Psychotherapy and Psychosomatics, 27*, 8-17.

Thornton, J. W. (1987). A test of subliminal symbiotic activation as a means of alleviating depression. *Psychoanalytic Psychology, 4*, 335-342.

Thornton, P. I., Igleheart, H. C., & Silverman, L. H. (1987). Subliminal stimulation of symbiotic fantasies as an aid in the treatment of drug abusers. *International Journal of the Addictions, 22*, 751-765.

Tilley, A. J. (1979). Sleep learning during Stage 2 and REM sleep. *Biological Psychology, 9*, 155-161.

Tisdall, P. (1983). Mixed messages. *Science, 7*, 84-85.

Tulving, E. (1972). Episodic and semantic memory. In E. Tulving & W. Donaldson (Eds.), *Organization of memory* (pp. 381-403). New York: Academic Press.

Tyrer, P., Lee, I., & Horn, S. (1978). Treatment of agoraphobia by subliminal and supraliminal exposure to phobic cine-film. *The Lancet, 1*, 358-360.

Vokey, J. R., & Read, J. D. (1985). Subliminal messages: Between the devil and the media. *American Psychologist, 40*, 1231-1239.

Weimer, W. B. (1977). A conceptual framework for cognitive psychology: Motor theories of the mind. In R. Shaw & J. Bransford (Eds.), *Perceiving, acting, and knowing: Toward an ecological psychology*. Hillsdale, NJ: Lawrence Erlbaum Associates.

Weinberger, J. (1989). Response to Balay and Shevrin: Constructive critique or misguided attack? *American Psychologist*, 1417-1419.

Weinberger, J., & Silverman, L. H. (1987). Subliminal psychodynamic activation: A method for studying psychoanalytic dynamic propositions. In R. Hogan & W. Jones (Eds.), *Perspectives in personality: Theory, measurement and interpersonal dynamics* (Vol. 2, pp. 251-287). Greenwich, CT: JAI Press.

Wheeler, B. L. (1985). Relationship of personal characteristics to mood and enjoyment after hearing live and recorded music and to musical taste. *Psychology of Music, 13*, 81-92.

Williams, H. C., Murlock, H. C., & Murlock, J. V. (1966). Instrumental behavior during sleep. *Psychophysiology, 2*, 208-216.

Wilson, W. R. (1979). Feeling more than we can know: Exposure effects without learning. *Journal of Personality and Social Psychology, 37*, 811-821.

Wolberg, L. R. (1964). *Hypnoanalysis*. New York: Grune & Stratton.

Wright, J. H., Jacisin, J. J., Radin, N. S., & Bell, R. A. (1978). Glucose metabolism in unipolar depression. *British Journal of Psychiatry, 132*, 386-393.

Wurtman, R. J., Hefti, F., & Melamed, E. (1981). Precursor control of neurotransmitter synthesis. *Pharmacological Reviews, 32*, 315-335.

Yates, A. J. (1980). *Biofeedback and the modification of behavior*. New York: Plenum.

Zajonc, R. B. (1980). Feeling and thinking: Preferences need no inferences. *American Psychologist, 35*, 151-175.

Zajonc, R. B. (1984). On the primacy of affect. *American Psychologist, 39*, 117-123.

Zenhausern, R., & Hansen, K. (1974). Differential effect of subliminal and supraliminal accessory stimulation on task components in problem-solving. *Perceptual and Motor Skills, 38*, 375-378.

Zenhausern, R., Pompo, C., & Ciaiola, M. (1974). Simple and complex reaction time as a function of subliminal and supraliminal stimulation. *Perceptual and Motor Skills, 38*, 417-418.

Zillmann, D. (1971). Excitation transfer in communication-mediated aggressive behavior. *Journal of Experimental Social Psychology, 7*, 419-434.

Zuckerman, M. (1960). The effects of subliminal and supraliminal suggestions on verbal productivity. *Journal of Abnormal and Social Psychology, 60,* 404-411.

Zung, W. W. K., & Wilson, W. P. (1961). Responses to auditory stimulation during sleep: Discrimination and arousal as indicated with electroencephalography. *Archives of General Psychiatry, 4,* 548-562.

Zwosta, M. F., & Zenhausern, R. (1969). Application of signal detection theory to subliminal and supraliminal accessory stimulation. *Perceptual and Motor Skills, 28,* 699-704.

Author Index

Subject Index

RELAXATION AND
SUBLIMINAL TREATMENT TAPES

The following audio cassette treatment tapes are available for purchase only by psychologists, physicians, and other licensed health care professionals whose licensure requires a doctoral degree. To order these tapes, please complete the *Tape Purchaser's Agreement* and order form on the next page.

TREATMENT TAPES

SUB/OCB Subliminal treatment for obsessive thoughts and/or compulsive behaviors. **SUB/OCB** is designed to be administered adjunctively with exposure and response prevention treatment procedures. Also useful when reducing patients' feelings of guilt, uncleanliness, and impurity is indicated.

SUB/AC Subliminal aversive conditioning, used in conjunction with **SUB/S** or **SUB/E** to reduce desire to smoke or to reduce desire for specific foods. May be used independently to reduce urges associated with habit disorders.

SUB/S Subliminal treatment to support the cessation or reduction of smoking. To be used in conjunction with **SUB/AC**.

SUB/E Subliminal treatment to support the modification of appetitive behavior. To be used in conjunction with **SUB/AC** to support reduced desire for specific appetitive substances. Useful for reducing desire for problematic foods in patients with allergic disorders.

SUB/AD Subliminal treatment for anxiety and/or depression. Messages to enhance feelings of peacefulness, relaxation, happiness, wellness, and contentment are embedded in music or white noise. Useful during early phases of therapy and as a post-treatment procedure to sustain therapeutic gains.

SUB/BS Subliminal slow wave treatment for the enhancement of sleep quality.

RELAXATION TAPES WITH
SUBLIMINAL MOOD MODIFIERS

PMR/APS Two progressive muscular relaxation exercises, one active and one passive. The passive exercise is followed by subliminal messages, embedded in white noise, to enhance feelings of happiness, relaxation, contentment, and wellness.

HYB/S One active volitional breathing exercise and one passive hypnotic relaxation exercise. The breathing exercise is followed by subliminal messages, embedded in white noise, to enhance feelings of happiness, relaxation, contentment, and wellness.

ORDER FORM AND
"TAPE PURCHASER'S AGREEMENT" ⟶

YES, please send me:

_____ Copies of the book, *Subliminal Treatment Procedures: A Clinician's Guide* at $24.95 per copy plus shipping.* $_____

ALSO send me the following individual tapes at $10.95 per tape (plus shipping*). **Quantity Discounts:** 26-50 = $8.95 each; 51-100 = $7.95 each; 101+ = $6.95 each (plus shipping*). To order these tapes, you <u>must read and sign</u> the *Tape Purchaser's Agreement* below.

_____ SUB/OCB	_____ SUB/AC	_____ SUB/S
_____ SUB/E	_____ SUB/AD	_____ SUB/BS x Price Each
_____ PMR/APS	_____ HYB/S	

$_____

_____ Complete Tape Sets (all 8 tapes above) for $74.95 plus shipping.*
(Save Over $12!) $_____

TAPE PURCHASER'S AGREEMENT: I hereby state that I am licensed in a health care profession that requires a doctoral degree as a condition for licensure, and have received appropriate training to enable me to competently use relaxation and subliminal treatment procedures. In consideration for the opportunity to purchase, I agree, covenant, and contract to use the tapes which I purchase in a clinically appropriate fashion; to supervise and assume full responsibility and liability for the use/misuse of these materials; and to indemnify, defend, protect, and save harmless the publisher and author of these materials and their employees and agents from and against any and all claims of damage (including losses, claims, suits, judgments, liabilities, court costs, and legal fees) arising from my negligence, misuse, or inappropriate use of the tapes and other materials that I purchase pursuant to this agreement. I further agree to carefully read and adhere to the *Information for the Professional* guide that accompanies each tape, and to fully comply with the directions contained in that guide.

Signature _____ Date _____

Name/Title (PLEASE PRINT) _____

Degree_____ License #_____ State_____ Exp. Date_____

---

*SHIPPING:	
To $15.99 Order, Add $1.75 in US, $3 Foreign	SUBTOTAL $_____
$16-$30.99, Add $2.75 in US, $4 Foreign	Florida residents, please add 7% sales tax $_____
$31-$45.99, Add $3.75 in US, $5 Foreign	
$46-$70.99, Add $4.25 in US, $6 Foreign	➤ SHIPPING $_____
Orders over $71, Add 7% in US, 10% Foreign	

TOTAL $_____

All orders from individuals and private institutions must be prepaid in full.

Payment method:

_____ Check enclosed payable to PRP (US funds only)

_____ Charge my (circle):   Visa   MasterCard   American Express   Discover

Account #_____ Expiration Date_____

Signature_____ Daytime Phone #(_____)_____

Please send my order to:

Name (PLEASE PRINT)_____

Address_____

_____

City/State/Zip_____

Send this form to:
Professional Resource Press
PO Box 15560
Sarasota FL 34277-1560
or
FAX 1-813-366-7971

Credit card orders only, 1-800-443-3364. Customer service, call 1-813-366-7913.